I0612056

STORIES, TRUE AND NOT SO TRUE

Hans Christian Andersen

Edited by
Dr. Vladimir Orel

Table of Contents

From the editor

Hans Christian Andersen (1805-1875) is probably the most famous Dane. We all meet with him in our childhood as a wonderful and touching story-teller. In our volume Andersen appears in two different roles — as a familiar teller of fairy tales and as an intriguing author of his own story, his life.

THE TRUE STORY OF MY LIFE

CHAPTER I

My life is a lovely story, happy and full of incident. If, when I was a boy, and went forth into the world poor and friendless, a good fairy had met me and said, "Choose now thy own course through life, and the object for which thou wilt strive, and then, according to the development of thy mind, and as reason requires, I will guide and defend thee to its attainment," my fate could not, even then, have been directed more happily, more prudently, or better. The history of my life will say to the world what it says to me — There is a loving God, who directs all things for the best.

My native land, Denmark, is a poetical land, full of popular traditions, old songs, and an eventful history, which has become bound up with that of Sweden and Norway. The Danish islands are possessed of beautiful beech woods, and corn and clover fields: they resemble gardens on a great scale. Upon one of these green islands, Funen, stands Odense, the place of my birth. Odense is called after the pagan god Odin, who, as tradition states, lived here: this place is the capital of the province, and lies twenty-two Danish miles from Copenhagen.

In the year 1805 there lived here, in a small mean room, a young married couple, who were extremely attached to each other; he was a shoemaker, scarcely twenty-two years old, a man of a richly gifted and truly poetical mind. His wife, a few years older than himself, was ignorant of life and of the world, but possessed a heart full of love. The young man had himself made his shoemaking bench, and the bedstead with which he began housekeeping; this bedstead he had made out of the wooden frame which had borne only a short time before the coffin of the deceased Count Trampe, as he lay in state, and the remnants of the black cloth on the wood work kept the fact still in remembrance.

Instead of a noble corpse, surrounded by crape and wax-lights, here lay, on the second of April, 1805, a living and weeping child, — that was myself, Hans Christian Andersen. During the first day of my existence my father is said to have sate by the bed and read aloud in Holberg, but I cried all the time. "Wilt thou go to sleep, or listen quietly?" it is reported that my father asked in joke; but I still cried on; and even in the church, when I was taken to be baptized, I cried so loudly that the preacher, who was a passionate man, said, "The young one screams like a cat!" which words my mother never forgot. A poor emigrant, Gomar, who stood as godfather, consoled her in the mean time by saying that the louder I cried as a child, all the more beautifully should I sing when I grew older.

Our little room, which almost filled with the shoemaker's bench, the bed, and my crib, was the abode of my childhood; the walls, however, were covered with pictures, and over the work-bench was a cupboard containing books and songs; the little kitchen was full of shining plates and metal pans, and by means of a ladder it was possible to go out on the roof, where, in the gutters between and the neighbor's house, there stood a great chest filled with soil, my mother's sole garden, and where she grew her vegetables. In my story of the Snow Queen that garden still blooms.

I was the only child, and was extremely spoiled, but I continually heard from my mother how very much happier I was than she had been, and that I was brought up like a nobleman's child. She, as a child, had been driven out by her parents to beg, and once when she was not able to do it, she had sate for a whole day under a bridge and wept. I have drawn her character in two different aspects, in old Dominica, in the Improvisatore, and in the mother of Christian, in Only a Fiddler.

My father gratified me in all my wishes. I possessed his whole heart; he lived for me. On Sundays, he made me perspective glasses, theatres, and pictures which could be changed; he read to me from Holberg's plays and the Arabian Tales; it was only in such moments as these that I can remember to have seen him really cheerful, for he never felt himself happy in his life and as a handicrafts-man. His parents had been country people in good circumstances, but upon whom many misfortunes had fallen; the cattle had died; the farm house had been burned down; and lastly, the husband had lost his reason. On this the wife had removed with him to Odense, and there put her son, whose mind was full of intelligence, apprentice to a shoemaker; it could not be otherwise, although it was his ardent wish to be able to attend the Grammar School, where he might have learned Latin. A few well-to-do citizens had at one time spoken of this, of clubbing together a sufficient sum to pay for his board and education, and thus giving him a start in life; but it never went beyond words. My poor father saw his dearest wish unfulfilled; and he never lost the remembrance of it. I recollect that once, as a child, I saw tears in his eyes, and it was when a youth from the Grammar School came to our house to be measured for a new pair of boots, and showed us his books and told us what he learned.

"That was the path upon which I ought to have gone!" said my father, kissed me passionately, and was silent the whole evening.

He very seldom associated with his equals. He went out into the woods on Sundays, when he took me with him; he did not talk much when he was out, but would sit silently, sunk in deep thought, whilst I ran about and strung strawberries on a straw, or bound garlands. Only twice in the year, and that in the month of May, when the woods were arrayed in their earliest green, did my mother go with us, and then she wore a cotton gown, which she put on only on these occasions, and when she partook of the Lord's Supper, and which, as long as I can remember, was her holiday gown. She always took home with her from the wood a great many fresh beech boughs, which were then planted behind the polished stone. Later in the year sprigs of St. John's wort were stuck into the chinks of the beams, and we considered their growth as omens whether our lives would be long or short. Green branches and pictures ornamented our little room, which my mother always kept neat and clean; she took great pride in always having the bed-linen and the curtains very white.

The mother of my father came daily to our house, were it only for a moment, in order to see her little grandson. I was her joy and her delight. She was a quiet and most amiable old woman, with mild blue eyes and a fine figure, which life had severely tried. From having been the wife of a countryman in easy circumstances she had now fallen into great poverty, and dwelt with her feeble-minded husband in a little house, which was the last, poor remains of their property. I never saw her shed a tear. But it made all the deeper impression upon me when she quietly sighed, and told me about her own mother's mother, how she had been a rich, noble lady in the city of Cassel, and that she had married a "comedy-player," that was as she expressed it, and run away from parents and home, for all of which her posterity had now to do penance. I never can recollect that I heard her mention the family name of her grandmother; but her own maiden name was Nommesen. She was employed to take care of the garden belonging to a lunatic asylum, and every Sunday evening she brought us some flowers, which they gave her permission to take home with her. These flowers adorned my mother's cupboard; but still they were mine, and to me it was allowed to put them in the glass of water. How great was this pleasure! She brought them all to me; she loved me with her whole soul. I knew it, and I understood it.

She burned, twice in the year, the green rubbish of the garden; on such occasions she took me with her to the asylum, and I lay upon the great heaps of green leaves and pea-straw. I had many flowers to play with, and — which was a circumstance upon which I set great importanceu I had here better food to eat than I could expect at home.

All such patients as were harmless were permitted to go freely about the court; they often came to us in the garden, and with curiosity and terror I listened to them and followed them about; nay, I even ventured so far as to go with the attendants to those who were raving mad. A long passage led to their cells. On one occasion, when the attendants were out of the way, I lay down upon the floor, and peeped through the crack of the door into one of these cells. I saw within a lady almost naked, lying on her straw bed; her hair hung down over her shoulders, and she sang with a very beautiful voice. All at once she sprang up, and threw herself against the door where I lay; the little valve through which she received her food burst open; she stared down upon me, and stretched out her long arm towards me. I screamed for terror — I felt the tips of her fingers touching my clothes — I was half dead when the attendant came; and even in later years that sight and that feeling remained within my soul.

Close beside the place where the leaves were burned, the poor old women had their spinning-room. I often went in there, and was very soon a favorite. When with these people, I found myself possessed of an eloquence which filled them with astonishment. I had accidentally heard about the internal mechanism of the human frame, of course without understanding anything about it; but all these mysteries were very captivating to me; and with chalk, therefore, I drew a quantity of flourishes on the door, which were to represent the intestines; and my description of the heart and the lungs made the deepest impression. I passed for a remarkably wise child, that would not live long; and they rewarded my eloquence by telling me tales in return; and thus a world as rich as that of the thousand and one nights was revealed to me. The stories told by these old ladies, and the insane figures which I saw around me in the asylum, operated in the meantime so powerfully upon me, that when it grew dark I scarcely dared to go out of the house. I was therefore permitted, generally at sunset, to lay me down in my parents' bed with its long flowered curtains, because the press-bed in which I slept could not conveniently be put down so early in the evening on account of the room it occupied in our small dwelling; and here, in the paternal bed, lay I in a waking dream, as if the actual world did not concern me. I was very much afraid of my weak-minded grandfather. Only once had he ever spoken to me, and then he had made use of the formal pronoun "you." He employed himself in cutting out of wood strange figures, men with beasts' heads, and beasts with wings; these he packed in a basket and carried them out into the country, where he was everywhere well received by the peasant women, because he gave to them and their children these strange toys. One day, when he was returning to Odense, I heard the boys in the street shouting after him; I hid myself behind a flight of steps in terror, for I knew that I was of his flesh and blood.

Every circumstance around me tended to excite my imagination. Odense itself, in those days in which there was not a single steamboat in existence, and when intercourse with other places was much more rare than now, was a totally different city to what it is in our day; a person might have fancied himself living hundreds of years ago, because so many customs prevailed then which belonged to an earlier age. The guilds walked in procession through the town with their harlequin before them with mace and bells; on Shrove Tuesday the butchers led the fattest ox through the streets adorned with garlands, whilst a boy in a white shirt and with great wings on his shoulders rode upon it; the sailors paraded through the city with music and all their flags flying, and then two of the boldest among them stood and wrestled upon a plank placed between two boats, and the one who was not thrown into the water was the victor.

That, however, which more particularly stamped itself upon my memory, and became refreshed by after often-repeated relations, was, the abode of the Spaniards in

Funen in 1808. It is true that at that time I was but three years old; still I nevertheless perfectly remember the brown foreign men who made disturbances in the streets, and the cannon which were fired. I saw the people lying on straw in a half-tumbledown church, which was near the asylum. One day, a Spanish soldier took me in his arms and pressed a silver image, which he wore upon his breast, to my lips. I remember that my mother was angry at it, because, she said, there was something papistical about it; but the image, and the strange man, who danced me about, kissed me and wept, pleased me: certainly he had children at home in Spain. I saw one of his comrades led to execution; he had killed a Frenchman. Many years afterwards this little circumstance occasioned me to write my little poem, "The Soldier," which Chamisso translated into German, and which afterwards was included in the illustrated people's books of soldier-songs. [Footnote: This same little song, sent to me by the author, was translated by me and published in the 19th No. of Howitt's Journal. — M. H.] I very seldom played with other boys; even at school I took little interest in their games, but remained sitting within doors. At home I had playthings enough, which my father made for me. My greatest delight was in making clothes for my dolls, or in stretching out one of my mother's aprons between the wall and two sticks before a currant-bush which I had planted in the yard, and thus to gaze in between the sun-illumined leaves. I was a singularly dreamy child, and so constantly went about with my eyes shut, as at last to give the impression of having weak sight, although the sense of sight was especially cultivated by me.

Sometimes, during the harvest, my mother went into the field to glean. I accompanied her, and we went, like Ruth in the Bible, to glean in the rich fields of Boaz. One day we went to a place, the bailiff of which was well known for being a man of a rude and savage disposition. We saw him coming with a huge whip in his hand, and my mother and all the others ran away. I had wooden shoes on my bare feet, and in my haste I lost these, and then the thorns pricked me so that I could not run, and thus I was left behind and alone. The man came up and lifted his whip to strike me, when I looked him in the face and involuntarily exclaimed, —

"How dare you strike me, when God can see it?"

The strong, stern man looked at me, and at once became mild; he patted me on my cheeks, asked me my name, and gave me money.

When I brought this to my mother and showed it her, she said to the others, "He is a strange child, my Hans Christian; everybody is kind to him: this bad fellow even has given him money."

I grew up pious and superstitious. I had no idea of want or need; to be sure my parents had only sufficient to live from day to day, but I at least had plenty of every thing; an old woman altered my father's clothes for me. Now and then I went with my parents to the theatre, where the first representations which I saw were in German. "Das Donauweibchen" was the favorite piece of the whole city; there, however, I saw, for the first time, Holberg's Village Politicians treated as an opera.

The first impression which a theatre and the crowd assembled there made upon me was, at all events, no sign of any thing poetical slumbering in me; for my first exclamation on seeing so many people, was, "Now, if we only had as many casks of butter as there are people here, then I would eat lots of butter!" The theatre, however, soon became my favorite place, but, as I could only very seldom go there, I acquired the friendship of the man who carried out the playbills, and he gave me one every day. With this I seated myself in a corner and imagined an entire play, according to the name of the piece and the characters in it. That was my first, unconscious poetising.

My father's favorite reading was plays and stories, although he also read works of history and the Scriptures. He pondered in silent thought afterwards upon that which he had read, but my mother did not understand him when he talked with her about them, and therefore he grew more and more silent. One day, he closed the Bible with the words, "Christ was a man like us, but an extraordinary man!" These words horrified my mother, and she burst into tears. In my distress I prayed to God that he would forgive this fearful blasphemy in my father. "There is no other devil than that which we have in our own hearts," I heard my father say one day and I made myself miserable about him and his soul; I was therefore entirely of the opinion of my mother and the neighbours, when my father, one morning, found three scratches on his arm, probably occasioned by a nail, that the devil had been to visit him in the night, in order to prove to him that he really existed. My father's rambles in the wood became more frequent; he had no rest. The events of the war in Germany, which he read in the newspapers with eager curiosity, occupied him completely. Napoleon was his hero: his rise from obscurity was the most beautiful example to him. At that time Denmark was in league with France; nothing was talked of but war; my father entered the service as a soldier, in hope of returning home a lieutenant. My mother wept. The neighbours shrugged their shoulders, and said that it was folly to go out to be shot when there was no occasion for it.

The morning on which the corps were to march I heard my father singing and talking merrily, but his heart was deeply agitated; I observed that by the passionate manner in which he kissed me when he took his leave. I lay sick of the measles and alone in the room, when the drums beat and my mother accompanied my father, weeping, to the city gate. As soon as they were gone my old grandmother came in; she looked at me with her mild eyes and said, it would be a good thing if I died; but that God's will was always the best.

That was the first day of real sorrow which I remember.

The regiment advanced no farther than Holstein, peace was concluded, and the voluntary soldier returned to his work-stool. Everything fell into its old course. I played again with my dolls, acted comedies, and always in German, because I had only seen them in this language; but my German was a sort of gibberish which I made up, and in which there occurred only one real German word, and that was *"Besen,"* a word which I had picked up out of the various dialects which my father brought home from Holstein.

"Thou hast indeed some benefit from my travels," said he in joke. "God knows whether thou wilt get as far; but that must be thy care. Think about it, Hans Christian!" But it was my mother's intention that as long as she had any voice in the matter, I should remain at home, and not lose my health as he had done.

That was the case with him; his health had suffered. One morning he woke in a state of the wildest excitement, and talked only of campaigns and Napoleon. He fancied that he had received orders from him to take the command. My mother immediately sent me, not to the physician,

17

but to a so-called wise woman some miles from Odense. I went to her. She questioned me, measured my arm with a woolen thread, made extraordinary signs, and at last laid a green twig upon my breast. It was, she said, a piece of the same kind of tree upon which the Saviour was crucified.

"Go now," said she, "by the river side towards home. If your father will die this time, then you will meet his ghost."

My anxiety and distress may be imagined, — I, who was so full of superstition, and whose imagination was so easily excited.

"And thou hast not met anything, hast thou?" inquired my mother when I got home. I assured her, with beating heart, that I had not.

My father died the third day after that. His corpse lay on the bed: I therefore slept with my mother. A cricket chirped the whole night through.

"He is dead," said my mother, addressing it; "thou needest not call him. The ice maiden has fetched him."

I understood what she meant. I recollected that, in the winter before, when our window panes were frozen, my father pointed to them and showed us a figure as that of a maiden with outstretched arms. "She is come to fetch me," said he, in jest. And now, when he lay dead on the bed, my mother remembered this, and it occupied my thoughts also.

He was buried in St. Knud's churchyard, by the door on the left hand side coming from the altar. My grandmother planted roses upon his grave. There are now in the selfsame place two strangers' graves, and the grass grows green upon them also.

After my father's death I was entirely left to myself. My mother went out washing. I sate alone at home with my little theatre, made dolls' clothes and read plays. It has been told me that I was always clean and nicely dressed. I had grown tall; my hair was long, bright, and almost yellow, and I always went bare-headed. There dwelt in our neighborhood the widow of a clergyman, Madame Bunkeflod, with the sister of her deceased husband. This lady opened to me her door, and hers was the first house belonging to the educated class into which I was kindly received. The deceased clergyman had written poems, and had gained a reputation in Danish literature. His spinning songs were at that time in the mouths of the people. In my vignettes to the Danish poets I thus sang of him whom my contemporaries had forgotten: —

Spindles rattle, wheels turn round, Spinning-songs depart; Songs which youth sings soon become Music of the heart.

Here it was that I heard for the first time the word *poet* spoken, and that with so much reverence, as proved it to be something sacred. It is true that my father had read Holberg's play to me; but here it was not of these that they spoke, but of verses and poetry. "My brother the poet," said Bunkeflod's sister, and her eyes sparkled as she said it. From her I learned that it was a something glorious, a something fortunate, to be a poet. Here, too, for the first time, I read Shakspeare, in a bad translation, to be sure; but the bold descriptions, the heroic incidents, witches, and ghosts were exactly to my taste. I immediately acted Shakspeare's plays on my little puppet theatre. I saw Hamlet's ghost, and lived upon the heath with Lear. The more persons died in a play, the more interesting I thought it. At this time I wrote my first piece: it was nothing less than a tragedy, wherein, as a matter of course, everybody died. The subject of it I borrowed from an old song about Pyramus and Thisbe; but I had increased the incidents through a hermit and his son, who both loved Thisbe, and who both killed themselves when she died. Many speeches of the hermit were passages from the Bible, taken out of the little catechism, especially from our duty to our neighbors. To the piece I gave the title "Abor and Elvira."

"It ought to be called 'Perch (Aborre) and Stockfish,'" said one of our neighbors wittily to me, as I came with it to her after having read it with great satisfaction and joy to all the people in our street. This entirely depressed me, because I felt that she was turning both me and my poem to ridicule. With a troubled heart I told it to my mother.

"She only said so," replied my mother, "because her son had not done it." I was comforted, and began a new piece, in which a king and queen were among the dramatis personae. I thought it was not quite right that these dignified personages, as in Shakspeare, should speak like other men and women. I asked my mother and different people how a king ought properly to speak, but no one knew exactly. They said that it was so many years since a king had been in Odense, but that he certainly spoke in a foreign language. I procured myself, therefore, a sort of lexicon, in which were German, French, and English words with Danish meanings, and this helped me. I took a word out of each language, and inserted them into the speeches of my king and queen. It was a regular Babel-like language, which I considered only suitable for such elevated personages.

I desired now that everybody should hear my piece. It was a real felicity to me to read it aloud, and it never occurred to me that others should not have the same pleasure in listening to it.

The son of one of our neighbors worked in a cloth manufactory, and every week brought home a sum of money. I was at a loose end, people said, and got nothing. I was also now to go to the manufactory, "not for the sake of the money," my mother said, "but that she might know where I was, and what I was doing."

My old grandmother took me to the place, therefore, and was very much affected, because, said she, she had not expected to live to see the time when I should consort with the poor ragged lads that worked there.

Many of the journeymen who were employed in the manufactory were Germans; they sang and were merry fellows, and many a coarse joke of theirs filled the place with loud laughter. I heard them, and I there learned that, to the innocent ears of a child, the impure remains very unintelligible. It took no hold upon my heart. I was possessed at that time of a remarkably beautiful and high soprano voice, and I knew it; because when I sang in my parents' little garden, the people in the street stood and listened, and the fine folks in the garden of the states-councillor, which adjoined ours, listened at the fence. When, therefore, the people at the manufactory asked me whether I could sing, I immediately began, and all the looms stood still: all the journeymen listened to me. I had to sing again and again, whilst the other boys had my work given them to do. I now told them that I also could act plays, and that I knew whole scenes of Holberg and Shakspeare. Everybody liked me; and in this way, the first days in the manufactory passed on very merrily. One day, however, when I was in my best singing vein, and everybody spoke of the extraordinary brilliancy of my voice, one of the journeymen said that I was a girl, and not a boy. He seized hold of me. I cried and screamed. The other journeymen thought it very amusing, and held me fast by my arms and legs. I screamed aloud, and was as much ashamed as a girl; and then, darting from them, rushed home to my mother, who immediately promised me that I should never go there again.

I again visited Madame Bunkeflod, for whose birthday I invented and made a white silk pincushion. I also made an acquaintance with another old clergyman's widow in the neighborhood. She permitted me to read aloud to her the works which she had from the circulating library. One of them began with these words: "It was a tempestuous night; the rain beat against the window-panes."

"That is an extraordinary book," said the old lady; and I quite innocently asked her how she knew that it was. "I can tell from the beginning," said she, "that it will turn out extraordinary."

I regarded her penetration with a sort of reverence.

Once in the harvest time my mother took me with her many miles from Odense to a nobleman's seat in the neighborhood of Bogense, her native place. The lady who lived there, and with whose parents my mother had lived, had said that some time she might come and see her. That was a great journey for me: we went most of the way on foot, and required, I believe, two days for the journey. The country here made such a strong impression upon me, that my most earnest wish was to remain in it, and become a countryman. It was just in the hop-picking season; my mother and I sat in the barn with a great many country people round a great binn, and helped to pick the hops. They told tales as they sat at their work, and every one related what wonderful things he had seen or experienced. One afternoon I heard an old man among them say that God knew every thing, both what had happened and what would happen. That idea occupied my whole mind, and towards evening, as I went alone from the court, where there was a deep pond, and stood upon some stones which were just within the water, the thought passed through my head, whether God actually knew everything which was to happen there. Yes, he has now determined that I should live and be so many years old, thought I; but, if I now were to jump into the water here and drown myself, then it would not be as he wished; and all at once I was firmly and resolutely determined to drown myself. I ran to where the water was deepest, and then a new thought passed through my soul. "It is the devil who wishes to have power over me!" I uttered a loud cry, and, running away from the place as if I were pursued, fell weeping into my mother's arms. But neither she nor any one else could wring from me what was amiss with me.

"He has certainly seen a ghost," said one of the women; and I almost believed so myself.

My mother married a second time, a young handicraftsman; but his family, who also belonged to the handicraft class, thought that he had married below himself, and neither my mother nor myself were permitted to visit them. My step-father was a young, grave man, who would have nothing to do with my education. I spent my time, therefore, over my peep show and my puppet theatre, and my greatest happiness consisted in collecting bright colored pieces of cloth and silk, which I cut out myself and sewed. My mother regarded it as good exercise preparatory to my becoming a tailor, and took up the idea that I certainly was born for it. I, on the contrary, said that I would go to the theatre and be an actor, a wish which my mother most sedulously opposed, because she knew of no other theatre than those of the strolling players and the rope-dancers. No, a tailor I must and should be. The only thing which in some measure reconciled me to this prospect was, that I should then get so many fragments to make up for my theatre.

My passion for reading, the many dramatic scenes which I knew by heart, and my remarkably fine voice, had turned upon me in some sort the attention of several of the more influential families of Odense. I was sent for to their houses, and the peculiar characteristics of my mind excited their interest. Among others who noticed me was the Colonel Hoegh-Guldberg, who with his family showed me the kindest sympathy; so much so, indeed, that he introduced me to the present king, then Prince Christian.

I grew rapidly, and was a tall lad, of whom my mother said that she could not let him any longer go about without any object in life. I was sent, therefore, to the charity school, but learned only religion, writing, and arithmetic, and the last badly enough; I could also scarcely spell a word correctly. On the master's birthday I always wove him a garland and wrote him a poem; he received them half with smiles and half as a joke; the last time, however, he scolded me. The street lads had also heard from their parents of my peculiar turn of mind, and that I was in the habit of going to the houses of the gentry. I was therefore one day pursued by a wild crowd of them, who shouted after me derisively, "There runs the play-writer!" I hid myself at home in a corner, wept, and prayed to God.

My mother said that I must be confirmed, in order that I might be apprenticed to the tailor trade, and thus do something rational. She loved me with her whole heart, but she did not understand my impulses and my endeavors, nor indeed at that time did I myself. The people about her always spoke against my odd ways, and turned me to ridicule.

We belonged to the parish of St. Knud, and the candidates for confirmation could either enter their names with the prevost or the chaplain. The children of the so-called superior families and the scholars of the grammar school went to the first, and the children of the poor to the second. I, however, announced myself as a candidate to the prevost, who was obliged to receive me, although he discovered vanity in my placing myself among his catechists, where, although taking the lowest place, I was still above those who were under the care of the chaplain. I would, however, hope that it was not alone vanity which impelled me. I had a sort of fear of the poor boys, who had laughed at me, and I always felt as it were an inward drawing towards the scholars of the grammar school, whom I regarded as far better than other boys. When I saw them playing in the church-yard, I would stand outside the railings, and wish that I were but among the fortunate ones, — not for the sake of play, but for the sake of the many books they had, and for what they might be able to become in the world. With the prevost, therefore, I should be able to come together with them, and be as they were; but I do not remember a single one of them now, so little intercourse would they hold with me. I had daily the feeling of having thrust myself in where people thought that I did not belong. One young girl, however, there was, and one who was considered too of the highest rank, whom I shall afterwards have to mention; she always looked gently and kindly at me, and even once gave me a rose. I returned home full of happiness, because there was one being who did not overlook and repel me.

An old female tailor altered my deceased father's great coat into a confirmation suit for me; never before had I worn so good a coat. I had also for the first time in my life a pair of boots. My delight was extremely great; my only fear was that everybody would not see them, and therefore I drew them up over my trousers, and thus marched through the church. The boots creaked, and that inwardly pleased me, for thus the congregation would hear that they were new. My whole devotion was disturbed; I was aware of it, and it caused me a horrible pang of conscience that my thoughts should be as much with my new boots as with God. I prayed him earnestly from my heart to forgive me, and then again I thought about my new boots.

During the last year I had saved together a little sum of money. When I counted it over I found it to be thirteen rix dollars banco (about thirty shillings) I was quite overjoyed at the possession of so much wealth, and as my mother now most resolutely required that I should be apprenticed to a tailor, I prayed and besought her that I might make a journey to Copenhagen, that I might see the greatest city in the world. "What wilt thou do there?" asked my mother.

"I will become famous," returned I, and I then told her all that I had read about extraordinary men. "People have," said I, "at first an immense deal of adversity to go through, and then they will be famous."

It was a wholly unintelligible impulse that guided me. I wept, I prayed, and at last my mother consented, after having first sent for a so-called wise woman out of the hospital, that she might read my future fortune by the coffee-grounds and cards.

"Your son will become a great man," said the old woman, "and in honor of him, Odense will one day be illuminated."

My mother wept when she heard that, and I obtained permission to travel. All the neighbors told my mother that it was a dreadful thing to let me, at only fourteen years of age, go to Copenhagen, which was such a long way off, and such a great and intricate city, and where I knew nobody.

"Yes," replied my mother, "but he lets me have no peace; I have therefore given my consent, but I am sure that he will go no further than Nyborg; when he gets sight of the rough sea, he will be frightened and turn back again."

During the summer before my confirmation, a part of the singers and performers of the Theatre Royal had been in Odense, and had given a series of operas and tragedies there. The whole city was taken with them. I, who was on good terms with the man who delivered the play-bills, saw the performances behind the scenes, and had even acted a part as page, shepherd, etc., and had spoken a few words. My zeal was so great on such occasions, that I stood there fully apparelled when the actors arrived to dress. By these means their attention was turned to me; my childlike manners and my enthusiasm amused them; they talked kindly with me, and I looked up to them as to earthly divinities. Everything which I had formerly heard about my musical voice, and my recitation of poetry, became intelligible to me. It was the theatre for which I was born: it was there that I should become a famous man, and for that reason Copenhagen was the goal of my endeavors. I heard a deal said about the large theatre in Copenhagen, and that there was to be soon what was called the ballet, a something which surpassed both the opera and the play; more especially did I hear the solo-dancer, Madame Schall, spoken of as the first of all. She therefore appeared to me as the queen of everything, and in my imagination I regarded her as the one who would be able to do everything for me, if I could only obtain her support. Filled with these thoughts, I went to the old printer Iversen, one of the most respectable citizens of Odense, and who, as I heard, had had considerable intercourse with the actors when they were in the town. He, I thought, must of necessity be acquainted with the famous dancer; him I would request to give me a letter of introduction to her, and then I would commit the rest to God.

The old man saw me for the first time, and heard my petition with much kindness; but he dissuaded me most earnestly from it, and said that I might learn a trade.

"That would actually be a great sin," returned I.

He was startled at the manner in which I said that, and it prepossessed him in my favor; he confessed that he was not personally acquainted with the dancer, but still that he would give me a letter to her. I received one from him, and now believed the goal to be nearly won.

My mother packed up my clothes in a small bundle, and made a bargain with the driver of a post carriage to take me back with him to Copenhagen for three rix dollars banco. The afternoon on which we were to set out came, and my mother accompanied me to the city gate. Here stood my old grandmother; in the last few years her beautiful hair had become grey; she fell upon my neck and wept, without being able to speak a word. I was myself deeply affected. And thus we parted. I saw her no more; she died in the following year.

I do not even know her grave; she sleeps in the poorhouse burial-ground.

The postilion blew his horn; it was a glorious sunny afternoon, and the sunshine soon entered into my gay child-like mind. I delighted in every novel object which met my eye, and I was journeying towards the goal of my soul's desires. When, however, I arrived at Nyborg on the great Belt, and was borne in the ship away from my native island, I then truly felt how alone and forlorn I was, and that I had no one else except God in heaven to depend upon.

As soon as I set foot on Zealand, I stepped behind a shed, which stood on the shore, and falling upon my knees, besought of God to help and guide me aright; I felt myself comforted by so doing, and I firmly trusted in God and my own good fortune. The whole day and the following night I travelled through cities and villages; I stood solitarily by the carriage, and ate my bread while it was repacked. — I thought I was far away in the wide world.

CHAPTER II

On Monday morning, September 5th, 1819, I saw from the heights of Frederiksburg, Copenhagen, for the first time. At this place I alighted from the carriage, and with my little bundle in my hand, entered the city through the castle garden, the long alley and the suburb.

The evening before my arrival had been made memorable by the breaking out of the so-called Jews quarrel, which spread through many European countries. The whole city was in commotion [Footnote: This remarkable disturbance makes a fine incident in Anderson's romance of "Only a Fiddler." — M. H.]; every body was in the streets; the noise and tumult of Copenhagen far exceeded, therefore, any idea which my imagination had formed of this, at that time, to me great city.

With scarcely ten dollars in my pocket, I turned into a small public-house. My first ramble was to the theatre. I went round it many times; I looked up to its walls, and regarded them almost as a home. One of the bill-sellers, who wandered about here each day, observed me, and asked me if I would have a bill. I was so wholly ignorant of the world, that I thought the man wished to give me one; I therefore accepted his offer with thankfulness. He fancied I was making fun of him and was angry; so that I was frightened, and hastened from the place which was to me the dearest in the city. Little did I then imagine that ten years afterwards my first dramatic piece would be represented there, and that in this manner I should make my appearance before the Danish public. On the following day I dressed myself in my confirmation suit, nor were the boots forgotten, although, this time, they were worn, naturally, under my trousers; and thus, in my best attire, with a hat on, which fell half over my eyes, I hastened to present my letter of introduction to the dancer, Madame Schall. Before I rung at the bell, I fell on my knees before the door and prayed God that I here might find help and support. A maid-servant came down the steps with her basket in her hand; she smiled kindly at me, gave me a skilling (Danish), and tripped on. Astonished, I looked at her and the money. I had on my confirmation suit, and thought I must look very smart. How then could she think that I wanted to beg? I called after her.

"Keep it, keep it!" said she to me, in return, and was gone.

At length I was admitted to the dancer; she looked at me in great amazement, and then heard what I had to say. She had not the slightest knowledge of him from whom the letter came, and my whole appearance and behavior seemed very strange to her. I confessed to her my heartfelt inclination for the theatre; and upon her asking me what characters I thought I could represent, I replied, Cinderella. This piece had been performed in Odense by the royal company, and the principal characters had so greatly taken my fancy, that I could play the part perfectly from memory. In the mean time I asked her permission to take off my boots, otherwise I was not

31

light enough for this character; and then taking up my broad hat for a tambourine, I began to dance and sing, —

"Here below, nor rank nor riches, Are exempt from pain and woe."

My strange gestures and my great activity caused the lady to think me out of my mind, and she lost no time in getting rid of me.

From her I went to the manager of the theatre, to ask for an engagement. He looked at me, and said that I was "too thin for the theatre."

"Oh," replied I, "if you will only engage me with one hundred rix dollars banco salary, then I shall soon get fat!" The manager bade me gravely go my way, adding, that they only engaged people of education.

I stood there deeply wounded. I knew no one in all Copenhagen who could give me either counsel or consolation. I thought of death as being the only thing, and the best thing for me; but even then my thoughts rose upwards to God, and with all the undoubting confidence of a child in his father, they riveted themselves upon Him. I wept bitterly, and then I said to myself, "When everything happens really miserably, then he sends help. I have always read so. People must first of all suffer a great deal before they can bring anything to accomplishment."

I now went and bought myself a gallery-ticket for the opera of Paul and Virginia. The separation of the lovers affected me to such a degree, that I burst into violent weeping. A few women, who sat near me, consoled me by saying that it was only a play, and nothing to trouble oneself about; and then they gave me a sausage sandwich. I had the greatest confidence in everybody, and therefore I told them, with the utmost openness, that I did not really weep about Paul and Virginia, but because I regarded the theatre as my Virginia, and that if I must be separated from it, I should be just as wretched as Paul. They looked at me, and seemed not to understand my meaning. I then told them why I had come to Copenhagen, and how forlorn I was there. One of the women, therefore, gave me more, bread and butter, with fruit and cakes.

On the following morning I paid my bill, and to my infinite trouble I saw that my whole wealth consisted in one rix dollar banco. It was necessary, therefore, either that I should find some vessel to take me home, or put myself to work with some handicraftsman. I considered that the last was the wiser of the two, because, if I returned to Odense, I must there also put myself to work of a similar kind; besides which, I knew very well that the people there would laugh at me if I came back again. It was to me a matter of indifference what handicraft trade I learned, — I only should make use of it to keep life within me in Copenhagen. I bought a newspaper, therefore. I found among the advertisements that a cabinet maker was in want of an apprentice. The man received me kindly, but said that before I was bound to him he must have an attestation, and my baptismal register from Odense; and that till these came I could remove to his house, and try how the business pleased me. At six o'clock the next morning I went to the workshop: several journeymen were there, and two or three apprentices; but the master was not come. They fell into merry and idle discourse. I was as bashful as a girl, and as they soon perceived this, I was unmercifully rallied upon it. Later in the day the rude jests of the young fellows went so far, that, in remembrance of the scene at the manufactory, I took the resolute determination not to remain a single day longer in the workshop. I went down to the master, therefore, and told him that I could not stand it; he tried to console me, but in vain: I was too much affected, and hastened away.

I now went through the streets; nobody knew me; I was quite forlorn. I then bethought myself of having read in a newspaper in Odense the name of an Italian, Siboni, who was the director of the Academy of Music in Copenhagen. Everybody had praised my voice; perhaps he would assist me for its sake; if not, then that very evening I must seek out the master of some vessel who would take me home again. At the thoughts of the journey home I became still more violently excited, and in this state of suffering I hastened to Siboni's house.

It happened that very day that he had a large party to dinner; our celebrated composer Weyse was there, the poet Baggesen, and other guests. The housekeeper opened the door to me, and to her I not only related my wish to be engaged as a singer, but also the whole history of my life. She listened to me with the greatest sympathy, and then she left me. I waited a long time, and she must have been repeating to the company the greater part of what I had said, for, in a while, the door opened, and all the guests came out and looked at me. They would have me to sing, and Siboni heard me attentively. I gave some scenes out of Holberg, and repeated a few poems; and then, all at once, the sense of my unhappy condition so overcame me that I burst into tears; the whole company applauded.

"I prophesy," said Baggesen, "that one day something will come out of him; but do not be vain when, some day, the

34

whole public shall applaud thee!" and then he added something about pure, true nature, and that this is too often destroyed by years and by intercourse with mankind. I did not understand it all.

Siboni promised to cultivate my voice, and that I therefore should succeed as singer at the Theatre Royal. It made me very happy; I laughed and wept; and as the housekeeper led me out and saw the excitement under which I labored, she stroked my cheeks, and said that on the following day I should go to Professor Weyse, who meant to do something for me, and upon whom I could depend.

I went to Weyse, who himself had risen from poverty; he had deeply felt and fully comprehended my unhappy situation, and had raised by a subscription seventy rix dollars banco for me. I then wrote my first letter to my mother, a letter full of rejoicing, for the good fortune of the whole world seemed poured upon me. My mother in her joy showed my letter to all her friends; many heard of it with astonishment; others laughed at it, for what was to be the end of it? In order to understand Siboni it was necessary for me to learn something of German. A woman of Copenhagen, with whom I travelled from Odense to this city, and who gladly, according to her means, would have supported me, obtained, through one of her acquaintance, a language-master, who gratuitously gave me some German lessons, and thus I learned a few phrases in that language. Siboni received me into his house, and gave me food and instruction; but half a year afterwards my voice broke, or was injured, in consequence of my being compelled to wear bad shoes through the winter, and having besides no warm under-clothing. There was no longer any prospect that I should become a fine singer. Siboni told me that candidly, and counselled me to go to Odense, and there learn a trade.

I, who in the rich colors of fancy had described to my mother the happiness which I actually felt, must now return home and become an object of derision! Agonized with this thought, I stood as if crushed to the earth. Yet, precisely amid this apparently great un-happiness lay the stepping-stones of a better fortune.

As I found myself again abandoned, and was pondering by myself upon what was best for me next to do, it occurred to me that the Poet Guldberg, a brother of the Colonel of that name in Odense, who had shown me so much kindness, lived in Copenhagen. He lived at that time near the new church-yard outside the city, of which he has so beautifully sung in his poems. I wrote to him, and related to him everything; afterwards I went to him myself, and found him surrounded with books and tobacco pipes. The strong, warm-hearted man received me kindly; and as he saw by my letter how incorrectly I wrote, he promised to give me instruction in the Danish tongue; he examined me a little in German, and thought that it would be well if he could improve me in this respect also. More than this, he made me a present of the profits of a little work which he had just then published; it became known, and I believe they exceeded one hundred rix dollars banco; the excellent Weyse and others also supported me.

It was too expensive for me to lodge at a public house; I was therefore obliged to seek for private lodgings. My ignorance of the world led me to a widow who lived in one of the most disreputable streets of Copenhagen; she was inclined to receive me into her house, and I never suspected what kind of world it was which moved around me. She was a stern, but active dame; she described to me the other people of the city in such horrible colors as made me suppose that I was in the only safe haven there. I was to pay twenty rix dollars monthly for one room, which was nothing but an empty store-room, without window and light, but I had permission to sit in her parlor. I was to make trial of it at first for two days, meantime on the following day she told me that I could decide to stay or immediately go. I, who so easily attach myself to people, already liked her, and felt myself at home with her; but more than sixteen dollars per month Weyse had told me I must not pay, and this was the sum which I had received from him and Guldberg, so that no surplus remained to me for my other expenses. This troubled me very much; when she was gone out of the room, I seated myself on the sofa, and contemplated the portrait of her deceased husband.

I was so wholly a child, that as the tears rolled down my own cheeks, I wetted the eyes of the portrait with my tears, in order that the dead man might feel how troubled I was, and influence the heart of his wife. She must have seen that nothing more was to be drained out of me, for when she returned to the room she said that she would receive me into her house for the sixteen rix dollars. I thanked God and the dead man. I found myself in the midst of the mysteries of Copenhagen, but I did not understand how to interpret them. There in the house in which I lived a friendly young lady, who lived alone, and often wept; every evening her old father came and paid her a visit. I opened the door to him frequently; he wore a plain sort of coat, had his throat very much tied up, and his hat pulled over his eyes. He always drank his tea with her, and nobody dared to be present, because he was not fond of company: she never seemed very glad at his coming. [Footnote: This character will be recognised in Steffen Margaret, in Only a Fiddler. — M. H.] Many years afterwards, when I had reached another step on the ladder of life, when the refined world of fashionable life was opened before me, I saw one evening, in the midst of a brilliantly lighted hall, a polite old gentleman covered with orders — that was the old father in the shabby coat, he whom I had let in. He had little idea that I had opened the door to him when he played his part as guest, but I, on my side, then had also no thought but for my own comedy-playing; that is to say, I was at that time so much of a child that I played with my puppet-theatre and made my dolls' clothes; and in order that I might obtain gaily-colored fragments for this purpose, I used to go to the shops and ask for patterns of various kinds of stuffs and ribbons. I myself did not possess a single farthing; my landlady received all the money each month in advance; only now and then, when I did any errands for her, she gave me something, and that went in the purchase of paper or for old play-books. I was now very happy, and was doubly so because Professor Guldberg had induced Lindgron, the first comic actor at the theatre, to give me instruction. He gave me several parts in Holberg to learn, such as Hendrik, and the Silly Boy, for which I had shown some talent. My desire, however, was to play the Correggio. I obtained permission to learn this piece in my own way, although Lindgron asked, with comic gravity, whether I expected to resemble the great painter? I, however, repeated to him the soliloquy in the picture gallery with so much feeling, that the old man clapped me on the shoulder and said, "Feeling you have; but you must not be an actor, though God knows what else. Speak to Guldberg about your learning Latin: that always opens the way for a student."

I a student! That was a thought which had never come before into my head. The theatre lay nearer to me, and was dearer too; but Latin I had also always wished to learn. But before I spoke on the subject to Guldberg, I mentioned it to the lady who gave me gratuitous instruction in German; but she told me that Latin was the most expensive language in the world, and that it was not possible to gain free instruction in it. Guldberg, however, managed it so that one of his friends, out of kindness, gave me two lessons a week.

The dancer, Dahlen, whose wife at that time was one of the first artistes on the Danish boards, opened his house to me. I passed many an evening there, and the gentle, warm-hearted lady was kind to me. The husband took me with him to the dancing-school, and that was to me one step nearer to the theatre. There stood I for whole mornings, with a long staff, and stretched my legs; but notwithstanding all my good-will, it was Dahlen's opinion that I should never get beyond a figurante. One advantage, however, I had gained; I might in an evening make my appearance behind the scenes of the theatre; nay, even sit upon the farthest bench in the box of the figurantes. It seemed to me as if I had got my foot just within the theatre, although I had never yet been upon the stage itself.

One night the little opera of the Two Little Savoyards was given; in the market scene every one, even the mechanists, might go up to help in filling the stage; I heard them say so, and rouging myself a little, I went happily up with the others. I was in my ordinary dress; the confirmation coat, which still held together, although, with regard to brushing and repairs, it looked but miserably, and the great hat which fell down over my face. I was very conscious of the ill condition of my attire, and would have been glad to have concealed it; but, through the endeavor to do so, my movements became still more angular. I did not dare to hold myself upright, because, by so doing, I exhibited all the more plainly the shortness of my waistcoat, which I had outgrown. I had the feeling very plainly that people would make themselves merry about me; yet, at this moment, I felt nothing but the happiness of stepping for the first time before the foot-lamps. My heart beat; I stepped forward; there came up one of the singers, who at that time was much thought of, but now is forgotten; he took me by the hand, and jeeringly wished me happiness on my d but. "Allow me to introduce you to the Danish public," said he, and drew me forward to the lamps. The people would laugh at me — I felt it; the tears rolled down my cheeks; I tore myself loose, and left the stage full of anguish.

Shortly after this, Dahlen arranged a ballet of Armida, in which I received a little part: I was a spirit. In this ballet I became acquainted with the lady of Professor Heiberg, the wife of the poet, and now a highly esteemed actress on the Danish stage; she, then a little girl, had also a part in it, and our names stood printed in the bill. That was a moment in my life, when my name was printed! I fancied I could see it a nimbus of immortality. I was continually looking at the printed paper. I carried the programme of the ballet with me at night to bed, lay and read my name by candle light — in short, I was happy.

I had now been two years in Copenhagen. The sum of money which had been collected for me was expended, but I was ashamed of making known my wants and my necessities. I had removed to the house of a woman whose husband, when living, was master of a trading-vessel, and there I had only lodging and breakfast. Those were heavy, dark days for me.

The lady believed that I went out to dine with various families, whilst I only ate a little bread on one of the benches in the royal garden. Very rarely did I venture into some of the lowest eating-houses, and choose there the least expensive dish. I was, in truth, very forlorn; but I did not feel the whole weight of my condition. Every person who spoke to me kindly I took for a faithful friend. God was with me in my little room; and many a night, when I have said my evening prayer, I asked of Him, like a child, "Will things soon be better with me?" I had the notion, that as it went with me on New Year's Day, so would it go with me through the whole year; and my highest wishes were to obtain a part in a play.

It was now New Year's Day. The theatre was closed, and only a half-blind porter sat at the entrance to the stage, on which there was not a soul. I stole past him with beating heart, got between the movable scenes and the curtain, and advanced to the open part of the stage. Here I fell down upon my knees, but not a single verse for declamation could I recall to my memory. I then said aloud the Lord's Prayer, and went out with the persuasion, that because I had spoken from the stage on New Year's Day, I should in the course of the year succeed in speaking still more, as well as in having a part assigned to me.

During the two years of my residence in Copenhagen I had never been out into the open country. Once only had I been in the park, and there I had been deeply engrossed by studying the diversions of the people and their gay tumult. In the spring of the third year, I went out for the first time amid the verdure of a spring morning. It was into the garden of the Fredericksberg, the summer residence of Frederick VI. I stood still suddenly under the first large budding beech tree. The sun made the leaves transparent — there was a fragrance, a freshness — the birds sang. I was overcome by it — I shouted aloud for joy, threw my arms around the tree and kissed it.

"Is he mad?" said a man close behind me. It was one of the servants of the castle. I ran away, shocked at what I had heard, and then went thoughtfully and calmly back to the city.

My voice had, in the mean time, in part regained its richness. The singing master of the choir-school heard it, offered me a place in the school, thinking that, by singing with the choir, I should acquire greater freedom in the exercise of my powers on the stage. I thought that I could see by this means a new way opened for me. I went from the dancing-school into the singing-school, and entered the choir, now as a shepherd, and now as a warrior. The theatre was my world. I had permission to go in the pit, and thus it fared ill with my Latin. I heard many people say that there was no Latin required for singing in the choir, and that without the knowledge of this language it was possible to become a great actor. I thought there was good sense in that, and very often, either with or without reason, excused myself from my Latin evening lesson. Guldberg became aware of this, and for the first time I received a reprimand which almost crushed me to the earth. I fancy that no criminal could suffer more by hearing the sentence of death pronounced upon him. My distress of mind must have expressed itself in my countenance, for he said "Do not act any more comedy." But it was no comedy to me.

I was now to learn Latin no longer. I felt my dependence upon the kindness of others in such a degree as I had never done before. Occasionally I had had gloomy and earnest thoughts in looking forward to my future, because

I was in want of the very necessaries of life; at other times I had the perfect thoughtlessness of a child.

The widow of the celebrated Danish statesman, Christian Colbjrnsen, and her daughter, were the first ladies of high rank who cordially befriended the poor lad; who listened to me with sympathy, and saw me frequently. Mrs. von Colbjrnsen resided, during the summer, at Bakkehus, where also lived the poet Rahbek and his interesting wife. Rahbek never spoke to me; but his lively and kind-hearted wife often amused herself with me. I had at that time again begun to write a tragedy, which I read aloud to her. Immediately on hearing the first scenes, she exclaimed, "But you have actually taken whole passages out of Oehlenschl ger and Ingemann."

"Yes, but they are so beautiful!" replied I in my simplicity, and read on.

One day, when I was going from her to Mrs. von Colbjrnsen, she gave me a handful of roses, and said, "Will you take them up to her? It will certainly give her pleasure to receive them from the hand of a poet." These words were said half in jest; but it was the first time that anybody had connected my name with that of poet. It went through me, body and soul, and tears filled my eyes. I know that, from this very moment, my mind was awoke to writing and poetry. Formerly it had been merely an amusement by way of variety from my puppet-theatre.

At Bakkehus lived also Professor Thiele, a young student at that time, but even then the editor of the Danish popular legends, and known to the public as the solver of Baggesen's riddle, and as the writer of beautiful poetry. He was possessed of sentiment, true inspiration, and heart. He had calmly and attentively watched the unfolding of my mind, until we now became friends. He was one of the few who, at that time, spoke the truth of me, when other people were making themselves merry at my expense, and having only eyes for that which was ludicrous in me. People had called me, in jest, the little orator, and, as such, I was an object of curiosity. They found amusement in me, and I mistook every smile for a smile of applause. One of my later friends has told me that it probably was about this period that he saw me for the first time. It was in the drawing-room of a rich tradesman, where people were making themselves very merry with me. They desired me to repeat one of my poems, and, as I did this with great feeling, the merriment was changed into sympathy with me.

I heard it said every day, what a good thing it would be for me if I could study. People advised me to devote myself to science, but no one moved one step to enable me to do so; it was labor enough for me to keep body and soul together. It therefore occurred to me to write a tragedy, which I would offer to the Theatre Royal, and would then begin to study with the money which I should thus obtain. Whilst Guldberg instructed me in Danish, I had written a tragedy from a German story, called The Chapel in the Wood; yet as this was done merely as an exercise in the language, and, as he forbade me in the most decided manner to bring it out, I would not do so. I originated my own material, therefore; and within fourteen days I wrote my national tragedy called the Robbers in Wissenberg (the name of a little village in Funen.) There was scarcely a word in it correctly written, as I had no person to help me, because I meant it to be anonymous; there was, nevertheless, one person admitted into the secret, namely, the young lady whom I had met with in Odense, during my preparation for confirmation, the only one who at that time showed me kindness and good-will. It was through her that I was introduced to the Colbjrnsen family, and thus known and received in all those circles of which the one leads into the other. She paid some one to prepare a legible copy of my piece, and undertook to present it for perusal. After an interval of six weeks, I received it back, accompanied by a letter which said the people did not frequently wish to retain works which betrayed, in so great a degree, a want of elementary knowledge.

It was just at the close of the theatrical season, in May, 1823, that I received a letter from the directors, by which I was dismissed from the singing and dancing school, the letter adding also, that my participation in the school-teaching could lead to no advantage for me, but that they wished some of my many friends would enable me to receive an education, without which, talent availed nothing. I felt myself again, as it were, cast out into the wide world without help and without support. It was absolutely necessary that I should write a piece for the theatre, and that *must* be accepted; there was no other salvation for me. I wrote, therefore, a tragedy founded on a passage in history, and I called it Alfsol. I was delighted with the first act, and with this I immediately went to the Danish translator of Shakspeare, Admiral Wulff, now deceased, who good-naturedly heard me read it. In after years I met with the most cordial reception in his family. At that time I also introduced myself to our celebrated physician Oersted, and his house has remained to me to this day an affectionate home, to which my heart has firmly attached itself, and where I find my oldest and most unchangeable friends.

A favorite preacher, the rural dean Gutfeldt, was living at that time, and he it was who exerted himself most earnestly for my tragedy, which was now finished; and having written a letter of recommendation, he sent it to the managers of the theatre. I was suspended between hope and fear. In the course of the summer I endured bitter want, but I told it to no one, else many a one, whose sympathy I had experienced, would have helped me to the utmost of their means. A false shame prevented me from confessing what I endured. Still happiness filled my heart. I read then for the first time the works of Walter Scott. A new world was opened to me: I forgot the reality, and gave to the circulating library that which should have provided me with a dinner.

The present conference councillor, Collin, one of the most distinguished men of Denmark, who unites with the greatest ability the noblest and best heart, to whom I looked up with confidence in all things, who has been a second father to me, and in whose children I have found brothers and sisters; — this excellent man I saw now for the first time. He was at that time director of the Theatre Royal, and people universally told me that it would be the best thing for me if he would interest himself on my behalf: it was either Oersted or Gutfeldt who first mentioned me to him; and now for the first time I went to that house which was to become so dear to me. Before the ramparts of Copenhagen were extended, this house lay outside the gate, and served as a summer residence to the Spanish Ambassador; now, however, it stands, a crooked, angular frame-work building, in a respectable street; an old-fashioned wooden balcony leads to the entrance, and a great tree spreads its green branches over the court and its pointed gables. It was to become a paternal house to me. Who does not willingly linger over the description of home?

I discovered only the man of business in Collin; his conversation was grave and in few words. I went away, without expecting any sympathy from this man; and yet it was precisely Collin who in all sincerity thought for my advantage, and who worked for it silently, as he had done for others, through the whole course of his active life. But at that time I did not understand the apparent calmness with which he listened, whilst his heart bled for the afflicted, and he always labored for them with zeal and success, and knew how to help them. He touched so lightly upon my tragedy, which had been sent to him, and on account of which many people had overwhelmed me with flattering speeches, that I regarded him rather as an enemy than a protector.

In a few day I was sent for by the directors of the theatre, when Rahbek gave me back my play as useless for the stage; adding, however, that there were so many grains of corn scattered in it, that it was hoped, that perhaps, by earnest study, after going to school and the previous knowledge of all that is requisite, I might, some time, be able to write a work which should be worthy of being acted on the Danish stage.

In order therefore to obtain the means for my support and the necessary instruction, Collin recommended me to King Frederick the Sixth, who granted to me a certain sum annually for some years; and, by means of Collin also, the directors of the high schools allowed me to receive free instruction in the grammar school at Slagelse, where just then a new, and, as was said, an active rector was appointed. I was almost dumb with astonishment: never had I thought that my life would take this direction, although I had no correct idea of the path which I had now to tread. I was to go with the earliest mail to Slagelse, which lay twelve Danish miles from Copenhagen, to the place where also the poets Baggesen and Ingemann had gone to school. I was to receive money quarterly from Collin; I was to apply to him in all cases, and he it was who was to ascertain my industry and my progress.

I went to him the second time to express to him my thanks. Mildly and kindly he said to me, "Write to me without restraint about everything which you require, and tell me how it goes with you." From this hour I struck root in his heart; no father could have been more to me than he was, and is; none could have more heartily rejoiced in my happiness, and my after reception with the public; none have shared my sorrow more kindly; and I am proud to say that one of the most excellent men which Denmark possesses feels towards me as towards his own child. His beneficence was conferred without his making me feel it painful either by word or look. That was not the case with every one to whom, in this change of my fortunes, I had to offer my thanks; I was told to think of my inconceivable happiness and my poverty; in Collin's words was expressed the warm-heartedness of a father, and to him it was that properly I was indebted for everything.

The journey was hastily determined upon, and I had yet for myself some business to arrange. I had spoken to an acquaintance from Odense who had the management of a small printing concern, for a widow, to get "Alfsal" printed, that I might, by the sale of the work, make a little money. Before, however, the piece was printed, it was necessary that I should obtain a certain number of subscribers; but these were not obtained, and the manuscript lay in the printing-office, which, at the time I went to fetch it away, was shut up. Some years afterwards, however, it suddenly made its appearance in print without my knowledge or my desire, in its unaltered shape, but without my name.

On a beautiful autumn day I set off with the mail from Copenhagen to begin my school-life in Slagelse. A young student, who a month before had passed his first examination, and now was travelling home to Jutland to exhibit himself there as a student, and to see once more his parents and his friends, sate at my side and exulted for joy over the new life which now lay before him; he assured me that he should be the most unhappy of human beings if he were in my place, and were again beginning to go to the grammar school. But I travelled with a good heart towards the little city of Zealand. My mother received a joyful letter from me. I only wished that my father and the old grandmother yet lived, and could hear that I now went to the grammar school.

CHAPTER III

When, late in the evening, I arrived at the inn in Slagelse, I asked the hostess if there were anything remarkable in the city.

"Yes," said she, "a new English fire-engine and Pastor Bastholm's library," and those probably were all the lions in the city. A few officers of the Lancers composed the fine-gentleman world. Everybody knew what was done in everybody's house, whether a scholar was elevated or degraded in his class, and the like. A private theatre, to which, at general rehearsal, the scholars of the grammar school and the maid-servants of the town had free entrance, furnished rich material for conversation. The place was remote from woods, and still farther from the coast; but the great post-road went through the city, and the post-horn resounded from the rolling carriage.

I boarded with a respectable widow of the educated class, and had a little chamber looking out into the garden and field. My place in the school was in the lowest class, among little boys: — I knew indeed nothing at all.

I was actually like a wild bird which is confined in a cage; I had the greatest desire to learn, but for the moment I floundered about, as if I had been thrown into the sea; the one wave followed another; grammar, geography, mathematics — I felt myself overpowered by them, and feared that I should never be able to acquire all these. The rector, who took a peculiar delight in turning everything to ridicule, did not, of course, make an exception in my case. To me he stood then as a divinity; I believed unconditionally every word which he spoke. One day, when I had replied incorrectly to his question, and he said that I was stupid, I mentioned it to Collin, and told him my anxiety, lest I did not deserve all that people had done for me; but he consoled me. Occasionally, however, on some subjects of instruction, I began to receive a good certificate, and the teachers were heartily kind to me; yet, notwithstanding that I advanced, I still lost confidence in myself more and more. On one of the first examinations, however, I obtained the praise of the rector. He wrote the same in my character-book; and, happy in this, I went a few days afterwards to Copenhagen. Guldberg, who saw the progress I had made, received me kindly, and commended my zeal; and his brother in Odense furnished me the next summer with the means of visiting the place of my birth, where I had not been since I left it to seek adventures. I crossed the Belt, and went on foot to Odense. When I came near enough to see the lofty old church tower, my heart was more and more affected; I felt deeply the care of God for me, and I burst into tears. My mother rejoiced over me. The families of Iversen and Guldberg received me cordially; and in the little streets I saw the people open their windows to look after me, for everybody knew how remarkably well things had fared with me; nay, I fancied I actually stood upon the pinnacle of fortune, when one of the principal citizens, who had built a high tower to his house, led me up there, and I looked out thence over the city, and the surrounding country, and some old women in the hospital below, who had known me from childhood, pointed up to me.

As soon, however, as I returned to Slagelse, this halo of glory vanished, as well as every thought of it. I may freely confess that I was industrious, and I rose, as soon as it was possible, into a higher class; but in proportion as I rose did I feel the pressure upon me more strongly, and that my endeavors were not sufficiently productive. Many an evening, when sleep overcame me, did I wash my head with cold water, or run about the lonely little garden, till I was again wakeful, and could comprehend the book anew. The rector filled up a portion of his hours of teaching with jests, nicknames, and not the happiest of witticisms. I was as if paralyzed with anxiety when he entered the room, and from that cause my replies often expressed the opposite of that which I wished to say, and thereby my anxiety was all the more increased. What was to become of me?

In a moment of ill-humor I wrote a letter to the head master, who was one of those who was most cordially opposed to me. I said in this letter that I regarded myself as a person so little gifted by nature, that it was impossible for me to study, and that the people in Copenhagen threw away the money which they spent upon me: I besought him therefore to counsel me what I should do. The excellent man strengthened me with mild words, and wrote to me a most friendly and consolatory letter; he said that the rector meant kindly by me — that it was his custom and way of acting — that I was making all the progress that people could expect from me, and that I need not doubt of my abilities. He told me that he himself was a peasant youth of three and twenty, older than I myself was, when he began his studies; the misfortune for me was, that I ought to have been treated differently to the other scholars, but that this could hardly be done in a school; but that things were progressing, and that I stood well both with the teachers and my fellow students.

Every Sunday we had to attend the church and hear an old preacher; the other scholars learned their lessons in history and mathematics while he preached; I learned my task in religion, and thought that, by so doing, it was less sinful. The general rehearsals at the private theatre were points of light in my school life; they took place in a back building, where the lowing of the cows might be heard; the street-decoration was a picture of the marketplace of the city, by which means the representation had something familiar about it; it amused the inhabitants to see their own houses.

On Sunday afternoons it was my delight to go to the castle of Antvorskov, at that time only half ruinous, and once a monastery, where I pursued the excavating of the ruined cellars, as if it had been a Pompeii. I also often rambled to the crucifix of St. Anders, which stands upon one of the heights of Slagelse, and which is one of the wooden crosses erected in the time of Catholicism in Denmark. St. Anders was a priest in Slagelse, and travelled to the Holy Land; on the last day he remained so long praying on the holy grave, that the ship sailed away without him. Vexed at this circumstance, he walked along the shore, where a man met him riding on an ass, and took him up with him. Immediately he fell asleep, and when he awoke he heard the bells of Slagelse ringing. He lay upon the (Hvilehi) hill of rest, where the cross now stands. He was at home a year and a day before the ship returned, which had sailed away without him, and an angel had borne him home. The legend, and the place where he woke, were both favorites of mine. From this spot I could see the ocean and Funen. Here I could indulge my fancies; when at home, my sense of duty chained my thoughts only to my books.

The happiest time, however, was when, once on a Sunday, whilst the wood was green, I went to the city of Sor, two (Danish) miles from Slagelse, and which lies in the midst of woods, surrounded by lakes. Here is an academy for the nobility, founded by the poet Holberg. Everything lay in a conventual stillness. I visited here the poet Ingemann, who had just married, and who held a situation as teacher; he had already received me kindly in Copenhagen; but here his reception of me was still more kind. His life in this place seemed to me like a beautiful story; flowers and vines twined around his window; the rooms were adorned with the portraits of distinguished poets, and other pictures. We sailed upon the lake with an Aeolian harp made fast to the mast. Ingemann talked so cheerfully, and his excellent, amiable wife treated me as if she were an elder sister: — I loved these people. Our friendship has grown with years. I have been from that time almost every summer a welcome guest there, and I have experienced that there are people in whose society one is made better, as it were; that which is bitter passes away, and the whole world appears in sunlight.

Among the pupils in the academy of nobles, there were two who made verses; they knew that I did the same, and they attached themselves to me. The one was Petit, who afterwards, certainly with the best intention, but not faithfully, translated several of my books; the other, the poet Karl Bagger, one of the most gifted of men who has come forward in Danish literature, but who has been unjustly judged. His poems are full of freshness and originality; his story, "The Life of my Brother," is a genial book, by the critique on which the Danish

Monthly Review of Literature has proved that it does not understand how to give judgment. These two academicians were very different from me: life rushed rejoicingly through their veins; I was sensitive and childlike. In my character-book I always received, as regarded my conduct, "remarkably good." On one occasion, however, I only obtained the testimony of "very good;" and so anxious and childlike was I, that I wrote a letter to Collin on that account, and assured him in grave earnestness, that I was perfectly innocent, although I had only obtained a character of "very good."

The rector grew weary of his residence in Slagelse; he applied for the vacant post of rector in the grammar-school of Helsingr, and obtained it. He told me of it, and added kindly, that I might write to Collin and ask leave to accompany him thither; that I might live in his house, and could even now remove to his family; I should then in half a year become a student, which could not be the case if I remained behind, and that then he would himself give me some private lessons in Latin and Greek. On this same occasion he wrote also to Collin; and this letter, which I afterwards saw, contained the greatest praise of my industry, of the progress I had made, and of my good abilities, which last I imagined that he thoroughly mistook, and for the want of which, I myself had so often wept. I had no conception that he judged of me so favorably; it would have strengthened and relieved me had I known it; whereas, on the contrary, his perpetual blame depressed me. I, of course, immediately received Collin's permission, and removed to the house of the rector. But that, alas! was an unfortunate house.

I accompanied him to Helsingr, one of the loveliest places in Denmark, close to the Sound, which is at this place not above a mile (Danish) broad, and which seems like a blue, swelling river between Denmark and Sweden. The ships of all nations sail past daily by hundreds; in winter the ice forms a firm bridge between the two countries, and when in spring this breaks up, it resembles a floating glacier. The scenery here made a lively impression upon me, but I dared only to cast stolen glances at it. When the school hours were over, the house door was commonly locked; I was obliged to remain in the heated school-room and learn my Latin, or else play with the children, or sit in my little room; I never went out to visit anybody. My life in this family furnishes the most evil dreams to my remembrance. I was almost overcome by it, and my prayer to God every evening was, that he would remove this cup from me and let me die. I possessed not an atom of confidence in myself. I never mentioned in my letters how hard it went with me, because the rector found his pleasure in making a jest of me, and turning my feelings to ridicule. I never complained of any one, with the exception of myself. I knew that they would say in Copenhagen, "He has not the desire to do any thing; a fanciful being can do no good with realities."

My letters to Collin, written at this time, showed such a gloomy despairing state of mind, that they touched him deeply; but people imagined that was not to be helped; they fancied that it was my disposition, and not, as was the case, that it was the consequence of outward influences. My temper of mind was thoroughly buoyant, and susceptible of every ray of sunshine; but only on one single holiday in the year, when I could go to Copenhagen, was I able to enjoy it.

What a change it was to get for a few days out of the rector's rooms into a house in Copenhagen, where all was elegance, cleanliness, and full of the comforts of refined life! This was at Admiral Wulff's, whose wife felt for me the kindness of a mother, and whose children met me with cordiality; they dwelt in a portion of the Castle of Amalienburg, and my chamber looked out into the square. I remember the first evening there; Aladdin's words passed through my mind, when he looked down from his splendid castle into the square, and said, "Here came I as a poor lad." My soul was full of gratitude.

During my whole residence in Slagelse I had scarcely written more than four or five poems; two of which, "The Soul," and "To my Mother," will be found printed in my collected works. During my school-time at Helsingr I wrote only one single poem, "The Dying Child;" a poem which, of all my after works, became most popular and most widely circulated. I read it to some acquaintance in Copenhagen; some were struck by it, but most of them only remarked my Funen dialect, which drops the d in every word. I was commended by many; but from the greater number I received a lecture on modesty, and that I should not get too great ideas of myself — I who really at that time thought nothing of myself. [Footnote: How beautifully is all this part of the author's experience reflected in that of Antonio, the Improvisatore, whose highly sensitive nature was too often wounded by the well-meant lectures of patrons and common-place minds. — M. H.]

At the house of Admiral Wulff I saw many men of the most distinguished talent, and among them all my mind paid the greatest homage to one — that was the poet Adam Oehlenschl ger. I heard his praise resound from every mouth around me; I looked up to him with the most pious faith: I was happy when one evening, in a large brilliantly-lighted drawing room — where I deeply felt that my apparel was the shabbiest there, and for that reason I concealed myself behind the long curtains — Oehlenschl ger came to me and offered me his hand. I could have fallen before him on my knees. I again saw Weyse, and heard him improvise upon the piano. Wulff himself read aloud his translations of Byron; and Oehlenschl ger's young daughter Charlotte surprised me by her joyous, merry humor.

From such a house as this, I, after a few days, returned to the rector, and felt the difference deeply. He also came direct from Copenhagen, where he had heard it said that I had read in company one of my own poems. He looked at me with a penetrating glance, and commanded me to bring him the poem, when, if he found in it one spark of poetry, he would forgive me. I tremblingly brought to him "The Dying Child;" he read it, and pronounced it to be sentimentality and idle trash. He gave way freely to his anger. If he had believed that I wasted my time in writing verses, or that I was of a nature which required a severe treatment, then his intention would have been good; but he could not pretend this. But from this day forward my situation was more unfortunate than ever; I suffered so severely in my mind that I was very near sinking under it. That was the darkest, the most unhappy time in my life.

Just then one of the masters went to Copenhagen, and related to Collin exactly what I had to bear, and immediately he removed me from the school and from the rector's house. When, in taking leave of him, I thanked him for the kindness which I had received from him, the passionate man cursed me, and ended by saying that I should never become a student, that my verses would grow mouldy on the floor of the bookseller's shop, and that I myself should end my days in a mad-house. I trembled to my innermost being, and left him.

Several years afterwards, when my writings were read, when the Improvisatore first came out, I met him in Copenhagen; he offered me his hand in a conciliatory manner, and said that he had erred respecting me, and had treated me wrong; but it now was all the same to me. The heavy, dark days had also produced their blessing in my life. A young man, who afterwards became celebrated in Denmark for his zeal in the Northern languages and in history, became my teacher. I hired a little garret; it is described in the Fiddler; and in The Picture Book without Pictures, people may see that I often received there visits from the moon. I had a certain sum allowed for my support; but as instruction was to be paid for, I had to make savings in other ways. A few families through the week-days gave me a place at their tables. I was a sort of boarder, as many another poor student in Copenhagen is still: there was a variety in it; it gave an insight into the several kinds of family life, which was not without its influence on me. I studied industriously; in some particular branches I had considerably distinguished myself in Helsingr, especially in mathematics; these were, therefore, now much more left to myself: everything tended to assist me in my Greek and Latin studies; in one direction, however, and that the one in which it would least have been expected, did my excellent teacher find much to do; namely, in religion. He closely adhered to the literal meaning of the Bible; with this I was acquainted, because from my first entrance in the school I had clearly understood what was said and taught by it. I received gladly, both with feeling and understanding, the doctrine, that God is love: everything which opposed this — a burning hell, therefore, whose fire endured forever — I could not recognize. Released from the distressing existence of the school-bench, I now expressed myself like a free man; and my teacher, who was one of the noblest and most amiable of human beings, but who adhered firmly to the letter, was often quite distressed about me. We disputed, whilst pure flames kindled within our hearts. It was nevertheless good for me that I came to this unspoiled, highly-gifted young man, who was possessed of a nature as peculiar as my own.

That which, on the contrary, was an error in me, and which became very perceptible, was a pleasure which I had, not in jesting with, but in playing with my best feelings, and in regarding the understanding as the most important thing in the world. The rector had completely mistaken my undisguisedly candid and sensitive character; my excitable feelings were made ridiculous, and thrown back upon themselves; and now, when I could freely advance upon the way to my object, this change showed itself in me. From severe suffering I did not rush into libertinism, but into an erroneous endeavor to appear other than I was. I ridiculed feeling, and fancied that I had quite thrown it aside; and yet I could be made wretched for a whole day, if I met with a sour countenance where I expected a friendly one. Every poem which I had formerly written with tears, I now parodied, or gave to it a ludicrous refrain; one of which I called "The Lament of the Kitten," another, "The Sick Poet." The few poems which I wrote at that time were all of a humorous character: a complete change had passed over me; the stunted plant was reset, and now began to put forth new shoots.

Wulff's eldest daughter, a very clever and lively girl, understood and encouraged the humor, which made itself evident in my few poems; she possessed my entire confidence; she protected me like a good sister, and had great influence over me, whilst she awoke in me a feeling for the comic.

At this time, also, a fresh current of life was sent through the Danish literature; for this the people had an interest, and politics played no part in it.

Heiberg, who had gained the acknowledged reputation of a poet by his excellent works, "Psyche" and "Walter the Potter," had introduced the vaudeville upon the Danish stage; it was a Danish vaudeville, blood of our blood, and was therefore received with acclamation, and supplanted almost everything else. Thalia kept carnival on the Danish stage, and Heiberg was her secretary. I made his acquaintance first at Oersted's. Refined, eloquent, and the hero of the day, he pleased me in a high degree; he was most kind to me, and I visited him; he considered one of my humorous poems worthy of a place in his most excellent weekly paper, "The Flying Post." Shortly before I had, after a deal of trouble, got my poem of "The Dying Child" printed in a paper; none of the many publishers of journals, who otherwise accept of the most lamentable trash, had the courage to print a poem by a schoolboy. My best known poem they printed at that time, accompanied by an excuse for it. Heiberg saw it, and gave it in his paper an honorable place. Two humorous poems, signed H., were truly my d but with him.

I remember the first evening when the "Flying Post" appeared with my verses in it. I was with a family who wished me well, but who regarded my poetical talent as quite insignificant, and who found something to censure in every line. The master of the house entered with the "Flying Post" in his hand.

"This evening," said he, "there are two excellent poems: they are by Heiberg; nobody else could write anything like them." And now my poems were received with rapture. The daughter, who was in my secret, exclaimed, in her delight, that I was the author. They were all struck into silence, and were vexed. That wounded me deeply.

One of our least esteemed writers, but a man of rank, who was very hospitable, gave me one day a seat at his table. He told me that a new year's gift would come out, and that he was applied to for a contribution. I said that a little poem of mine, at the wish of the publisher, would appear in the same new year's gift.

"What, then, everybody and anybody are to contribute to this book!" said the man in vexation: "then he will need nothing from me; I certainly can hardly give him anything."

My teacher dwelt at a considerable distance from me. I went to him twice each day, and on the way there my thoughts were occupied with my lessons. On my return, however, I breathed more freely, and then bright poetical ideas passed through my brain, but they were never committed to paper; only five or six humorous poems were written in the course of the year, and these disturbed me less when they were laid to rest on paper than if they had remained in my mind.

In September, 1828, I was a student; and when the examination was over, the thousand ideas and thoughts, by which I was pursued on the way to my teacher, flew like a swarm of bees out into the world, and, indeed, into my first work, "A Journey on Foot to Amack;" a peculiar, humorous book, but one which fully exhibited my own individual character at that time, my disposition to sport with everything, and to jest in tears over my own feelings — a fantastic, gaily-colored tapestry-work. No publisher had the courage to bring out that little book; I therefore ventured to do it myself, and, in a few days after its appearance, the impression was sold. Publisher Keitzel bought from me the second edition; after a while he had a third; and besides this, the work was reprinted in Sweden.

Everybody read my book; I heard nothing but praise; I was "a student," — I had attained the highest goal of my wishes. I was in a whirl of joy; and in this state I wrote my first dramatic work, "Love on the Nicholas Tower, or, What says the Pit?" It was unsuccessful, because it satirized that which no longer existed amongst us, namely, the shows of the middle ages; besides which, it rather ridiculed the enthusiasm for the vaudeville. The subject of it was, in short, as follows: — The watchman of the Nicholas Tower, who always spoke as a knight of the castle, wished to give his daughter to the watchman of the neighboring church-tower; but she loved a young tailor, who had made a journey to the grave of Eulenspiegel, and was just now returned, as the punch-bowl steamed, and was to be emptied in honor of the young lady's consent being given. The lovers escape together to the tailor's herberg, where dancing and merriment are going forward. The watchman, however, fetches back his daughter; but she had lost her senses, and she assured them that she never would recover them, unless she had her tailor. The old watchman determines that Fate should decide the affair; but, then, who was Fate? The idea then comes into his head that the public shall be his Pythia, and that the public shall decide whether she should have the tailor or the watchman. They determine, therefore, to send to one of the youngest of the poets, and beg him to write the history in the style of the vaudeville, a kind of writing which was the most successful at that time, and when the piece was brought upon the stage, and the public either whistled or hissed, it should be in no wise considered that the work of the young author had been unsuccessful, but that it should be the voice of Fate, which said, "She shall marry the watchman." If, on the contrary, the piece was successful, it indicated that she should have the tailor; and this last, remarked the father, must be said in prose, in order that the public may understand it. Now every one of the characters thought himself on the stage, where in the epilogue the lovers besought the public for their applause, whilst the watchman begged them either to whistle, or at least to hiss.

My fellow students received the piece with acclamation; they were proud of me. I was the second of their body who in this year had brought out a piece on the Danish stage; the other was Arnesen, student at the same time with me, and author of a vaudeville called "The Intrigue in the People's Theatre," a piece which had a great run. We were the two young authors of the October examination, two of the sixteen poets which this year produced, and whom people in jest divided into the four great and the twelve small poets.

I was now a happy human being; I possessed the soul of a poet, and the heart of youth; all houses began to be open to me; I flew from circle to circle. Still, however, I devoted myself industriously to study, so that in September, 1829, I passed my *Examen philologicum et philosophicum*, and brought out the first collected edition of my poems, which met with great praise. Life lay bright with sunshine before me.

CHAPTER IV

Until now I had only seen a small part of my native land, that is to say, a few points in Funen and Zealand, as well as Moen's Klint, which last is truly one of our most beautiful places; the beechwoods there hang like a garland over the white chalk cliffs, from which a view is obtained far over the Baltic. I wished, therefore, in the summer of 1830, to devote my first literary proceeds to seeing Jutland, and making myself more thoroughly acquainted with my own Funen. I had no idea how much solidity of mind I should derive from this summer excursion, or what a change was about to take place in my inner life.

Jutland, which stretches between the German Ocean and the Baltic, until it ends at Skagen in a reef of quicksands, possesses a peculiar character. Towards the Baltic extend immense woods and hills; towards the North Sea, mountains and quicksands, scenery of a grand and solitary character; and between the two, infinite expanses of brown heath, with their wandering gipsies, their wailing birds, and their deep solitude, which the Danish poet, Steen Blicher, has described in his novels.

This was the first foreign scenery which I had ever seen, and the impression, therefore, which it made upon me was very strong. [Footnote: This impressive and wild scenery, with its characteristic figures, of gipsies etc., is most exquisitely introduced into the author's novel of "O. T."; indeed it gives a coloring and tone to the whole work, which the reader never can forget. In my opinion Andersen never wrote anything finer in the way of description than many parts of this work, though as a story it is not equal to his others. — M. H.] In the cities, where my "Journey on Foot" and my comic poems were known, I met with a good reception. Funen revealed her rural life to me; and, not far from my birth-place of Odense, I passed several weeks at the country seat of the elder Iversen as a welcome guest. Poems sprung forth upon paper, but of the comic fewer and fewer. Sentiment, which I had so often derided, would now be avenged. I arrived, in the course of my journey, at the house of a rich family in a small city; and here suddenly a new world opened before me, an immense world, which yet could be contained in four lines, which I wrote at that time: —

A pair of dark eyes fixed my sight, They were my world, my home, my delight, The soul beamed in them, and childlike peace, And never on earth will their memory cease.

New plans of life occupied me. I would give up writing poetry, — to what could it lead? I would study theology, and become a preacher; I had only one thought, and that was *she*. But it was self-delusion: she loved another; she married him. It was not till several years later that I felt and acknowledged that it was best, both for her and for myself, that things had fallen out as they were. She had no idea, perhaps, how deep my feeling for her had been, or what an influence it produced in me. She had become the excellent wife of a good man, and a happy mother. God's blessing rest upon her!

66

In my "Journey on Foot," and in most of my writings, satire had been the prevailing characteristic. This displeased many people, who thought that this bent of mind could lead to no good purpose. The critics now blamed me precisely for that which a far deeper feeling had expelled from my breast. A new collection of Poetry, "Fancies and Sketches," which was published for the new year, showed satisfactorily what my heart suffered. A paraphrase of the history of my own heart appeared in a serious vaudeville, "Parting and Meeting," with this difference only, that here the love was mutual: the piece was not presented on the stage till five years later.

Among my young friends in Copenhagen at that time was Orla Lehmann, who afterwards rose higher in popular favor, on account of his political efforts than any man in Denmark. Full of animation, eloquent and undaunted, his character of mind was one which interested me also. The German language was much studied at his father's; they had received there Heine's poems, and they were very attractive for young Orla. He lived in the country, in the neighborhood of the castle of Fredericksberg. I went there to see him, and he sang as I came one of Heine's verses, "Thalatta, Thalatta, du eviges Meer." We read Heine together; the afternoon and the evening passed, and I was obliged to remain there all night; but I had on this evening made the acquaintance of a poet, who, as it seemed to me, sang from the soul; he supplanted Hoffman, who, as might be seen by my "Journey on Foot," had formerly had the greatest influence on me. In my youth there were only three authors who as it were infused themselves into my blood, — Walter Scott, Hoffman, and Heine.

I betrayed more and more in my writings an unhealthy turn of mind. I felt an inclination to seek for the melancholy in life, and to linger on the dark side of things. I became sensitive and thought rather of the blame than the praise which was lavished on me. My late school education, which was forced, and my impulse to become an author whilst I was yet a student, make it evident that my first work, the "Journey on Foot," was not without grammatical errors. Had I only paid some one to correct the press, which was a work I was unaccustomed to, then no charge of this kind could have been brought against me. Now, on the contrary, people laughed at these errors, and dwelt upon them, passing over carelessly that in the book which had merit. I know people who only read my poems to find out errors; they noted down, for instance, how often I used the word *beautiful,* or some similar word. A gentleman, now a clergyman, at that time a writer of vaudevilles and a critic, was not ashamed, in a company where I was, to go through several of my poems in this style; so that a little girl of six years old, who heard with amazement that he discovered everything to be wrong, took the book, and pointing out the conjunction *and,* said, "There is yet a little word about which you have not scolded." He felt what a reproof lay in the remark of the child; he looked ashamed and kissed the little one. All this wounded me; but I had, since my school-days, become somewhat timid, and that caused me to take it all quietly: I was morbidly sensitive, and I was good-natured to a fault. Everybody knew it, and some were on that account almost cruel to me. Everybody wished to teach me; almost everybody said that I was spoiled by praise, and therefore they would speak the truth to me. Thus I heard continually of my faults, the real and the ideal weaknesses. In the mean time, however, my feelings burst forth; and then I said that I would become a poet whom they should see honored. But this was regarded only as the crowning mark of the most unbearable vanity; and from house to house it was repeated. I was a good man, they said, but one of the vainest in existence; and in that very time I was often ready wholly to despair of my abilities, and had, as in the darkest days of my school-life, a feeling, as if my whole talents were a self-deception. I almost believed so; but it was more than I could bear, to hear the same thing said, sternly and jeeringly, by others; and if I then uttered a proud, an inconsiderate word, it was addressed to the scourge with which I was smitten; and when those who smite are those we love, then do the scourges become scorpions.

For this reason Collin thought that I should make a little journey, — for instance, to North Germany, — in order to divert my mind and furnish me with new ideas.

In the spring of 1831, I left Denmark for the first time. I saw L bek and Hamburg. Everything astonished me and occupied my mind. I saw mountains for the first time, — the Harzgebirge. The world expanded so astonishingly before me. My good humor returned to me, as to the bird of passage. Sorrow is the flock of sparrows which remains behind, and builds in the nests of the birds of passage. But I did not feel myself wholly restored.

In Dresden I made acquaintance with Tieck. Ingemann had given me a letter to him. I heard him one evening read aloud one of Shakspeare's plays. On taking leave of him, he wished me a poet's success, embraced and kissed me; which made the deepest impression upon me. The expression of his eyes I shall never forget. I left him with tears, and prayed most fervently to God for strength to enable me to pursue the way after which my whole soul strove — strength, which should enable to express that which I felt in my soul; and that when I next saw Tieck, I might be known and valued by him. It was not until several years afterwards, when my later works were translated into German, and well received in his country, that we saw each other again; I felt the true hand-pressure of him who had given to me, in my second father-land, the kiss of consecration.

In Berlin, a letter of Oersted's procured me the acquaintance of Chamisso. That grave man, with his long locks and honest eyes, opened the door to me himself, read the letter, and I know not how it was, but we understood each other immediately. I felt perfect confidence in him, and told him so, though it was in bad German. Chamisso understood Danish; I gave him my poems, and he was the first who translated any of them, and thus introduced me into Germany. It was thus he spoke of me at that time in the *Morgenblatt*: "Gifted with wit, fancy, humor, and a national na vet , Andersen has still in his power tones which awaken deeper echoes. He understands, in particular, how with perfect ease, by a few slight but graphic touches, to call into existence little pictures and landscapes, but which are often so peculiarly local as not to interest those who are unfamiliar with the home of the poet. Perhaps that which may be translated from him, or which is so already, may be the least calculated to give a proper idea of him."

Chamisso became a friend for my whole life. The pleasure which he had in my later writings may be seen by the printed letters addressed to me in the collected edition of his works.

The little journey in Germany had great influence upon me, as my Copenhagen friends acknowledged. The impressions of the journey were immediately written down, and I gave them forth under the title of "Shadow Pictures." Whether I were actually improved or not, there still prevailed at home the same petty pleasure in dragging out my faults, the same perpetual schooling of me; and I was weak enough to endure it from those who were officious meddlers. I seldom made a joke of it; but if I did so, it was called arrogance and vanity, and it was asserted that I never would listen to rational people. Such an instructor once asked me whether I wrote *Dog* with a little *d*; — he had found such an error of the press in my last work. I replied, jestingly, "Yes, because I here spoke of a little dog."

But these are small troubles, people will say. Yes, but they are drops which wear hollows in the rock. I speak of it here; I feel a necessity to do so; here to protest against the accusation of vanity, which, since no other error can be discovered in my private life, is seized upon, and even now is thrown at me like an old medal.

From the end of the year 1828, to the beginning of 1839, I maintained myself alone by my writings. Denmark is a small country; but few books at that time went to Sweden and Norway; and on that account the profit could not be great. It was difficult for me to pull through, — doubly difficult, because my dress must in some measure accord with the circles into which I went. To produce, and always to be producing, was destructive, nay, impossible. I translated a few pieces for the theatre, — *La Quarantaine*, and *La Reine de seize ans*; and as, at that time, a young composer of the name of Hartmann, a grandson of him who composed the Danish folks-song of "King Christian stood by the tall, tall mast," wished for text to an opera, I was of course ready to write it. Through the writings of Hoffman, my attention had been turned to the masked comedies of Gozzi: I read *Il Corvo*,

71

and finding that it was an excellent subject, I wrote, in a few weeks, my opera-text of the Raven. It will sound strange to the ears of countrymen when I say that I, at that time, recommended Hartmann; that I gave my word for it, in my letter to the theatrical directors, for his being a man of talent, who would produce something good. He now takes the first rank among the living Danish composers.

I worked up also Walter Scott's "Bride of Lammermoor" for another young composer, Bredal. Both operas appeared on the stage; but I was subjected to the most merciless criticism, as one who had stultified the labors of foreign poets. What people had discovered to be good in me before seemed now to be forgotten, and all talent was denied to me. The composer Weyse, my earliest benefactor, whom I have already mentioned, was, on the contrary, satisfied in the highest degree with my treatment of these subjects. He told me that he had wished for a long time to compose an opera from Walter Scott's "Kenilworth." He now requested me to commence the joint work, and write the text. I had no idea of the summary justice which would be dealt to me. I needed money to live, and, what still more determined me to it, I felt flattered to have to work with Weyse our most celebrated composer. It delighted me that he, who had first spoken in my favor at Siboni's house, now, as artist, sought a noble connection with me. I had scarcely half finished the text, when I was already blamed for having made use of a well-known romance. I wished to give it up; but Weyse consoled me, and encouraged me to proceed. Afterwards, before he had finished the music, when I was about to travel abroad, I committed my fate, as regarded the text, entirely to his hands. He wrote whole verses of it, and the altered conclusion is wholly his own. It was a peculiarity of that singular man that he liked no book which ended sorrowfully. For that reason, Amy must marry Leicester, and Elizabeth say, "Proud England, I am thine." I opposed this at the beginning; but afterwards I yielded, and the piece was really half-created by Weyse. It was brought on the stage, but was not printed, with the exception of the songs. To this followed anonymous attacks: the city post brought me letters in which the unknown writers scoffed at and derided me. That same year I published a new collection of poetry, "The Twelve Months of the Year;" and this book, though it was afterwards pronounced to contain the greater part of my best lyrical poems, was then condemned as bad.

At that time "The Monthly Review of Literature," though it is now gone to its grave, was in its full bloom. At its first appearance, it numbered among its co-workers some of the most distinguished names. Its want, however, was men who were qualified to speak ably on aesthetic works. Unfortunately, everybody fancies himself able to give an opinion upon these; but people may write excellently on surgery or pedagogical science, and may have a name in those things, and yet be dolts in poetry: of this proofs may be seen. By degrees it became more and more difficult for the critical bench to find a judge for poetical works. The one, however, who, through his extraordinary zeal for writing and speaking, was ready at hand, was the historian and states-councillor Molbeck, who played, in our time, so great a part in the history of Danish criticism, that I must speak of him rather more fully. He is an industrious collector, writes extremely correct Danish, and his Danish dictionary, let him be reproached with whatever want he may, is a most highly useful work; but, as a judge of aesthetic works, he is one-sided, and even fanatically devoted to party spirit. He belongs, unfortunately, to the men of science, who are only one sixty-fourth of a poet, and who are the most incompetent judges of aesthetics. He has, for example, by his critiques on Ingemann's romances, shown how far he is below the poetry which he censures. He has himself published a volume of poems, which belong to the common run of books, "A Ramble through Denmark," written in the *fade*, flowery style of those times, and "A Journey through Germany, France, and Italy," which seems to be made up out of books, not out of life. He sate in his study, or in the Royal Library, where he has a post, when suddenly he became director of the theatre and censor of the pieces sent in. He was sickly, one-sided in judgment, and irritable: people may imagine the result. He spoke of my first poems very favorably; but my star soon sank for another, who was in the ascendant, a young lyrical poet, Paludan M ller; and, as he no longer loved, he hated me. That is the short history; indeed, in the selfsame Monthly Review the very poems which had formerly been praised were now condemned by the same judge, when they appeared in a new increased edition. There is a Danish proverb, "When the carriage drags, everybody pushes behind;" and I proved the truth of it now.

It happened that a new star in Danish literature ascended at this time. Heinrich Hertz published his "Letters from the Dead" anonymously: it was a mode of driving all the unclean things out of the temple. The deceased Baggesen sent polemical letters from Paradise, which resembled in the highest degree the style of that author. They contained a sort of apotheosis of Heiberg, and in part attacks upon Oehlenschl ger and Hauch. The old story about my orthographical errors was again revived; my name and my school-days in Slagelse were brought into connection with St. Anders.

I was ridiculed, or if people will, I was chastised. Hertz's book went through all Denmark; people spoke of nothing but him. It made it still more piquant that the author of the work could not be discovered. People were enraptured, and justly. Heiberg, in his "Flying Post," defended a few aesthetical insignificants, but not me. I felt the wound of the sharp knife deeply. My enemies now regarded me as entirely shut out from the world of spirits. I however in a short time published a little book, "Vignettes to the Danish Poets," in which I characterized the dead and the living authors in a few lines each, but only spoke of that which was good in them. The book excited attention; it was regarded as one of the best of my works; it was imitated, but the critics did not meddle with it. It was evident, on this occasion, as had already been the case, that the critics never laid hands on those of my works which were the most successful.

My affairs were now in their worst condition; and precisely in that same year in which a stipend for travelling had been conferred upon Hertz, I also had presented a petition for the same purpose. The universal opinion was that I had reached the point of culmination, and if I was to succeed in travelling it must be at this present time. I felt, what since then has become an acknowledged fact, that travelling would be the best school for me. In the mean time I was told that to bring it under consideration I must endeavor to obtain from the most distinguished poets and men of science a kind of recommendation; because this very year there were so many distinguished young men who were soliciting a stipend, that it would be difficult among these to put in an available claim. I therefore obtained recommendations for myself; and I am, so far as I know, the only Danish poet who was obliged to produce recommendations to prove that he was a poet.

And here also it is remarkable, that the men who recommended me have each one made prominent some very different qualification which gave me a claim: for instance, Oehlenschl ger, my lyrical power, and the earnestness that was in me; Ingemann, my skill in depicting popular life; Heiberg declared that, since the days of Wessel, no Danish poet had possessed so much humor as myself; Oersted remarked, every one, they who were against me as well as those who were for me, agreed on one subject, and this was that I was a *true* poet. Thiele expressed himself warmly and enthusiastically about the power which he had seen in me, combating against the oppression and the misery of life. I received a stipend for travelling; Hertz a larger and I a smaller one: and that also was quite in the order of things.

"Now be happy," said my friends, "make yourself aware of your unbounded good fortune! Enjoy the present moment, as it will probably be the only time in which you will get abroad. You shall hear what people say about you while you are travelling, and how we shall defend you; sometimes, however, we shall not be able to do that."

It was painful to me to hear such things said; I felt a compulsion of soul to be away, that I might, if possible, breathe freely; but sorrow is firmly seated on the horse of the rider. More than one sorrow oppressed my heart, and although I opened the chambers of my heart to the world, one or two of them I keep locked, nevertheless. On setting out on my journey, my prayer to God was that I might die far away from Denmark, or return strengthened for activity, and in a condition to produce works which should win for me and my beloved ones joy and honor.

Precisely at the moment of setting out on my journey, the form of my beloved arose in my heart. Among the few whom I have already named, there are two who exercised a great influence upon my life and my poetry, and these I must more particularly mention. A beloved mother, an unusually liberal-minded and well educated lady, Madame L ss c, had introduced me into her agreeable circle of friends; she often felt the deepest sympathy with me in my troubles; she always turned my attention to the beautiful in nature and the poetical in the details of life, and as almost everyone regarded me as a poet, she elevated my mind; yes, and if there be tenderness and purity in anything which I have written, they are among those things for which I have especially to be thankful to her. Another character of great importance to me was Collin's son Edward. Brought up under fortunate circumstances of life, he was possessed of that courage and determination which I wanted. I felt that he sincerely loved me, and I full of affection, threw myself upon him with my whole soul; he passed on calmly and practically through the business of life. I often mistook him at the very moment when he felt for me most deeply, and when he would gladly have infused into me a portion of his own character, — to me who was as a reed shaken by the wind. In the practical part of life, he, the younger, stood actively by my side, from the assistance which he gave in my Latin exercises, to the arranging the business of bringing out editions of my works. He has always remained the same; and were I to enumerate my friends, he would be placed by me as the first on the list. When the traveller leaves the mountains behind him, then for the first time he sees them in their true form: so is it also with friends.

I arrived at Paris by way of Cassel and the Rhine. I retained a vivid impression of all that I saw. The idea for a poem fixed itself firmer and firmer in my mind; and I hoped, as it became more clearly worked out, to propitiate by it my enemies. There is an old Danish folks-song of Agnete and the Merman, which bore an affinity to my own state of mind, and to the treatment of which I felt an inward impulse. The song tells that Agnete wandered solitarily along the shore, when a merman rose up from the waves and decoyed her by his speeches. She followed him to the bottom of the sea, remained there seven years, and bore him seven children. One day, as she sat by the cradle, she heard the church bells sounding down to her in the depths of the sea, and a longing seized her heart to go to church. By her prayers and tears she induced the merman to conduct her to the upper world again, promising soon to return. He prayed her not to forget his children, more especially the little one in the cradle; stopped up her ears and her mouth, and then led her upwards to the sea-shore. When, however, she entered the church, all the holy images, as soon as they saw her, a daughter of sin and from the depths of the sea, turned themselves round to the walls. She was affrighted, and would not return, although the little ones in her home below were weeping.

I treated this subject freely, in a lyrical and dramatic manner. I will venture to say that the whole grew out of my heart; all the recollections of our beechwoods and the open sea were blended in it.

In the midst of the excitement of Paris I lived in the spirit of the Danish folks-songs. The most heartfelt gratitude to God filled my soul, because I felt that all which I had, I had received through his mercy; yet at the same time I took a lively interest in all that surrounded me. I was present at one of the July festivals, in their first freshness; it was in the year 1833. I saw the unveiling of Napoleon's pillar. I gazed on the world-experienced King Louis Philippe, who is evidently defended by Providence. I saw the Duke of Orleans, full of health and the enjoyment of life, dancing at the gay people's ball, in the gay Maison de Ville. Accident led in Paris to my first meeting with Heine, the poet, who at that time occupied the throne in my poetical world. When I told him how happy this meeting and his kind words made me, he said that this could not very well be the case, else I should have sought him out. I replied, that I had not done so precisely because I estimated him so highly. I should have feared that he might have thought it ridiculous in me, an unknown Danish poet, to seek him out; "and," added I, "your sarcastic smile would deeply have wounded me." In reply, he said something friendly.

Several years afterwards, when we again met in Paris, he gave me a cordial reception, and I had a view into the brightly poetical portion of his soul.

Paul D port met me with equal kindness. Victor Hugo also received me.

During my journey to Paris, and the whole month that I spent there, I heard not a single word from home. Could my friends perhaps have nothing agreeable to tell me? At length, however, a letter arrived; a large letter, which cost a large sum in postage. My heart beat with joy and yearning impatience; it was, indeed, my first letter. I opened it, but I discovered not a single written word, nothing but a Copenhagen newspaper, containing a lampoon upon me, and that was sent to me all that distance with postage unpaid, probably by the anonymous writer himself. This abominable malice wounded me deeply. I have never discovered who the author was, perhaps he was one of those who afterwards called me friend, and pressed my hand. Some men have base thoughts: I also have mine.

It is a weakness of my country-people, that commonly, when abroad, during their residence in large cities, they almost live exclusively in company together; they must dine together, meet at the theatre, and see all the lions of the place in company. Letters are read by each other; news of home is received and talked over, and at last they hardly know whether they are in a foreign land or their own. I had given way to the same weakness in Paris; and in leaving it, therefore, determined for one month to board myself in some quiet place in Switzerland, and live only among the French, so as to be compelled to speak their language, which was necessary to me in the highest degree.

In the little city of Lodi, in a valley of the Jura mountains, where the snow fell in August, and the clouds floated below us, was I received by the amiable family of a wealthy watchmaker. They would not hear a word about payment. I lived among them and their friends as a relation, and when we parted the children wept. We had become friends, although I could not understand their patois; they shouted loudly into my ear, because they fancied I must be deaf, as I could not understand them. In the evenings, in that elevated region, there was a repose and a stillness in nature, and the sound of the evening bells ascended to us from the French frontier. At some distance from the city, stood a solitary house, painted white and clean; on descending through two cellars, the noise of a millwheel was heard, and the rushing waters of a river which flowed on here, hidden from the world. I often visited this place in my solitary rambles, and here I finished my poem of "Agnete and the Merman," which I had begun in Paris.

I sent home this poem from Lodi; and never, with my earlier or my later works, were my hopes so high as they were now. But it was received coldly. People said I had done it in imitation of Oehlenschl ger, who at one time sent home masterpieces. Within the last few years, I fancy, this poem has been somewhat more read, and has met with its friends. It was, however, a step forwards, and it decided, as it were, unconsciously to me, my pure lyrical phasis. It has been also of late critically adjudged in Denmark, that, notwithstanding that on its first appearance it excited far less attention than some of my earlier and less successful works, still that in this the poetry is of a deeper, fuller, and more powerful character than anything which I had hitherto produced.

This poem closes one portion of my life.

CHAPTER V

On the 5th of September, 1833, I crossed the Simplon on my way to Italy. On the very day, on which, fourteen years before, I had arrived poor and helpless in Copenhagen, did I set foot in this country of my longing and of my poetical happiness. It happened in this case, as it often does, by accident, without any arrangement on my part, as if I had preordained lucky days in the year; yet good fortune has so frequently been with me, that I perhaps only remind myself of its visits on my own self-elected days.

All was sunshine — all was spring! The vine hung in long trails from tree to tree; never since have I seen Italy so beautiful. I sailed on Lago Maggiore; ascended the cathedral of Milan; passed several days in Genoa, and made from thence a journey, rich in the beauties of nature, along the shore to Carrara. I had seen statues in Paris, but my eyes were closed to them; in Florence, before the Venus de Medici, it was for the first time as if scales fell from my eyes; a new world of art disclosed itself before me; that was the first fruit of my journey. Here it was that I first learned to understand the beauty of form — the spirit which reveals itself in form. The life of the people — nature — all was new to me; and yet as

82

strangely familiar as if I were come to a home where I had lived in my childhood. With a peculiar rapidity did I seize upon everything, and entered into its life, whilst a deep northern melancholy — it was not home-sickness, but a heavy, unhappy feeling — filled my breast. I received the news in Rome, of how little the poem of Agnete, which I had sent home, was thought of there; the next letter in Rome brought me the news that my mother was dead. I was now quite alone in the world.

It was at this time, and in Rome, that my first meeting with Hertz took place. In a letter which I had received from Collin, he had said that it would give him pleasure to hear that Hertz and I had become friends; but even without this wish it would have happened, for Hertz kindly offered me his hand, and expressed sympathy with my sorrow. He had, of all those with whom I was at that time acquainted, the most variously cultivated mind. We had often disputations together, even about the attacks which had been made upon me at home as a poet. He, who had himself given me a wound, said the following words, which deeply impressed themselves on my memory: "Your misfortune is, that you have been obliged to print everything; the public has been able to follow you step by step. I believe that even, a Goethe himself must have suffered the same fate, had he been in your situation." And then he praised my talent for seizing upon the characteristics of nature, and giving, by a few intuitive sketches, pictures of familiar life. My intercourse with him was very instructive to me, and I felt that I had one merciful judge more. I travelled in company with him to Naples, where we dwelt together in one house.

In Rome I also became first acquainted with Thorwaldsen. Many years before, when I had not long been in Copenhagen, and was walking through the streets

83

as a poor boy, Thorwaldsen was there too: that was on his first return home. We met one another in the street. I knew that he was a distinguished man in art; I looked at him, I bowed; he went on, and then, suddenly turning round, came back to me, and said, "Where have I seen you before? I think we know one another." I replied, "No, we do not know one another at all." I now related this story to him in Rome; he smiled, pressed my hand, and said, "Yet we felt at that time that we should become good friends." I read Agnete to him; and that which delighted me in his judgment upon it was the assertion, "It is just," said he, "as if I were walking at home in the woods, and heard the Danish lakes;" and then he kissed me.

One day, when he saw how distressed I was, and I related to him about the pasquinade which I had received from home in Paris, he gnashed his teeth violently, and said, in momentary anger, "Yes, yes, I know the people; it would not have gone any better with me if I had remained there; I should then, perhaps, not even have obtained permission to set up a model. Thank God that I did not need them, for then they know how to torment and to annoy." He desired me to keep up a good heart, and then things could not fail of going well; and with that he told me of some dark passages in his own life, where he in like manner had been mortified and unjustly condemned.

After the Carnival, I left Rome for Naples; saw at Capri the blue Grotto, which was at that time first discovered; visited the temple at Paestum, and returned in the Easter week to Rome, from whence I went through Florence and Venice to Vienna and Munich; but I had at that time neither mind nor heart for Germany; and when I thought on Denmark, I felt fear and distress of mind about the bad reception which I expected to find there. Italy, with its scenery and its people's life, occupied my soul, and towards this land I felt a yearning. My earlier life, and what I had now seen, blended themselves together into an image — into poetry, which I was compelled to write down, although I was convinced that it would occasion me more trouble than joy, if my necessities at home should oblige me to print it. I had written already in Rome the first chapter. It was my novel of "The Improvisatore."

At one of my first visits to the theatre at Odense, as a little boy, where, as I have already mentioned, the representations were given in the German language, I saw the Donauweibchen, and the public applauded the actress of the principal part. Homage was paid to her, and she was honored; and I vividly remember thinking how happy she must be.

Many years afterwards, when, as a student, I visited Odense, I saw, in one of the chambers of the hospital where the poor widows lived and where one bed stood by another, a female portrait hanging over one bed in a gilt frame. It was Lessing's Emilia Galotti, and represented her as pulling the rose to pieces; but the picture was a portrait. It appeared singular in contrast with the poverty by which it was surrounded.

"Whom does it represent?" asked I.

"Oh!" said one of the old women, "it is the face of the German lady, the poor lady who once was an actress!" And then I saw a little delicate woman, whose face was covered with wrinkles, and in an old silk gown that once had been black. That the once celebrated Singer, who, as the Donauweibchen, had been applauded by every one. This circumstance made an indelible impression upon me, and often occurred to my mind.

In Naples I heard Malibran for the first time. Her singing and acting surpassed anything which I had hitherto either heard or seen; and yet I thought the while of the miserably poor singer in the hospital of Odense: the two figures blended into the Annunciata of the novel. Italy was the back ground for that which had been experienced and that which was imagined. In August of 1834 I returned to Denmark. I wrote the first part of the book at Ingemann's, in Sor, in a little chamber in the roof, among fragrant lime-trees. I finished it in Copenhagen.

At this time my best friends, even, had almost given me up as a poet; they said that they had erred with regard to my talents. It was with difficulty that I found a publisher for the book. I received a miserable sum of money for it, and the "Improvisatore" made its appearance; was read, sold out, and again published. The critics were silent; the newspapers said nothing; but I heard all around me of the interest which was felt for the work, and the delight that it occasioned. At length the poet Carl Bagger, who was at that time the editor of a newspaper, wrote the first critique upon it, and began ironically, with the customary tirade against me — "that it was all over with this author, who had already passed his heyday;" — in short, he went the whole length of the tobacco and tea criticism, in order suddenly to dash out, and to express his extremely warm enthusiasm for me; and my book. People now laughed at me, but I wept. This was my mood of mind. I wept freely, and felt gratitude to God and man.

"To the Conference Councillor Collin and to his noble wife, in whom I found parents, whose children were brethren and sisters to me, whose house was my home, do

I here present the best of which I am possessed." — So ran the dedication. Many who formerly had been my enemy, now changed their opinion; and among these one became my friend, who, I hope, will remain so through the whole of my life. That was Hauch the poet, one of the noblest characters with whom I am acquainted. He had returned home from Italy after a residence of several years abroad, just at the time when Heiberg's vaudevilles were intoxicating the inhabitants of Copenhagen, and when my "Journey on Foot" was making me a little known. He commenced a controversy with Heiberg, and somewhat scoffed at me. Nobody called his attention to my better lyrical writings; I was described to him as a spoiled, petulant child of fortune. He now read my Improvisatore, and feeling that there was something good in me, his noble character evinced itself by his writing a cordial letter to me, in which he said, that he had done me an injustice, and offered me now the hand of reconciliation. From that time we became friends. He used his influence for me with the utmost zeal, and has watched my onward career with heartfelt friendship. But so little able have many people been to understand what is excellent in him, or the noble connection of heart between us two, that not long since, when he wrote a novel, and drew in it the caricature of a poet, whose vanity ended in insanity, the people in Denmark discovered that he had treated me with the greatest injustice, because he had described in it my weakness. People must not believe that this was the assertion of one single person, or a misapprehension of my character; no; and Hauch felt himself compelled to write a treatise upon me as a poet, that he might show what a different place he assigned to me.

But to return to the "Improvisatore." This book raised my sunken fortunes; collected my friends again around me, nay, even obtained for me new ones. For the first time I felt that I had obtained a due acknowledgment. The book was translated into German by Kruse, with a long title, *"Jugendleben und Tr ume eines italienischen Dichter's."* I objected to the title; but he declared that it was necessary in order to attract attention to the book.

Bagger had, as already stated, been the first to pass judgment on the work; after an interval of some time a second critique made its appearance, more courteous, it is true, than I was accustomed to, but still passing lightly over the best things in the book and dwelling on its deficiencies, and on the number of incorrectly written Italian words. And, as Nicolai's well-known book, "Italy as it really is," came out just then, people universally said, "Now we shall be able to see what it is about which Andersen has written, for from Nicolai a true idea of Italy may be obtained for the first time."

It was from Germany that resounded the first decided acknowledgment of the merits of my work, or rather perhaps its over estimation. I bow myself in joyful gratitude, like a sick man toward the sunshine, when my heart is grateful. I am not, as the Danish Monthly Review, in its critique of the "Improvisatore," condescended to assert, an unthankful man, who exhibits in his work a want of gratitude towards his benefactors. I was indeed myself poor Antonio who sighed under the burden which I had to bear, — *I,* the poor lad who ate the bread of charity. From Sweden also, later, resounded my praise, and the Swedish newspapers contained articles in praise of this work, which within the last two years has been equally warmly received in England, where Mary Howitt, the poetess, has translated it into English; the same good fortune also is said to have attended the book in Holland and Russia. Everywhere abroad resounded the loudest acknowledgments of its excellence.

There exists in the public a power which is stronger than all the critics and cliques. I felt that I stood at home on firmer ground, and my spirit again had moments in which it raised its wings for flight. In this alternation of feeling between gaiety and ill humor, I wrote my next novel, "O. T.," which is regarded by many persons in Denmark as my best work; — an estimation which I cannot myself award to it. It contains characteristic features of town life. My first Tales appeared before "O. T;" but this is not the place in which to speak of them. I felt just at this time a strong mental impulse to write, and I believed that I had found my true element in novel-writing. In the following year, 1837, I published "Only a Fiddler," a book which on my part had been deeply pondered over, and the details of which sprang fresh to the paper. My design was to show that talent is not genius, and that if the sunshine of good fortune be withheld, this must go to the ground, though without losing its nobler, better nature. This book likewise had its partisans; but still the critics would not vouchsafe to me any encouragement; they forgot that with years the boy becomes a man, and that people may acquire knowledge in other than the ordinary ways. They could not separate themselves from their old preconceived opinions. Whilst "O. T." was going through the press it was submitted sheet by sheet to a professor of the university, who had himself offered to undertake this work, and by two other able men also; notwithstanding all this, the Reviews said, "We find the usual grammatical negligence, which we always find in Andersen, in this work also." That which contributed likewise to place this book in the shade was the circumstance of Heiberg having at that time published his Every-day Stories, which were written in excellent language, and with good taste and truth. Their own merits, and the recommendation of their being Heiberg's, who was the beaming star of literature, placed them in the highest rank.

I had however advanced so far, that there no longer existed any doubt as to my poetical ability, which people had wholly denied to me before my journey to Italy. Still not a single Danish critic had spoken of the characteristics which are peculiar to my novels. It was not until my works appeared in Swedish that this was done, and then several Swedish journals went profoundly into the subject and analyzed my works with good and honorable intentions. The case was the same in Germany; and from this country too my heart was strengthened to proceed. It was not until last year that in Denmark, a man of influence, Hauch the poet, spoke of the novels in his already mentioned treatise, and with a few touches brought their characteristics prominently forward.

"The principal thing," says he, "in Andersen's best and most elaborate works, in those which are distinguished for the richest fancy, the deepest feeling, the most lively poetic spirit, is, of talent, or at least of a noble nature, which will struggle its way out of narrow and depressing circumstances. This is the case with his three novels, and with this purpose in view, it is really an important state of existence which he describes, — an inner world, which no one understands better than he, who has himself, drained out of the bitter cup of suffering and renunciation, painful and deep feelings which are closely related to those of his own experience, and from which Memory, who, according to the old significant myth, is the mother of the Muses, met him hand in hand with them. That which he, in these his works, relates to the world, deserves assuredly to be listened to with attention; because, at the same time that it may be only the most secret inward life of the individual, yet it is also the common lot of men of talent and genius, at least when these are in needy circumstances, as is the case of those who are here placed before our eyes. In so far as in his 'Improvisatore,' in 'O. T.,' and in 'Only a Fiddler,' he represents not only himself, in his own separate individuality, but at the same time the momentous combat which so many have to pass through, and which he understands so well, because in it his own life has developed itself; therefore in no instance can he be said to present to the reader what belongs to the world of illusion, but only that which bears witness to truth, and which, as is the case with all such testimony, has a universal and enduring worth.

"And still more than this, Andersen is not only the defender of talent and genius, but, at the same time, of every human heart which is unkindly and unjustly treated. And whilst he himself has so painfully suffered in that deep combat in which the Laocoon-snakes seize upon the outstretched hand; whilst he himself has been compelled to drink from that wormwood-steeped bowl which the cold-blooded and arrogant world so constantly offers to those who are in depressed circumstances, he is fully capable of giving to his delineations in this respect a truth and an earnestness, nay, even a tragic and a pain-awakening pathos that rarely fails of producing its effect on the sympathizing human heart. Who can read that scene in his 'Only a Fiddler,' in which the 'high-bred hound,' as the poet expresses it, 'turned away with disgust from the broken victuals which the poor youth received as alms, without recognizing, at the same time, that this is no game in which vanity seeks for a triumph, but that it expresses much more — human nature wounded to its inmost depths, which here speaks out its sufferings.'"

Thus is it spoken in Denmark of my works, after an interval of nine or ten years; thus speaks the voice of a noble, venerated man. It is with me and the critics as it is with wine, — the more years pass before it is drunk the better is its flavor.

During the year in which "The Fiddler" came out, I visited for the first time the neighboring country of Sweden. I went by the Gta canal to Stockholm. At that time nobody understood what is now called Scandinavian sympathies; there still existed a sort of mistrust inherited from the old wars between the two neighbor nations. Little was known of Swedish literature, and there were only very few Danes who could easily read and understand the Swedish language; — people scarcely knew Tegn r's Frithiof and Axel, excepting through translations. I had, however, read a few other Swedish authors, and the deceased, unfortunate Stagnelius pleased me more as a poet than Tegn r, who represented poetry in Sweden. I, who hitherto had only travelled into Germany and southern countries, where by this means, the departure from Copenhagen was also the departure from my mother tongue, felt, in this respect, almost at home in Sweden: the languages are so much akin, that of two persons each might read in the language of his own country, and yet the other understand him. It seemed to me, as a Dane, that Denmark expanded itself; kinship with the people exhibited itself, in many ways, more and more; and I felt, livingly, how near akin are Swedes, Danes, and Norwegians.

I met with cordial, kind people, — and with these I easily made acquaintance. I reckon this journey among the happiest I ever made. I had no knowledge of the character of Swedish scenery, and therefore I was in the highest degree astonished by the Trollh tta-voyage, and by the extremely picturesque situation of Stockholm. It sounds to the uninitiated half like a fairy-tale, when one says that the steam-boat goes up across the lakes over the mountains, from whence may be seen the outstretched pine and beechwoods below. Immense sluices heave up and lower the vessel again, whilst the travellers ramble through the woods. None of the cascades of Switzerland, none in Italy, not even that of Terni, have in them anything so imposing as that of Trollh tta. Such is the impression, at all events, which it made on me.

On this journey, and at this last-mentioned place, commenced a very interesting acquaintance, and one which has not been without its influence on me, — an acquaintance with the Swedish authoress, Fredrika Bremer. I had just been speaking with the captain of the steam-boat and some of the passengers about the Swedish authors living in Stockholm, and I mentioned my desire to see and converse with Miss Bremer.

"You will not meet with her," said the Captain, "as she is at this moment on a visit in Norway."

"She will be coming back while I am there," said I in joke; "I always am lucky in my journeys, and that which I most wish for is always accomplished.

"Hardly this time, however," said the captain.

A few hours after this he came up to me laughing, with the list of the newly arrived passengers in his hand. "Lucky fellow," said he aloud, "you take good fortune with you; Miss Bremer is here, and sails with us to Stockholm."

I received it as a joke; he showed me the list, but still I was uncertain. Among the new arrivals, I could see no one who resembled an authoress. Evening came on, and about midnight we were on the great Wener lake. At sunrise I wished to have a view of this extensive lake, the shores of which could scarcely be seen; and for this purpose I left the cabin. At the very moment that I did so, another passenger was also doing the same, a lady neither young nor old, wrapped in a shawl and cloak. I thought to myself, if Miss Bremer is on board, this must be she, and fell into discourse with her; she replied politely, but still distantly, nor would she directly answer my question, whether she was the authoress of the celebrated novels. She asked after my name; was acquainted with it, but confessed that she had read none of my works. She then inquired whether I had not some of them with me, and I lent her a copy of the "Improvisatore," which I had destined for Beskow. She vanished immediately with the volumes, and was not again visible all morning.

When I again saw her, her countenance was beaming, and she was full of cordiality; she pressed my hand, and said that she had read the greater part of the first volume, and that she now knew me.

The vessel flew with us across the mountains, through quiet inland lakes and forests, till it arrived at the Baltic Sea, where islands lie scattered, as in the Archipelago, and where the most remarkable transition takes place from naked cliffs to grassy islands, and to those on which stand trees and houses. Eddies and breakers make it here necessary to take on board a skilful pilot; and there are indeed some places where every passenger must sit quietly on his seat, whilst the eye of the pilot is riveted upon one point. On shipboard one feels the mighty power of nature, which at one moment seizes hold of the vessel and the next lets it go again.

Miss Bremer related many legends and many histories, which were connected with this or that island, or those farm-premises up aloft on the mainland.

In Stockholm, the acquaintance with her increased, and year after year the letters which have passed between us have strengthened it. She is a noble woman; the great truths of religion, and the poetry which lies in the quiet circumstances of life, have penetrated her being.

It was not until after my visit to Stockholm that her Swedish translation of my novel came out; my lyrical poems only, and my "Journey on Foot," were known to a few authors; these received me with the utmost kindness, and the lately deceased Dahlgr n, well known by his humorous poems, wrote a song in my honor — in short, I met with hospitality, and countenances beaming with Sunday gladness. Sweden and its inhabitants became dear to me. The city itself, by its situation and its whole picturesque appearance, seemed to me to emulate Naples. Of course, this last has the advantage of fine atmosphere, and the sunshine of the south; but the view of Stockholm is just as imposing; it has also some resemblance to Constantinople, as seen from Pera, only that the minarets are wanting. There prevails a great variety of coloring in the capital of Sweden; white painted buildings; frame-work houses, with the wood-work painted red; barracks of turf, with flowering plants; fir tree and birches look out from among the houses, and the churches with their balls and towers. The streets in Sdermalm ascend by flights of wooden steps up from the M lar lake, which is all active with smoking steam-vessels, and with boats rowed by women in gay-colored dresses.

I had brought with me a letter of introduction from Oersted, to the celebrated Berzelius, who gave me a good reception in the old city of Upsala. From this place I returned to Stockholm. City, country, and people, were all dear to me; it seemed to me, as I said before, that the boundaries of my native land had stretched themselves out, and I now first felt the kindredship of the three peoples, and in this feeling I wrote a Scandinavian song, a hymn of praise for all the three nations, for that which was peculiar and best in each one of them.

"One can see that the Swedes made a deal of him," was the first remark which I heard at home on this song.

Years pass on; the neighbors understand each other better; Oehlenschl ger. Fredrika Bremer, and Tegn r, caused them mutually to read each other's authors, and the foolish remains of the old enmity, which had no other foundation than that they did not know each other, vanished. There now prevails a beautiful, cordial relationship between Sweden and Denmark. A Scandinavian club has been established in Stockholm; and with this my song came to honor; and it was then said, "it will outlive everything that Andersen has written:" which was as unjust as when they said that it was only the product of flattered vanity. This song is now sung in Sweden as well as in Denmark.

On my return home I began to study history industriously, and made myself still further acquainted with the literature of foreign countries. Yet still the volume which afforded me the greatest pleasure was that of nature; and in a summer residence among the country-seats of Funen, and more especially at Lykkesholm, with its highly romantic site in the midst of woods, and at the

96

noble seat of Glorup, from whose possessor I met with the most friendly reception, did I acquire more true wisdom, assuredly, in my solitary rambles, than I ever could have gained from the schools.

The house of the Conference Councillor Collin in Copenhagen was at that time, as it has been since, a second father's house to me, and there I had parents, and brothers and sisters. The best circles of social life were open to me, and the student life interested me: here I mixed in the pleasures of youth. The student life of Copenhagen is, besides this, different from that of the German cities, and was at this time peculiar and full of life. For me this was most perceptible in the students' clubs, where students and professors were accustomed to meet each other: there was there no boundary drawn between the youthful and elder men of letters. In this club were to be found the journals and books of various countries; once a week an author would read his last work; a concert or some peculiar burlesque entertainment would take place. It was here that what may be called the first Danish people'scomedies took their origin, — comedies in which the events of the day were worked up always in an innocent, but witty and amusing manner. Sometimes dramatic representations were given in the presence of ladies for the furtherance of some noble purpose, as lately to assist Thorwaldsen's Museum, to raise funds for the execution of Bissen's statue in marble, and for similar ends. The professors and students were the actors. I also appeared several times as an actor, and convinced myself that my terror at appearing on the stage was greater than the talent which I perhaps possessed. Besides this, I wrote and arranged several pieces, and thus gave my assistance. Several scenes from this time, the scenes in the students' club, I have worked up in my romance of "O. T." The humor and love of life observable in various passages of this book, and in the little dramatic pieces written about this time, are owing to the influence of the family of Collin, where much good was done me in that respect, so that my morbid turn of mind was unable to gain the mastery of me. Collin's eldest married daughter, especially, exercised great influence over me, by her merry humor and wit. When the mind is yielding and elastic, like the expanse of ocean, it readily, like the ocean, mirrors its environments.

My writings, in my own country, were now classed among those which were always bought and read; therefore for each fresh work I received a higher payment. Yet, truly, when you consider what a circumscribed world the Danish reading world is, you will see that this payment could not be the most liberal. Yet I had to live. Collin, who is one of the men who do more than they promise, was my help, my consolation, my support.

At this time the late Count Conrad von Rantzau-Breitenburg, a native of Holstein, was Prime Minister in Denmark. He was of a noble, amiable nature, a highly educated man, and possessed of a truly chivalrous disposition. He carefully observed the movements in German and Danish literature. In his youth he had travelled much, and spent a long time in Spain and Italy, He read my "Improvisatore" in the original; his imagination was powerfully seized by it, and he spoke both at court and in his own private circles of my book in the warmest manner. He did not stop here; he sought me out, and became my benefactor and friend. One forenoon, whilst I was sitting solitarily in my little chamber, this friendly man stood before me for the first time. He belonged to that class of men who immediately inspire you with confidence; he besought me to visit him, and frankly asked me whether there were no means by which he could be of use to me. I hinted how oppressive it was to be *forced* to write in order to live, always to be forced to think of the morrow, and not move free from care, to be able to develop your mind and thoughts. He pressed my hand in a friendly manner, and promised to be an efficient friend. Collin and Oersted secretly associated themselves with him, and became my intercessors.

Already for many years there had existed, under Frederick VI., an institution which does the highest honor to the Danish government, namely, that beside the considerable sum expended yearly, for the travelling expenses of young literary men and artists, a small pension shall be awarded to such of them as enjoy no office emoluments. All our most important poets have had a share of this assistance, — Oehlenschl ger, Ingemann, Heiberg, C. Winther, and others. Hertz had just then received such a pension, and his future life made thus the more secure. It was my hope and my wish that the same good fortune might be mine — and it was. Frederick VI. granted me two hundred rix dollars banco yearly. I was filled with gratitude and joy. I was nolonger *forced* to write in order to live; I had a sure support in the possible event of sickness. I was less dependent upon the people about me. A new chapter of my life began.

CHAPTER VI

From this day forward, it was as if a more constant sunshine had entered my heart. I felt within myself more repose, more certainty; it was clear to me, as I glanced back over my earlier life, that a loving Providence watched over me, that all was directed for me by a higher Power; and the firmer becomes such a conviction, the more secure does a man feel himself. My childhood lay behind me, my youthful life began properly from this period; hitherto it had been only an arduous swimming against the stream. The spring of my life commenced; but still the spring had its dark days, its storms, before it advanced to settled summer; it has these in order to develop what shall then ripen. That which one of my dearest friends wrote to me on one of my later travels abroad, may serve as an introduction to what I have here to relate. He wrote in his own peculiar style: — "It is your vivid imagination which creates the idea of your being despised in Denmark; it is utterly untrue. You and Denmark agree admirably, and you would agree still better, if there were in Denmark no theatre — *Hinc illae lacrymae!* This cursed theatre. Is this, then, Denmark? and are you, then, nothing but a writer for the theatre?"

Herein lies a solid truth. The theatre has been the cave out of which most of the evil storms have burst upon me. They are peculiar people, these people of the theatre, — as different, in fact, from others, as Bedouins from Germans; from the first pantomimist to the first lover, everyone places himself systematically in one scale, and puts all the world in the other. The Danish theatre is a good theatre, it may indeed be placed on a level with the Burg theatre in Vienna; but the theatre in Copenhagen plays too great a part in conversation, and possesses in most circles too much importance. I am not sufficiently acquainted with the stage and the actors in other great cities, and therefore cannot compare them with our theatre; but ours has too little military discipline, and this is absolutely necessary where many people have to form a whole, even when that whole is an artistical one. The most distinguished dramatic poets in Denmark — that is to say, in Copenhagen, for there only is a theatre — have their troubles. Those actors and actresses who, through talent or the popular favor, take the first rank, very often place themselves above both the managers and authors. These must pay court to them, or they may ruin a part, or what is still worse, may spread abroad an unfavorable opinion of the piece previous to its being acted; and thus you have a coffee-house criticism before any one ought properly to know anything of the work. It is moreover characteristic of the people of Copenhagen, that when a new piece is announced, they do not say, "I am glad of it," but, "It will probably be good for nothing; it will be hissed off the stage." That hissing-off plays a great part, and is an amusement which fills the house; but it is not the bad actor who is hissed, no, the author and the composer only are the criminals; for them the scaffold is erected. Five minutes is the usual time, and the whistles resound, and the lovely women smile and felicitate themselves, like the Spanish ladies at their bloody

101

bullfights. All our most eminent dramatic writers have been whistled down, — as Oehlenschl ger, Heiberg, Oversko, and others; to say nothing of foreign classics, as Moli re. In the mean time the theatre is the most profitable sphere of labor for the Danish writer, whose public does not extend far beyond the frontiers. This had induced me to write the opera-text already spoken of, on account of which I was so severely criticised; and an internal impulse drove me afterwards to add some other works. Collin was no longer manager of the theatre, Councillor of Justice Molbeck had taken his place; and the tyranny which now commenced degenerated into the comic. I fancy that in course of time the manuscript volumes of the censorship, which are preserved in the theatre, and in which Molbeck has certainly recorded his judgments on received and rejected pieces, will present some remarkable characteristics. Over all that I wrote the staff was broken! One way was open to me by which to bring my pieces on the stage; and that was to give them to those actors who in summer gave representations at their own cost. In the summer of 1839 I wrote the vaudeville of "The Invisible One on Sprog," to scenery which had been painted for another piece which fell through; and the unrestrained merriment of the piece gave it such favor with the public, that I obtained its acceptance by the manager; and that light sketch still maintains itself on the boards, and has survived such a number of representations as I had never anticipated.

This approbation, however, procured me no further advantage, for each of my succeeding dramatic works received only rejection, and occasioned me only mortification. Nevertheless, seized by the idea and the circumstances of the little French narrative, "*Les paves,*" I determined to dramatise it; and as I had often heard that I did not possess the assiduity sufficient to work my mat riel well, I resolved to labor this drama — "The Mulatto" — from the beginning to the end, in the most diligent manner, and to compose it in alternately rhyming verse, as was then the fashion. It was a foreign subject of which I availed myself; but if verses are music, I at least endeavored to adapt my music to the text, and to let the poetry of another diffuse itself through my spiritual blood; so that people should not be heard to say, as they had done before, regarding the romance of Walter Scott, that the composition was cut down and fitted to the stage.

The piece was ready, and declared by able men, old friends, and actors who were to appear in it, to be excellent; a rich dramatic capacity lay in the mat riel, and my lyrical composition clothed this with so fresh a green, that people appeared satisfied. The piece was sent in, and was rejected by Molbeck. It was sufficiently known that what he cherished for the boards, withered there the first evening; but what he cast away as weeds were flowers for the garden — a real consolation for me. The assistant-manager, Privy Counsellor of State, Adler, a man of taste and liberality, became the patron of my work; and since a very favorable opinion of it already prevailed with the public, after I had read it to many persons, it was resolved on for representation. I had the honor to read it before my present King and Queen, who received me in a very kind and friendly manner, and from whom, since that time, I have experienced many proofs of favor and cordiality. The day of representation arrived; the bills were posted; I had not closed my eyes through the whole night from excitement and expectation; the people already stood in throngs before the theatre, to procure tickets, when royal messengers galloped through the streets, solemn groups collected, the minute guns pealed, — Frederick VI. had died this morning!

For two months more was the theatre closed, and was opened under Christian VIII., with my drama — "The Mulatto;" which was received with the most triumphant acclamation; but I could not at once feel the joy of it, I felt only relieved from a state of excitement, and breathed more freely.

This piece continued through a series of representations to receive the same approbation; many placed this work far above all my former ones, and considered that with it began my proper poetical career. It was soon translated into the Swedish, and acted with applause at the royal theatre in Stockholm. Travelling players introduced it into the smaller towns in the neighboring country; a Danish company gave it in the original language, in the Swedish city Malm, and a troop of students from the university town of Lund, welcomed it with enthusiasm. I had been for a week previous on a visit at some Swedish country houses, where I was entertained with so much cordial kindness that the recollection of it will never quit my bosom; and there, in a foreign country, I received the first public testimony of honor, and which has left upon me the deepest and most inextinguishable impression. I was invited by some students of Lund to visit their ancient town. Here a public dinner was given to me; speeches were made, toasts were pronounced; and as I was in the evening in a family circle, I was informed that the students meant to honor me with a serenade.

I felt myself actually overcome by this intelligence; my heart throbbed feverishly as I descried the thronging troop, with their blue caps, and arm-in-arm approaching the house. I experienced a feeling of humiliation; a most lively consciousness of my deficiencies, so that I seemed bowed to the very earth at the moment others were

104

elevating me. As they all uncovered their heads while I stepped forth, I had need of all my thoughts to avoid bursting into tears. In the feeling that I was unworthy of all this, I glanced round to see whether a smile did not pass over the face of some one, but I could discern nothing of the kind; and such a discovery would, at that moment, have inflicted on me the deepest wound.

After an hurrah, a speech was delivered, of which I clearly recollect the following words: — "When your native land, and the natives of Europe offer you their homage, then may you never forget that the first public honors were conferred on you by the students of Lund."

When the heart is warm, the strength of the expression is not weighed. I felt it deeply, and replied, that from this moment I became aware that I must assert a name in order to render myself worthy of these tokens of honor. I pressed the hands of those nearest to me, and returned them thanks so deep, so heartfelt, — certainly never was an expression of thanks more sincere. When I returned to my chamber, I went aside, in order to weep out this excitement, this overwhelming sensation. "Think no more of it, be joyous with us," said some of my lively Swedish friends; but a deep earnestness had entered my soul. Often has the memory of this time come back to me; and no noble-minded man, who reads these pages will discover a vanity in the fact, that I have lingered so long over this moment of life, which scorched the roots of pride rather than nourished them.

My drama was now to be brought on the stage at Malm; the students wished to see it; but I hastened my departure, that I might not be in the theatre at the time. With gratitude and joy fly my thoughts towards the Swedish University city, but I myself have not been there again since. In the Swedish newspapers the honors paid me were mentioned, and it was added that the Swedes were not unaware that in my own country there was a clique which persecuted me; but that this should not hinder my neighbors from offering me the honors which they deemed my due.

It was when I had returned to Copenhagen that I first truly felt how cordially I had been received by the Swedes; amongst some of my old and tried friends I found the most genuine sympathy. I saw tears in their eyes, tears of joy for the honors paid me; and especially, said they, for the manner in which I had received them. There is but one manner for me; at once, in the midst of joy, I fly with thanks to God.

There were certain persons who smiled at the enthusiasm; certain voices raised themselves already against "The Mulatto;" — "the mat riel was merely borrowed;" the French narrative was scrupulously studied. That exaggerated praise which I had received, now made me sensitive to the blame; I could bear it less easily than before, and saw more clearly, that it did not spring out of an interest in the matter, but was only uttered in order to mortify me. For the rest, my mind was fresh and elastic; I conceived precisely at this time the idea of "The Picture-Book without Pictures," and worked it out. This little book appears, to judge by the reviews and the number of editions, to have obtained an extraordinary popularity in Germany; it was also translated into Swedish, and dedicated to myself; at home, it was here less esteemed; people talked only of The Mulatto; and finally, only of the borrowed mat riel of it. I determined, therefore to produce a new dramatic work, in which both subject and development, in fact, everything should be of my own conception. I had the idea, and now wrote the tragedy of

The Moorish Maiden, hoping through this to stop the mouths of all my detractors, and to assert my place as a dramatic poet. I hoped, too, through the income from this, together with the proceeds of The Mulatto, to be able to make a fresh journey, not only to Italy, but to Greece and Turkey. My first going abroad had more than all besides operated towards my intellectual development; I was therefore full of the passion for travel, and of the endeavor to acquire more knowledge of nature and of human life.

My new piece did not please Heiberg, nor indeed my dramatic endeavors at all; his wife — for whom the chief part appeared to me especially to be written — refused, and that not in the most friendly manner, to play it. Deeply wounded, I went forth. I lamented this to some individuals. Whether this was repeated, or whether a complaint against the favorite of the public is a crime, enough: from this hour Heiberg became my opponent, — he whose intellectual rank I so highly estimated, — he with whom I would so willingly have allied myself, — and he who so often — I will venture to say it — I had approached with the whole sincerity of my nature. I have constantly declared his wife to be so distinguished an actress, and continue still so entirely of this opinion, that I would not hesitate one moment to assert that she would have a European reputation, were the Danish language as widely diffused as the German or the French. In tragedy she is, by the spirit and the geniality with which she comprehends and fills any part, a most interesting object; and in comedy she stands unrivalled.

The wrong may be on my side or not, — no matter: a party was opposed to me. I felt myself wounded, excited by many coincident annoyances there. I felt uncomfortable in my native country, yes, almost ill. I therefore left my piece to its fate, and, suffering and disconcerted, I hastened forth. In this mood I wrote a prologue to The Moorish Maiden; which betrayed my irritated mind far too palpably. If I would represent this portion of my life more clearly and reflectively it would require me to penetrate into the mysteries of the theatre, to analyze our aesthetic cliques, and to drag into conspicuous notice many individuals, who do not belong to publicity. Many persons in my place would, like me, have fallen ill, or would have resented it vehemently: perhaps the latter would have been the most sensible.

At my departure, many of my young friends amongst the students prepared a banquet for me; and amongst the elder ones who were present to receive me were Collin, Oehlenschl ger and Oersted. This was somewhat of sunshine in the midst of my mortification; songs by Oehlenschl ger and Hillerup were sung; and I found cordiality and friendship, as I quitted my country in distress. This was in October of 1840.

For the second time I went to Italy and Rome, to Greece and Constantinople — a journey which I have described after my own manner in A Poet's Bazaar.

In Holstein I continued some days with Count Rantzau-Breitenburg, who had before invited me, and whose ancestral castle I now for the first time visited. Here I became acquainted with the rich scenery of Holstein, heath and moorland, and then hastened by Nuremberg to Munich, where I again met with Cornelius and Schelling, and was kindly received by Kaulbach and Schelling. I cast a passing glance on the artistic life in Munich, but for the most part pursued my own solitary course, sometimes filled with the joy of life, but oftener despairing of my powers. I possessed a peculiar talent, that of lingering on the gloomy side of life, of extracting the bitter from it, of tasting it; and understood well, when the whole was exhausted, how to torment myself.

In the winter season I crossed the Brenner, remained some days in Florence, which I had before visited for a longer time, and about Christmas reached Rome. Here again I saw the noble treasures of art, met old friends, and once more passed a Carnival and Moccoli. But not alone was I bodily ill; nature around me appeared likewise to sicken; there was neither the tranquillity nor the freshness which attended my first sojourn in Rome. The rocks quaked, the Tiber twice rose into the streets, fever raged, and snatched numbers away. In a few days Prince Borghese lost his wife and three sons. Rain and wind prevailed; in short, it was dismal, and from home cold lotions only were sent me. My letters told me that The Moorish Maiden had several times been acted through, and had gone quietly off the stage; but, as was seen beforehand, a small public only had been present, and therefore the manager had laid the piece aside. Other Copenhagen letters to our countrymen in Rome spoke with enthusiasm of a new work by Heiberg; a satirical poem — A Soul after Death. It was but just out, they wrote; all Copenhagen was full of it, and Andersen was famously handled in it. The book was admirable, and I was made ridiculous in it. That was the whole which I heard, — all that I knew. No one told me what really was said of me; wherein lay the amusement and the ludicrous. It is doubly painful to be ridiculed when we don't know wherefore we are so. The information operated like molten lead dropped into a wound, and agonized me cruelly. It was not till after my return to Denmark that I read this book, and found that what was said of me in it, was really nothing in itself which was worth laying to heart. It was a jest over my celebrity "from Schonen to

Hundsr ck", which did not please Heiberg; he therefore sent my Mulatto and The Moorish Maiden to the infernal regions, where — and that was the most witty conceit — the condemned were doomed to witness the performance of both pieces in one evening; and then they could go away and lay themselves down quietly. I found the poetry, for the rest, so excellent, that I was half induced to write to Heiberg, and to return him my thanks for it; but I slept upon this fancy, and when I awoke and was more composed, I feared lest such thanks should be misunderstood; and so I gave it up.

In Rome, as I have said, I did not see the book; I only heard the arrows whizz and felt their wound, but I did not know what the poison was which lay concealed in them. It seemed to me that Rome was no joy-bringing city; when I was there before, I had also passed dark and bitter days. I was ill, for the first time in my life, truly and bodily ill, and I made haste to get away.

The Danish poet Holst was then in Rome; he had received this year a travelling pension. Hoist had written an elegy on King Frederick VI., which went from mouth to mouth, and awoke an enthusiasm, like that of Becker's contemporaneous Rhine song in Germany. He lived in the same house with me in Rome, and showed me much sympathy: with him I made the journey to Naples, where, notwithstanding it was March, the sun would not properly shine, and the snow lay on the hills around. There was fever in my blood; I suffered in body and in mind; and I soon lay so severely affected by it, that certainly nothing but a speedy blood-letting, to which my excellent Neapolitan landlord compelled me, saved my life.

In a few days I grew sensibly better; and I now proceeded by a French war steamer to Greece. Holst accompanied me on board. It was now as if a new life had risen for me; and in truth this was the case; and if this does not appear legibly in my later writings, yet it manifested itself in my views of life, and in my whole inner development. As I saw my European home lie far behind me, it seemed to me as if a stream of forgetfulness flowed of all bitter and rankling remembrances: I felt health in my blood, health in my thoughts, and freshly and courageously I again raised my head.

Like another Switzerland, with a loftier and clearer heaven than the Italian, Greece lay before me; nature made a deep and solemn impression upon me; I felt the sentiment of standing on the great battle field of the world, where nation had striven with nation, and had perished. No single poem can embrace such greatness; every scorched-up bed of a stream, every height, every stone, has mighty memoirs to relate. How little appear the inequalities of daily life in such a place! A kingdom of ideas streamed through me, and with such a fulness, that none of them fixed themselves on paper. I had a desire to express the idea, that the godlike was here on earth to maintain its contest, that it is thrust backward, and yet advances again victoriously through all ages; and I found in the legend of the Wandering Jew an occasion for it. For twelve months this fiction had been emerging from the sea of my thoughts; often did it wholly fill me; sometimes I fancied with the alchemists that I had dug up the treasure; then again it sank suddenly, and I despaired of ever being able to bring it to the light. I felt what a mass of knowledge of various kinds I must first acquire. Often at home, when I was compelled to hear reproofs on what they call a want of study, I had sat deep into the night, and had studied history in Hegel's Philosophy of

History. I said nothing of this, or other studies, or they would immediately have been spoken of, in the manner of an instructive lady, who said, that people justly complained that I did not possess learning enough. "You have really no mythology" said she; "in all your poems there appears no single God. You must pursue mythology; you must read Racine and Corneille." That she called learning; and in like manner every one had something peculiar to recommend. For my poem of Ahasuerus I had read much and noted much, but yet not enough; in Greece, I thought, the whole will collect itself into clearness. The poem is not yet ready, but I hope that it will become so to my honor; for it happens with the children of the spirit, as with the earthly ones, — they grow as they sleep.

In Athens I was heartily welcomed by Professor Ross, a native of Holstein, and by my countrymen. I found hospitality and a friendly feeling in the noble Prokesch-Osten; even the king and queen received me most graciously. I celebrated my birthday in the Acropolis.

From Athens I sailed to Smyrna, and with me it was no childish pleasure to be able to tread another quarter of the globe. I felt a devotion in it, like that which I felt as a child when I entered the old church at Odense. I thought on Christ, who bled on this earth; I thought on Homer, whose song eternally resounds hence over the earth. The shores of Asia preached to me their sermons, and were perhaps more impressive than any sermon in any church can be.

In Constantinople I passed eleven interesting days; and according to my good fortune in travel, the birthday of Mahomet itself fell exactly during my stay there. I saw the grand illumination, which completely transported me into the Thousand and One Nights.

Our Danish ambassador lived several miles from Constantinople, and I had therefore no opportunity of seeing him; but I found a cordial reception with the Austrian internuntius, Baron von St rmer. With him I had a German home and friends. I contemplated making my return by the Black Sea and up the Danube; but the country was disturbed; it was said there had been several thousand Christians murdered. My companions of the voyage, in the hotel where I resided, gave up this route of the Danube, for which I had the greatest desire, and collectively counselled me against it. But in this case I must return again by Greece and Italy — it was a severe conflict.

I do not belong to the courageous; I feel fear, especially in little dangers; but in great ones, and when an advantage is to be won, then I have a will, and it has grown firmer with years. I may tremble, I may fear; but I still do that which I consider the most proper to be done. I am not ashamed to confess my weakness; I hold that when out of our own true conviction we run counter to our inborn fear, we have done our duty. I had a strong desire to become acquainted with the interior of the country, and to traverse the Danube in its greatest expansion. I battled with myself; my imagination pointed to me the most horrible circumstances; it was an anxious night. In the morning I took counsel with Baron St rmer; and as he was of opinion that I might undertake the voyage, I determined upon it. From the moment that I had taken my determination, I had the most immovable reliance on Providence, and flung myself calmly on my fate. Nothing happened to me. The voyage was prosperous, and after the quarantine on the Wallachian frontier, which was painful enough to me, I arrived at Vienna on the twenty-first day of the journey. The sight of its towers, and the meeting with numerous Danes, awoke in me the thought of being speedily again at home. The idea bowed down my heart, and sad recollections and mortifications rose up within me once more.

In August, 1841, I was again in Copenhagen. There I wrote my recollections of travel, under the title of A Poet's Bazaar, in several chapters, according to the countries. In various places abroad I had met with individuals, as at home, to whom I felt myself attached. A poet is like the bird; he gives what he has, and he gives a song. I was desirous to give every one of those dear ones such a song. It was a fugitive idea, born, may I venture to say, in a grateful mood. Count Rantzau-Breitenburg, who had resided in Italy, who loved the land, and was become a friend and benefactor to me through my Improvisatore, must love that part of the book which treated of his country. To Liszt and Thalberg, who had both shown me the greatest friendship, I dedicated the portion which contained the voyage up the Danube, because one was a Hungarian and the other an Austrian. With these indications, the reader will easily be able to trace out the thought which influenced me in the choice of each dedication. But these appropriations were, in my native country, regarded as a fresh proof of my vanity; — "I wished to figure with great names, to name distinguished people as my friends."

The book has been translated into several languages, and the dedications with it. I know not how they have been regarded abroad; if I have been judged there as in Denmark, I hope that this explanation will change the opinion concerning them. In Denmark my Bazaar procured me the most handsome remuneration that I have as yet received, — a proof that I was at length read there. No regular criticism appeared upon it, if we except notices in some daily papers, and afterwards in the poetical attempt of a young writer who, a year before, had testified to me in writing his love, and his wish to do me honor; but who now, in his first public appearance, launched his satirical poem against his friend. I was personally attached to this young man, and am so still. He assuredly thought more on the popularity he would gain by sailing in the wake of Heiberg, than on the pain he would inflict on me. The newspaper criticism in Copenhagen was infinitely stupid. It was set down as exaggerated, that I could have seen the whole round blue globe of the moon in Smyrna at the time of the new moon. That was called fancy and extravagance, which there every one sees who can open his eyes. The new moon has a dark blue and perfectly round disk.

The Danish critics have generally no open eye for nature: even the highest and most cultivated monthly periodical of literature in Denmark censured me once because, in a poem I had described a rainbow by moonlight. That too was my fancy, which, said they, carried me too far. When I said in the Bazaar, "if I were a painter, I would paint this bridge; but, as I am no painter, but a poet, I must therefore speak," &c. Upon this the critic says, "He is so vain, that he tells us himself that he is a poet." There is something so pitiful in such criticism, that one cannot be wounded by it; but even when we are the most peaceable of men, we feel a desire to flagellate such wet dogs, who come into our rooms and lay themselves down in the best place in them. There might be a whole Fool's Chronicle written of all the absurd and shameless things which, from my first appearance before the public till this moment, I have been compelled to hear.

In the meantime the Bazaar was much read, and made what is called a hit. I received, connected with this book, much encouragement and many recognitions from individuals of the highest distinction in the realms of intellect in my native land.

The journey had strengthened me both in mind and body; I began to show indications of a firmer purpose, a more certain judgment. I was now in harmony with myself and with mankind around me.

Political life in Denmark had, at that time, arrived at a higher development, producing both good and evil fruits. The eloquence which had formerly accustomed itself to the Demosthenic mode, that of putting little pebbles in the mouth, the little pebbles of every day life, now exercised itself more freely on subjects of greater interest. I felt no call thereto, and no necessity to mix myself up in such matters; for I then believed that the politics of our times were a great misfortune to many a poet. Madame, politics are like Venus; they whom she decoys into her castle perish. It fares with the writings of these poets as with the newspapers: they are seized upon, read, praised, and forgotten. In our days every one wishes to rule; the subjective makes its power of value; people forget that that which is thought of cannot always be carried out, and that many things look very different when contemplated from the top of the tree, to what they did when seen from its roots. I will bow myself before him who is influenced by a noble conviction, and who only desires that which is conducive to good, be he prince or man of the people. Politics are no affair of mine. God has imparted to me another mission: that I felt, and that I feel still. I met in the so-called first families of the country a number of friendly, kind-hearted men, who valued the good that was in me, received me into their circles, and permitted me to participate in the happiness of their opulent summer residences; so that, still feeling independent, I could thoroughly give myself up to the pleasures of nature, the solitude of woods, and country life. There for the first time I lived wholly among the scenery of Denmark, and there I wrote the greater number of my fairy tales. On the banks of quiet lakes, amid the woods, on the green grassy pastures, where the game sprang past me and the stork paced along on his red legs, I heard nothing of politics, nothing of polemics; I heard no one practising himself in Hagel's phraseology. Nature, which was around me and within me, preached to me of my calling. I spent many happy days at the old house of Gisselfeld, formerly a monastery, which stands in the deepest solitude of the woods, surrounded with lakes and hills. The possessor of this fine place, the old Countess Danneskjold, mother of the Duchess of Augustenburg, was an agreeable and excellent lady, I was there not as a poor child of the people, but as a cordially-received guest. The beeches now overshadow her grave in the midst of that pleasant scenery to which her heart was allied.

Close by Gisselfeld, but in a still finer situation, and of much greater extent, lies the estate of Bregentoed, which belongs to Count Moltke, Danish Minister of Finance. The hospitality which I met with in this place, one of the richest and most beautiful of our country, and the happy, social life which surrounded me here, have diffused a sunshine over my life.

It may appear, perhaps, as if I desired to bring the names of great people prominently forward, and make a parade of them; or as if I wished in this way to offer a kind of thanks to my benefactors. They need it not, and I should be obliged to mention many other names still if this were my intention. I speak, however, only of these two places, and of Nys, which belongs to Baron Stampe, and which has become celebrated through Thorwaldsen. Here I lived much with the great sculptor, and here I became acquainted with one of my dearest young friends, the future possessor of the place.

Knowledge of life in these various circles has had great influence on me: among princes, among the nobility, and among the poorest of the people, I have met with specimens of noble humanity. We all of us resemble each other in that which is good and best.

Winter life in Denmark has likewise its attractions and its rich variety. I spent also some time in the country during this season, and made myself acquainted with its peculiar characteristics. The greatest part of my time, however, I passed in Copenhagen. I felt myself at home with the married sons and daughters of Collin, where a number of amiable children were growing up. Every year strengthened the bond of friendship between myself and the nobly-gifted composer, Hartmann: art and the freshness of nature prospered in his house. Collin was my counsellor in practical life, and Oersted in my literary affairs. The theatre was, if I may so say, my club. I visited it every evening, and in this very year I had received a place in the so-called court stalls. An author must, as a matter of course, work himself up to it. After the first accepted piece he obtains admission to the pit; after the second greater work, in the stalls, where the actors have their seats; and after three larger works, or a succession of lesser pieces, the poet is advanced to the best places. Here were to be found Thorwaldsen, Oehlenschl ger, and several older poets; and here also, in 1840, I obtained a place, after I had given in seven pieces. Whilst Thorwaldsen lived, I often, by his own wish, sate at his side. Oehlenschl ger was also my neighbor, and in many an evening hour, when no one dreamed of it, my soul was steeped in deep humility, as I sate between these great spirits. The different periods of my life passed before me; the time when I sate on the hindmost bench in the box of the female figurantes, as well as that in which, full of childish superstition, I knelt down there upon the stage and repeated the Lord's Prayer, just before the very place where I now sate among the first and the most distinguished men. At the time, perhaps, when a countryman of mine thus thought of and passed judgment upon me, — "there he sits, between the two great spirits, full of arrogance and pride;" he may now perceive by this acknowledgment how unjustly he has judged me. Humility, and prayer to God for strength to deserve my happiness, filled my heart. May He always enable me to preserve these feelings? I enjoyed the friendship of Thorwaldsen as well as of Oehlenschl ger, those two most distinguished stars in the horizon of the North. I may here bring forward their reflected glory in and around me.

There is in the character of Oehlenschl ger, when he is not seen in the circles of the great, where he is quiet and reserved, something so open and child-like, that no one can help becoming attached to him. As a poet, he holds in the North a position of as great importance as Goethe did in Germany. He is in his best works so penetrated by the spirit of the North, that through him it has, as it were, ascended upon all nations. In foreign countries he is not so much appreciated. The works by which he is best known are "Correggio" and "Aladdin;" but assuredly his masterly poem of "The Northern Gods" occupied a far higher rank: it is our "Iliad." It possesses power, freshness — nay, any expression of mine is poor. It is possessed of grandeur; it is the poet Oehlenschl ger in the bloom of

119

his soul. Hakon, Jarl, and Palnatoke will live in the poetry of Oehlenschl ger as long as mankind endures. Denmark, Norway, and Sweden have fully appreciated him, and have shown him that they do so, and whenever it is asked who occupies the first place in the kingdom of mind, the palm is always awarded to him. He is the true-born poet; he appears always young, whilst he himself, the oldest of all, surpasses all in the productiveness of his mind. He listened with friendly disposition to my first lyrical outpourings; and he acknowledged with earnestness and cordiality the poet who told the fairy-tales. My Biographer in the Danish Pantheon brought me in contact with Oehlenschl ger, when he said, "In our days it is becoming more and more rare for any one, by implicitly following those inborn impulses of his soul, which make themselves irresistibly felt, to step forward as an artist or a poet. He is more frequently fashioned by fate and circumstances than apparently destined by nature herself for this office. With the greater number of our poets an early acquaintance with passion, early inward experience, or outward circumstances, stand instead of the original vein of nature, and this cannot in any case be more incontestably proved in our own literature than by instancing Oehlenschl ger and Andersen. And in this way it may be explained why the former has been so frequently the object for the attacks of the critics, and why the latter was first properly appreciated as a poet in foreign countries where civilization of a longer date has already produced a disinclination for the compulsory rule of schools, and has occasioned a reaction towards that which is fresh and natural; whilst we Danes, on the contrary, cherish a pious respect for the yoke of the schools and the worn-out wisdom of maxims."

Thorwaldsen, whom, as I have already said, I had become acquainted with in Rome in the years 1833 and 1834, was expected in Denmark in the autumn of 1838, and great festive preparations were made in consequence. A flag was to wave upon one of the towers of Copenhagen as soon as the vessel which brought him should come in sight. It was a national festival. Boats decorated with flowers and flags filled the Rhede; painters, sculptors, all had their flags with emblems; the students' bore a Minerva, the poets' a Pegasus. It was misty weather, and the ship was first seen when it was already close by the city, and all poured out to meet him. The poets, who, I believe, according to the arrangement of Heiberg, had been invited, stood by their boat; Oehlenschl ger and Heiberg alone had not arrived. And now guns were fired from the ship, which came to anchor, and it was to be feared that Thorwaldsen might land before we had gone out to meet him. The wind bore the voice of singing over to us: the festive reception had already begun.

I wished to see him, and therefore cried out to the others, "Let us put off!"

"Without Oehlenschl ger and Heiberg?" asked some one.

"But they are not arrived, and it will be all over."

One of the poets declared that if these two men were not with us, I should not sail under that flag, and pointed up to Pegasus.

"We will throw it in the boat," said I, and took it down from the staff; the others now followed me, and came up just as Thorwaldsen reached land. We met with Oehlenschl ger and Heiberg in another boat, and they came over to us as the enthusiasm began on shore.

The people drew Thorwaldsen's carriage through the streets to his house, where everybody who had the slightest acquaintance with him, or with the friends of a friend of his, thronged around him. In the evening the artists gave him a serenade, and the blaze of the torches illumined the garden under the large trees, there was an exultation and joy which really and truly was felt. Young and old hastened through the open doors, and the joyful old man clasped those whom he knew to his breast, gave them his kiss, and pressed their hands. There was a glory round Thorwaldsen which kept me timidly back: my heart beat for joy of seeing him who had met me when abroad with kindness and consolation, who had pressed me to his heart, and had said that we must always remain friends. But here in this jubilant crowd, where thousands noticed every movement of his, where I too by all these should be observed and criticised — yes, criticised as a vain man who now only wished to show that he too was acquainted with Thorwaldsen, and that this great man was kind and friendly towards him — here, in this dense crowd, I drew myself back, and avoided being recognized by him. Some days afterwards, and early in the morning, I went to call upon him, and found him as a friend who had wondered at not having seen me earlier.

In honor of Thorwaldsen a musical-poetic academy was established, and the poets, who were invited to do so by Heiberg, wrote and read each one a poem in praise of him who had returned home. I wrote of Jason who fetched the golden fleece — that is to say, Jason-Thorwaldsen, who went forth to win golden art. A great dinner and a ball closed the festival, in which, for the first time in Denmark, popular life and a subject of great interest in the realms of art were made public.

From this evening I saw Thorwaldsen almost daily in company or in his studio: I often passed several weeks together with him at Nys, where he seemed to have firmly taken root, and where the greater number of his works, executed in Denmark, had their origin. He was of a healthful and simple disposition of mind, not without humor, and, therefore, he was extremely attached to Holberg the poet: he did not at all enter into the troubles and the disruptions of the world.

One morning at Nys — at the time when he was working at his own statue — I entered his work-room and bade him good morning; he appeared as if he did not wish to notice me, and I stole softly away again. At breakfast he was very parsimonious in the use of words, and when somebody asked him to say something at all events, he replied in his dry way: —

"I have said more during this morning than in many whole days, but nobody heard me. There I stood, and fancied that Andersen was behind me, for he came, and said good morning — so I told him a long story about myself and Byron. I thought that he might give one word in reply, and turned myself round; and there had I been standing a whole hour and chattering aloud to the bare walls."

We all of us besought him to let us hear the whole story yet once more; but we had it now very short.

"Oh, that was in Rome," said he, "when I was about to make Byron's statue; he placed himself just opposite to me, and began immediately to assume quite another countenance to what was customary to him. 'Will not you sit still?' said I; 'but you must not make these faces.' 'It is my expression,' said Byron. 'Indeed?' said I, and then

I made him as I wished, and everybody said, when it was finished, that I had hit the likeness. When Byron, however, saw it, he said, 'It does not resemble me at all; I look more unhappy.'"

"He was, above all things, so desirous of looking extremely unhappy," added Thorwaldsen, with a comic expression.

It afforded the great sculptor pleasure to listen to music after dinner with half-shut eyes, and it was his greatest delight when in the evening the game of lotto began, which the whole neighborhood of Nys was obliged to learn; they only played for glass pieces, and on this account I am able to relate a peculiar characteristic of this otherwise great man — that he played with the greatest interest on purpose to win. He would espouse with warmth and vehemence the part of those from whom he believed that he had received an injustice; he opposed himself to unfairness and raillery, even against the lady of the house, who for the rest had the most childlike sentiments towards him, and who had no other thought than how to make everything most agreeable to him. In his company I wrote several of my tales for children — for example, "Ole Luck Oin," ("Ole Shut Eye,") to which he listened with pleasure and interest. Often in the twilight, when the family circle sate in the open garden parlor, Thorwaldsen would come softly behind me, and, clapping me on the shoulder, would ask, "Shall we little ones hear any tales tonight?"

In his own peculiarly natural manner he bestowed the most bountiful praise on my fictions, for their truth; it delighted him to hear the same stories over and over again. Often, during his most glorious works, would he stand with laughing countenance, and listen to the stories of the Top and the Ball, and the Ugly Duckling. I possess a certain talent of improvising in my native tongue little poems and songs. This talent amused Thorwaldsen very much; and as he had modelled, at Nys, Holberg's portrait in clay, I was commissioned to make a poem for his work, and he received, therefore, the following impromptu: —

"No more shall Holberg live," by Death was said, "I crush the clay, his soul's bonds heretofore." "And from the formless clay, the cold, the dead," Cried Thorwaldsen, "shall Holberg live once more."

One morning, when he had just modelled in clay his great bas-relief of the Procession to Golgotha, I entered his study.

"Tell me," said he, "does it seem to you that I have dressed Pilate properly?"

"You must not say anything to him," said the Baroness, who was always with him: "it is right; it is excellent; go away with you!"

Thorwaldsen repeated his question.

"Well, then," said I, "as you ask me, I must confess that it really does appear to me as if Pilate were dressed rather as an Egyptian than as a Roman."

"It seems to me so too," said Thorwaldsen, seizing the clay with his hand, and destroying the figure.

"Now you are guilty of his having annihilated an immortal work," exclaimed the Baroness to me with warmth.

"Then we can make a new immortal work," said he, in a cheerful humor, and modelled Pilate as he now remains in the bas-relief in the Ladies' Church in Copenhagen.

His last birth-day was celebrated there in the country. I had written a merry little song, and it was hardly dry on the paper, when we sang it, in the early morning, before his door, accompanied by the music of jingling fire-irons, gongs, and bottles rubbed against a basket. Thorwaldsen himself, in his morning gown and slippers, opened his door, and danced round his chamber; swung round his Raphael's cap, and joined in the chorus. There was life and mirth in the strong old man.

On the last day of his life I sate by him at dinner; he was unusually good-humored; repeated several witticisms which he had just read in the Corsair, a well-known Copenhagen newspaper, and spoke of the journey which he should undertake to Italy in the summer. After this we parted; he went to the theatre, and I home.

On the following morning the waiter at the hotel where I lived said, "that it was a very remarkable thing about Thorwaldsen — that he had died yesterday."

"Thorwaldsen!" exclaimed I; "he is not dead, I dined with him yesterday."

"People say that he died last evening at the theatre," returned the waiter. I fancied that he might be taken ill; but still I felt a strange anxiety, and hastened immediately over to his house. There lay his corpse stretched out on the bed; the chamber was filled with strangers; the floor wet with melted snow; the air stifling; no one said a word: the Baroness Stampe sate on the bed and wept bitterly. I stood trembling and deeply agitated.

A farewell hymn, which I wrote, and to which Hartmann composed the music, was sung by Danish students over his coffin.

CHAPTER VII

In the summer of 1842, I wrote a little piece for the summer theatre, called, "The Bird in the Pear-tree," in which several scenes were acted up in the pear-tree. I had called it a dramatic trifle, in order that no one might expect either a great work or one of a very elaborate character. It was a little sketch, which, after being performed a few times, was received with so much applause, that the directors of the theatre accepted it; nay, even Mrs. Heiberg, the favorite of the public, desired to take a part in it. People had amused themselves; had thought the selection of the music excellent. I knew that the piece had stood its rehearsal — and then suddenly it was hissed. Some young men, who gave the word to hiss, had said to some others, who inquired from them their reasons for doing so, that the trifle had too much luck, and then Andersen would be getting too mettlesome.

I was not, on this evening, at the theatre myself, and had not the least idea of what was going on. On the following I went to the house of one of my friends. I had headache, and was looking very grave. The lady of the house met me with a sympathizing manner, took my hand, and said, "Is it really worth while to take it so much to heart?

There were only two who hissed, the whole house beside took your part."

"Hissed! My part! Have I been hissed?" exclaimed I.

It was quite comic; one person assured me that this hissing had been a triumph for me; everybody had joined in acclamation, and "there was only one who hissed."

After this, another person came, and I asked him of the number of those who hissed. "Two," said he. The next person said "three," and said positively there were no more. One of my most veracious friends now made his appearance, and I asked him upon his conscience, how many he had heard; he laid his hand upon his heart, and said that, at the very highest, they were five.

"No," said I, "now I will ask nobody more; the number grows just as with Falstaff; here stands one who asserts that there was only one person who hissed."

Shocked, and yet inclined to set it all right again, he replied, "Yes, that is possible, but then it was a strong, powerful hiss."

By my last works, and through a rational economy, I had now saved a small sum of money, which I destined to the purposes of a new journey to Paris, where I arrived in the winter of 1843, by way of D sseldorf, through Belgium.

Marmier had already, in the *R vue de Paris*, written an article on me, *La Vie d'un Po te*. He had also translated several of my poems into French, and had actually honored me with a poem which is printed in the above-named *R vue*. My name had thus reached, like a sound, the ears of some persons in the literary world, and I here met with a surprisingly friendly reception.

At Victor Hugo's invitation, I saw his abused *Burggraves*. Mr. and Mrs. Ancelot opened their house to me, and there I met Martinez della Rosa and other remarkable men of these times. Lamart ne seemed to me, in his domestic, and in his whole personal appearance, as the prince of them all. On my apologizing because I spoke such bad French, he replied, that he was to blame, because he did not understand the northern languages, in which, as he had discovered in late years, there existed a fresh and vigorous literature, and where the poetical ground was so peculiar that you had only to stoop down to find an old golden horn. He asked about the Trollh tta canal, and avowed a wish to visit Denmark and Stockholm. He recollected also our now reigning king, to whom, when as prince he was in Castellamare, he had paid his respects; besides this, he exhibited for a Frenchman, an extraordinary acquaintance with names and places in Denmark. On my departure he wrote a little poem for me, which I preserve amongst my dearest relics.

I generally found the jovial Alexander Dumas in bed, even long after mid-day: here he lay, with paper, pen, and ink, and wrote his newest drama. I found him thus one day; he nodded kindly to me, and said, "Sit down a minute; I have just now a visit from my muse; she will be going directly." He wrote on; spoke aloud; shouted a *viva!* sprang out of bed, and said, "The third act is finished!"

One evening he conducted me round into the various theatres, that I might see the life behind the scenes. We wandered about, arm in arm, along the gay Boulevard.

I also have to thank him for my acquaintance with Rachel. I had not seen her act, when Alexander Dumas asked me whether I had the desire to make her acquaintance. One evening, when she was to come out as Phedra he led me to the stage of the Th atre Fran ais. The Representation had begun, and behind the scenes, where a folding screen had formed a sort of room, in which stood a table with refreshments, and a few ottomans, sate the young girl who, as an author has said, understands how to chisel living statues out of Racine's and Corneille's blocks of marble. She was thin and slenderly formed, and looked very young. She looked to me there, and more particularly so afterwards in her own house, as an image of mourning; as a young girl who has just wept out her sorrow, and will now let her thoughts repose in quiet. She accosted us kindly in a deep powerful voice. In the course of conversation with Dumas, she forgot me. I stood there quite superfluous. Dumas observed it, said something handsome of me, and on that I ventured to take part in the discourse, although I had a depressing feeling that I stood before those who perhaps spoke the most beautiful French in all France. I said that I truly had seen much that was glorious and interesting, but that I had never yet seen a Rachel, and that on her account especially had I devoted the profits of my last work to a journey to Paris; and as, in conclusion, I added an apology on account of my French, she smiled and said, "When you say anything so polite as that which you have just said to me, to a Frenchwoman, she will always think that you speak well."

When I told her that her fame had resounded to the North, she declared that it was her intention to go to Petersburg and Copenhagen: "and when I come to your city", she said, "you must be my defender, as you are the only one there whom I know; and in order that we may become acquainted, and as you, as you say, are come to Paris especially on my account, we must see each other frequently. You will be welcome to me. I see my friends at my house every Thursday. But duty calls," said she, and offering us her hand, she nodded kindly, and then stood a few paces from us on the stage, taller, quite different, and with the expression of the tragic muse herself. Joyous acclamations ascended to where we sat.

As a Northlander I cannot accustom myself to the French mode of acting tragedy. Rachel plays in this same style, but in her it appears to be nature itself; it is as if all the others strove to imitate her. She is herself the French tragic muse, the others are only poor human beings. When Rachel plays people fancy that all tragedy must be acted in this manner. It is in her truth and nature, but under another revelation to that with which we are acquainted in the north.

At her house everything is rich and magnificent, perhaps too *recherch* . The innermost room was blue-green, with shaded lamps and statuettes of French authors. In the salon, properly speaking, the color which prevailed principally in the carpets, curtains, and bookcases was crimson. She herself was dressed in black, probably as she is represented in the well-known English steel engraving of her. Her guests consisted of gentlemen, for the greater part artists and men of learning. I also heard a few titles amongst them. Richly apparelled servants announced the names of the arrivals; tea was drunk and refreshments handed round, more in the German than the French style.

Victor Hugo had told me that he found she understood the German language. I asked her, and she replied in German, "ich kann es lesen; ich bin ja in Lothringen geboren; ich habe deutsche B cher, sehn Sie hier!" and she showed me Grillparzer's "Sappho," and then immediately continued the conversation in French. She expressed her pleasure in acting the part of Sappho, and then spoke of Schiller's "Maria Stuart," which character she has personated in a French version of that play. I saw her in this part, and she gave the last act especially with such a composure and tragic feeling, that she might have been one of the best of German actresses; but it was precisely in this very act that the French liked her least.

"My countrymen," said she, "are not accustomed to this manner, and in this manner alone can the part be given. No one should be raving when the heart is almost broken with sorrow, and when he is about to take an everlasting farewell of his friends."

Her drawing-room was, for the most part, decorated with books which were splendidly bound and arranged in handsome book-cases behind glass. A painting hung on the wall, which represented the interior of the theatre in London, where she stood forward on the stage, and flowers and garlands were thrown to her across the orchestra. Below this picture hung a pretty little book-shelf, holding what I call "the high nobility among the poets," — Goethe, Schiller, Calderon, Shakspeare, &c.

She asked me many questions respecting Germany and Denmark, art, and the theatre; and she encouraged me with a kind smile around her grave mouth, when I stumbled in French and stopped for a moment to collect myself, that I might not stick quite fast.

"Only speak," said she. "It is true that you do not speak French well. I have heard many foreigners speak my native language better; but their conversation has not been nearly as interesting as yours. I understand the sense of your words perfectly, and that is the principal thing which interests me in you."

The last time we parted she wrote the following words in my album: "L'art c'est le vrai! J'esp re que cet aphorisme ne semblera pas paradoxal un crivain si distingu comme M. Andersen."

I perceived amiability of character in Alfred de Vigny. He has married an English lady, and that which is best in both nations seemed to unite in his house. The last evening which I spent in Paris, he himself, who is possessed of intellectual status and worldly wealth, came almost at midnight to my lodging in the Rue Richelieu, ascended the many steps, and brought me his works under his arm. So much cordiality beamed in his eyes and he seemed to be so full of kindness towards me, that I felt affected by our separation.

I also became acquainted with the sculptor David. There was a something in his demeanor and in his straightforward manner that reminded me of Thorwaldsen and Bissen, especially of the latter. We did not meet till towards the conclusion of my residence in Paris. He lamented it, and said that he would execute a bust of me if I would remain there longer.

When I said, "But you know nothing of me as a poet, and cannot tell whether I deserve it or not," he looked earnestly in my face, clapped me on the shoulder, and said, "I have, however, read you yourself before your books. You are a poet."

At the Countess — — 's, where I met with Balzac, I saw an old lady, the expression of whose countenance attracted my attention. There was something so animated, so cordial in it, and everybody gathered about her. The Countess introduced me to her, and I heard that she was Madame Reybaud, the authoress of Les Epaves, the little story which I had made use of for my little drama of The Mulatto. I told her all about it, and of the representation of the piece, which interested her so much, that she became from this evening my especial protectress. We went out one evening together and exchanged ideas. She corrected my French and allowed me to repeat what did not appear correct to her. She is a lady of rich mental endowments, with a clear insight into the world, and she showed maternal kindness towards me.

I also again met with Heine. He had married since I was last here. I found him in indifferent health; but full of energy, and so friendly and so natural in his behavior towards me, that I felt no timidity in exhibiting myself to him as I was. One day he had been relating to his wife my story of the Constant Tin Soldier, and, whilst he said that I was the author of this story, he introduced me to her. She was a lively, pretty young lady. A troop of children, who, as Heine says, belonged to a neighbor, played about in their room. We two played with them whilst Heine copied out one of his last poems for me.

I perceived in him no pain-giving, sarcastic smile; I only heard the pulsation of a German heart, which is always perceptible in the songs, and which *must* live.

Through the means of the many people I was acquainted with here, among whom I might enumerate many others, as, for instance, Kalkbrenner, Gathy, &c., my residence in Paris was made very cheerful and rich in pleasure. I did not feel myself like a stranger there: I met with a friendly reception among the greatest and best. It was like a payment by anticipation of the talent which was in me, and through which they expected that I would some time prove them not to have been mistaken.

Whilst I was in Paris, I received from Germany, where already several of my works were translated and read, a delightful and encouraging proof of friendship. A German family, one of the most highly cultivated and amiable with whom I am acquainted, had read my writings with interest, especially the little biographical sketch prefixed to Only a Fiddler, and felt the heartiest goodwill towards me, with whom they were then not personally acquainted. They wrote to me, expressed their thanks for my works and the pleasure they had derived from them, and offered me a kind welcome to their house if I would visit it on my return home. There was a something extremely cordial and natural in this letter, which was the first that I received of this kind in Paris, and it also formed a remarkable contrast to that which was sent to me from my native land in the year 1833, when I was here for the first time.

In this way I found myself, through my writings, adopted, as it were, into a family to which since then I gladly betake myself, and where I know that it is not only as the poet, but as the man, that I am beloved. In how many instances have I not experienced the same kindness in foreign countries! I will mention one for the sake of its peculiarity.

There lived in Saxony a wealthy and benevolent family; the lady of the house read my romance of Only a Fiddler, and the impression of this book was such that she vowed that, if ever, in the course of her life, she should meet with a poor child which was possessed of great musical talents, she would not allow it to perish as the poor Fiddler had done. A musician who had heard her say this, brought to her soon after, not one, but two poor boys, assuring her of their talent, and reminding her of her promise. She kept her word: both boys were received into her house, were educated by her, and are now in the Conservatorium; the youngest of them played before me, and I saw that his countenance was happy and joyful. The same thing perhaps might have happened; the same excellent lady might have befriended these children without my book having been written: but notwithstanding this, my book is now connected with this as a link in the chain.

On my return home from Paris, I went along the Rhine; I knew that the poet Frieligrath, to whom the King of Prussia had given a pension, was residing in one of the Rhine towns. The picturesque character of his poems had delighted me extremely, and I wished to talk with him. I stopped at several towns on the Rhine, and inquired after him. In St. Goar, I was shown the house in which he lived. I found him sitting at his writing table, and he appeared annoyed at being disturbed by a stranger. I did not mention my name; but merely said that I could not pass St. Goar without paying my respects to the poet Frieligrath.

"That is very kind of you," said he, in a very cold tone; and then asked who I was.

"We have both of us one and the same friend, Chamisso!" replied I, and at these words he leapt up exultantly.

"You are then Andersen!" he exclaimed; threw his arms around my neck, and his honest eyes beamed with joy.

137

"Now you will stop several days here," said he. I told him that I could only stay a couple of hours, because I was travelling with some of my countrymen who were waiting for me.

"You have a great many friends in little St. Goar," said he; "it is but a short time since I read aloud your novel of O. T. to a large circle; one of these friends I must, at all events, fetch here, and you must also see my wife. Yes, indeed, you do not know that you had something to do in our being married."

He then related to me how my novel, Only a Fiddler, had caused them to exchange letters, and then led to their acquaintance, which acquaintance had ended in their being a married couple. He called her, mentioned to her my name, and I was regarded as an old friend. Such moments as these are a blessing; a mercy of God, a happiness — and how many such, how various, have I not enjoyed!

I relate all these, to me, joyful occurrences; they are facts in my life: I relate them, as I formerly have related that which was miserable, humiliating, and depressing; and if I have done so, in the spirit which operated in my soul, it will not be called pride or vanity; — neither of them would assuredly be the proper name for it. But people may perhaps ask at home, Has Andersen then never been attacked in foreign countries? I must reply, — no!

No regular attack has been made upon me, at least they have never at home called my attention to any such, and therefore there certainly cannot have been anything of the kind; — with the exception of one which made its appearance in Germany, but which originated in Denmark, at the very moment when I was in Paris.

A certain Mr. Boas made a journey at that time through Scandinavia, and wrote a book on the subject. In this he gave a sort of survey of Danish literature, which he also published in the journal called Die Grenzboten; in this I was very severely handled as a man and as a poet. Several other Danish poets also, as for instance, Christian Winter, have an equally great right to complain. Mr. Boas had drawn his information out of the miserable gossip of every-day life; his work excited attention in Copenhagen, and nobody there would allow themselves to be considered as his informants; nay even Holst the poet, who, as may be seen from the work, travelled with him through Sweden, and had received him at his house in Copenhagen, on this occasion published, in one of the most widely circulated of our papers, a declaration that he was in no way connected with Mr. Boas.

Mr. Boas had in Copenhagen attached himself to a particular clique consisting of a few young men; he had heard them full of lively spirits, talking during the day, of the Danish poets and their writings; he had then gone home, written down what he had heard and afterwards published it in his work. This was, to use the mildest term, inconsiderate. That my Improvisatore and Only a Fiddler did not please him, is a matter of taste, and to that I must submit myself. But when he, before the whole of Germany, where probably people will presume that what he has written is true, if he declare it to be, as is the case, the universal judgment against me in my native land; when he, I say, declared me before the whole of Germany, to be the most haughty of men, he inflicts upon me a deeper wound than he perhaps imagined. He conveyed the voice of a party, formerly hostile to me, into foreign countries. Nor is he true even in that which he represents; he gives circumstances as facts, which never took place.

In Denmark what he has written could not injure me, and many have declared themselves afraid of coming into contact with any one, who printed everything which he heard. His book was read in Germany, the public of which is now also mine; and I believe, therefore, that I may here say how faulty is his view of Danish literature and Danish poets; in what manner his book was received in my native land and that people there know in what way it was put together. But after I have expressed myself thus on this subject I will gladly offer Mr. Boas my hand; and if, in his next visit to Denmark, no other poet will receive him, I will do my utmost for him; I know that he will not be able to judge me more severely when we know each other, than when we knew each other not. His judgment would also have been quite of another character had he come to Denmark but one year later; things changed very much in a year's time. Then the tide had turned in my favor; I then had published my new children's stories, of which from that moment to the present there prevailed, through the whole of my native land, but one unchanging honorable opinion. When the edition of my collection of stories came out at Christmas 1843, the reaction began; acknowledgment of my merits were made, and favor shown me in Denmark, and from that time I have no cause for complaint. I have obtained and I obtain in my own land that which I deserve, nay perhaps, much more.

I will now turn to those little stories which in Denmark have been placed by every one, without any hesitation, higher than anything else I had hitherto written.

In the year 1835, some months after I published the Improvisatore, I brought out my first volume of Stories for Children, [Footnote: I find it very difficult to give a correct translation of the original word. The Danish is *Eventyr*, equivalent to the German *Abentheur*, or adventure; but adventures give in English a very different idea to this class of stories. The German word *M rchen*, gives the meaning completely, and this we may English by *fairy tale* or *legend*, but then neither of these words are fully correct with regard to Andersen's stories. In my translation of his "Eventyr fortalte for Born," I gave as an equivalent title, "Wonderful Stories for Children," and perhaps this near as I could come. — M. H.] which at that time was not so very much thought of. One monthly critical journal even complained that a young author who had just published a work like the Improvisatore, should immediately come out with anything so childish as the tales. I reaped a harvest of blame, precisely where people ought to have acknowledged the advantage of my mind producing something in a new direction. Several of my friends, whose judgment was of value to me, counselled me entirely to abstain from writing tales, as these were a something for which I had no talent. Others were of opinion that I had better, first of all, study the French fairy tale. I would willingly have discontinued writing them, but they forced themselves from me.

In the volume which I first published, I had, like Mus us, but in my own manner, related old stories, which I had heard as a child. The volume concluded with one which was original, and which seemed to have given the greatest pleasure, although it bore a tolerably near affinity to a story of Hoffman's. In my increasing disposition for children's stories, I therefore followed my own impulse, and invented them mostly myself. In the following year a new volume came out, and soon after that a third, in which the longest story, The Little Mermaid, was my own invention. This story, in an especial manner, created an interest which was only increased by the following volumes. One of these came out every Christmas, and before long no Christmas tree could exist without my stones.

Some of our first comic actors made the attempt of relating my little stories from the stage; it was a complete change from the declamatory poetry which had been heard to satiety. The Constant Tin Soldier, therefore, the Swineherd, and the Top and Ball, were told from the Royal stage, and from those of private theatres, and were well received. In order that the reader might be placed in the proper point of view, with regard to the manner in which I told the stories, I had called my first volume Stories told for Children. I had written my narrative down upon paper, exactly in the language, and with the expressions in which I had myself related them, by word of mouth, to the little ones, and I had arrived at the conviction that people of different ages were equally amused with them. The children made themselves merry for the most part over what might be called the actors, older people, on the contrary, were interested in the deeper meaning. The stories furnished reading for children and grown people, and that assuredly is a difficult task for those who will write children's stories. They met with open doors and open hearts in Denmark; everybody read them. I now removed the words "told for children," from my title, and published three volumes of "New Stories," all of which were of my own invention, and which were received in my own country with the greatest favor. I could not wish it greater; I felt a real anxiety in consequence, a fear of not being able to justify afterwards such an honorable award of praise.

A refreshing sunshine streamed into my heart; I felt courage and joy, and was filled, with a living desire of still more and more developing my powers in this direction,

— of studying more thoroughly this class of writing, and of observing still more attentively the rich wells of nature out of which I must create it. If attention be paid to the order in which my stories are written, it certainly will be seen that there is in them a gradual progression, a clearer working out of the idea, a greater discretion in the use of agency, and, if I may so speak, a more healthy tone and a more natural freshness may be perceived.

At this period of my life, I made an acquaintance which was of great moral and intellectual importance to me. I have already spoken of several persons and public characters who have had influence on me as the poet; but none of these have had more, nor in a nobler sense of the word, than the lady to whom I here turn myself; she, through whom I, at the same time, was enabled to forget my own individual self, to feel that which is holy in art, and to become acquainted with the command which God has given to genius.

I now turn back to the year 1840. One day in the hotel in which I lived in Copenhagen, I saw the name of Jenny Lind among those of the strangers from Sweden. I was aware at that time that she was the first singer in Stockholm. I had been that same year, in this neighbor country, and had there met with honor and kindness: I thought, therefore, that it would not be unbecoming in me to pay a visit to the young artist. She was, at this time, entirely unknown out of Sweden, so that I was convinced that, even in Copenhagen, her name was known only by few. She received me very courteously, but yet distantly, almost coldly. She was, as she said, on a journey with her father to South Sweden, and was come over to Copenhagen for a few days in order that she might see this city. We again parted distantly, and I had the impression of a very ordinary character which soon passed away from my mind.

In the autumn of 1843, Jenny Lind came again to Copenhagen. One of my friends, our clever ballet-master, Bournonville, who has married a Swedish lady, a friend of Jenny Lind, informed me of her arrival here and told me that she remembered me very kindly, and that now she had read my writings. He entreated me to go with him to her, and to employ all my persuasive art to induce her to take a few parts at the Theatre Royal; I should, he said, be then quite enchanted with what I should hear.

I was not now received as a stranger; she cordially extended to me her hand, and spoke of my writings and of Miss Fredrika Bremer, who also was her affectionate friend. The conversation was soon turned to her appearance in Copenhagen, and of this Jenny Lind declared that she stood in fear.

"I have never made my appearance," said she, "out of Sweden; everybody in my native land is so affectionate and kind to me, and if I made my appearance in Copenhagen and should be hissed! — I dare not venture on it!"

I said, that I, it was true, could not pass judgment on her singing, because I had never heard it, neither did I know how she acted, but nevertheless, I was convinced that such was the disposition at this moment in Copenhagen, that only a moderate voice and some knowledge of acting would be successful; I believed that she might safely venture.

Bournonville's persuasion obtained for the Copenhageners the greatest enjoyment which they ever had.

Jenny Lind made her first appearance among them as Alice in Robert le Diable — it was like a new revelation in the realms of art, the youthfully fresh voice forced itself into every heart; here reigned truth and nature; everything was full of meaning and intelligence. At one concert Jenny Lind sang her Swedish songs; there was something so peculiar in this, so bewitching; people thought nothing about the concert room; the popular melodies uttered by a being so purely feminine, and bearing the universal stamp of genius, exercised their omnipotent sway — the whole of Copenhagen was in raptures. Jenny Lind was the first singer to whom the Danish students gave a serenade: torches blazed around the hospitable villa where the serenade was given: she expressed her thanks by again singing some Swedish songs, and I then saw her hasten into the darkest corner and weep for emotion.

"Yes, yes," said she, "I will exert myself; I will endeavor, I will be better qualified than I am when I again come to Copenhagen."

On the stage, she was the great artiste, who rose above all those around her; at home, in her own chamber, a sensitive young girl with all the humility and piety of a child.

Her appearance in Copenhagen made an epoch in the history of our opera; it showed me art in its sanctity — I had beheld one of its vestals. She journeyed back to Stockholm, and from there Fredrika Bremer wrote to me: — "With regard to Jenny Lind as a singer, we are both of us perfectly agreed; she stands as high as any artist of our time can stand; but as yet you do not know her in her full greatness. Speak to her about her art, and you will wonder at the expansion of her mind, and will see her countenance beaming with inspiration. Converse then with her of God, and of the holiness of religion, and you will see tears in those innocent eyes; she is great as an artist, but she is still greater in her pure human existence!"

In the following year I was in Berlin; the conversation with Meyerbeer turned upon Jenny Lind; he had heard her sing the Swedish songs, and was transported by them.

"But how does she act?" asked he.

I spoke in raptures of her acting, and gave him at the same time some idea of her representation of Alice. He said to me that perhaps it might be possible for him to determine her to come to Berlin.

It is sufficiently well known that she made her appearance there, threw every one into astonishment and delight, and won for herself in Germany a European name. Last autumn she came again to Copenhagen, and the enthusiasm was incredible; the glory of renown makes genius perceptible to every one. People bivouacked regularly before the theatre, to obtain a ticket. Jenny Lind appeared still greater than ever in her art, because they had an opportunity of seeing her in many and such extremely different parts. Her Norma is plastic; every attitude might serve as the most beautiful model to a sculptor, and yet people felt that these were the inspiration of the moment, and had not been studied before the glass; Norma is no raving Italian; she is the suffering, sorrowing woman — the woman possessed of a heart to sacrifice herself for an unfortunate rival — the woman to whom, in the violence of the moment, the thought may suggest itself of murdering the children of a faithless lover, but who is immediately disarmed when she gazes into the eyes of the innocent ones.

"Norma, thou holy priestess," sings the chorus, and Jenny Lind has comprehended and shows to us this holy priestess in the aria, *Casta diva*. In Copenhagen she sang all her parts in Swedish, and the other singers sang theirs in Danish, and the two kindred languages mingled very beautifully together; there was no jarring; even in the Daughter of the Regiment where there is a deal of dialogue, the Swedish had something agreeable — and what acting! nay, the word itself is a contradiction — it was nature; anything as true never before appeared on the stage. She shows us perfectly the true child of nature grown up in the camp, but an inborn nobility pervades every movement. The Daughter of the Regiment and the Somnambule are certainly Jenny Land's most unsurpassable parts; no second can take their places in these beside her. People laugh, — they cry; it does them as much good as going to church; they become better for it. People feel that God is in art; and where God stands before us face to face there is a holy church.

"There will not in a whole century," said Mendelssohn, speaking to me of Jenny Lind, "be born another being so gifted as she;" and his words expressed my full conviction; one feels as she makes her appearance on the stage, that she is a pure vessel, from which a holy draught will be presented to us.

There is not anything which can lessen the impression which Jenny Lind's greatness on the stage makes, except her own personal character at home. An intelligent and child-like disposition exercises here its astonishing power;

147

she is happy; belonging, as it were, no longer to the world, a peaceful, quiet home, is the object of her thoughts — and yet she loves art with her whole soul, and feels her vocation in it. A noble, pious disposition like hers cannot be spoiled by homage. On one occasion only did I hear her express her joy in her talent and her self-consciousness. It was during her last residence in Copenhagen. Almost every evening she appeared either in the opera or at concerts; every hour was in requisition. She heard of a society, the object of which was, to assist unfortunate children, and to take them out of the hands of their parents by whom they were misused, and compelled either to beg or steal, and to place them in other and better circumstances. Benevolent people subscribed annually a small sum each for their support, nevertheless the means for this excellent purpose were small.

"But have I not still a disengaged evening?" said she; "let me give a night's performance for the benefit of these poor children; but we will have double prices!"

Such a performance was given, and returned large proceeds; when she was informed of this, and, that by this means, a number of poor children would be benefited for several years, her countenance beamed, and the tears filled her eyes.

"It is however beautiful," said she, "that I can sing so!"

I value her with the whole feeling of a brother, and I regard myself as happy that I know and understand such a spirit. God give to her that peace, that quiet happiness which she wishes for herself!

Through Jenny Lind I first became sensible of the holiness there is in art; through her I learned that one must forget oneself in the service of the Supreme. No books, no men have had a better or a more ennobling influence on me as the poet, than Jenny Lind, and I therefore have spoken of her so long and so warmly here.

I have made the happy discovery by experience, that inasmuch as art and life are more clearly understood by me, so much more sunshine from without has streamed into my soul. What blessings have not compensated me for the former dark days! Repose and certainty have forced themselves into my heart. Such repose can easily unite itself with the changing life of travel; I feel myself everywhere at home, attach myself easily to people, and they give me in return confidence and cordiality.

In the summer of 1844 I once more visited North Germany. An intellectual and amiable family in Oldenburg had invited me in the most friendly manner to spend some time at their house. Count von Rantzau-Breitenburg repeated also in his letters how welcome I should be to him. I set out on the journey, and this journey was, if not one of my longest, still one of my most interesting.

I saw the rich marsh-land in its summer luxuriance, and made with Rantzau several interesting little excursions. Breitenburg lies in the middle of woods on the river Str; the steam-voyage to Hamburg gives animation to the little river; the situation is picturesque, and life in the castle itself is comfortable and pleasant. I could devote myself perfectly to reading and poetry, because I was just as free as the bird in the air, and I was as much cared for as if I had been a beloved relation of the family. Alas it was the last time that I came hither; Count Rantzau had, even then, a presentiment of his approaching death. One day we met in the garden; he seized my hand, pressed it warmly, expressed his pleasure in my talents being acknowledged abroad, and his friendship for me, adding, in conclusion, "Yes, my dear young friend, God only knows but I have the firm belief that this year is the last time when we two shall meet here; my days will soon have run out their full course." He looked at me with so grave an expression, that it touched my heart deeply, but I knew not what to say. We were near to the chapel; he opened a little gate between some thick hedges, and we stood in a little garden, in which was a turfed grave and a seat beside it.

"Here you will find me, when you come the next time to Breitenburg," said he, and his sorrowful words were true. He died the following winter in Wiesbaden. I lost in him a friend, a protector, a noble excellent heart.

When I, on the first occasion, went to Germany, I visited the Hartz and the Saxon Switzerland. Goethe was still living. It was my most heartfelt wish to see him. It was not far from the Hartz to Weimar, but I had no letters of introduction to him, and, at that time, not one line of my writings was translated. Many persons had described Goethe to me as a very proud man, and the question arose whether indeed he would receive me. I doubted it, and determined not to go to Weimar until I should have written some work which would convey my name to Germany. I succeeded in this, but alas, Goethe was already dead.

I had made the acquaintance of his daughter-in-law Mrs. von Goethe, born at Pogwitsch, at the house of Mendelssohn Bartholdy, in Leipsig, on my return from Constantinople; this *spirituelle* lady received me with much kindness. She told me that her son Walter had been my friend for a long time; that as a boy he had made a whole play out of my Improvisatore; that this piece had been performed in Goethe's house; and lastly, that Walter, had once wished to go to Copenhagen to make my acquaintance. I thus had now friends in Weimar.

An extraordinary desire impelled me to see this city where Goethe, Schiller, Wieland, and Herder had lived, and from which so much light had streamed forth over the world. I approached that land which had been rendered sacred by Luther, by the strife of the Minnesingers on the Wartburg, and by the memory of many noble and great events.

On the 24th of June, the birthday of the Grand Duke, I arrived a stranger in the friendly town. Everything indicated the festivity which was then going forward, and the young prince was received with great rejoicing in the theatre, where a new opera was being given. I did not think how firmly, the most glorious and the best of all those whom I here saw around me, would grow into my heart; how many of my future friends sat around me here — how dear this city would become to me — in Germany my second home. I was invited by Goethe's worthy friend, the excellent Chancellor M ller, and I met with the most cordial reception from him. By accident I here met on my first call, with the Kammerherr Beaulieu de Marconnay, whom I had known in Oldenburg; he was now placed in Weimar. He invited me to remove to his house. In the course of a few minutes I was his stationary guest, and I felt "it is good to be here."

There are people whom it only requires a few days to know and to love; I won in Beaulieu, in these few days, a friend, as I believe, for my whole life. He introduced me

151

into the family circle, the amiable chancellor received me equally cordially; and I who had, on my arrival, fancied myself quite forlorn, because Mrs. von Goethe and her son Walter were in Vienna, was now known in Weimar, and well received in all its circles.

The reigning Grand Duke and Duchess gave me so gracious and kind a reception as made a deep impression upon me. After I had been presented, I was invited to dine, and soon after received an invitation to visit the hereditary Grand Duke and his lady, at the hunting seat of Ettersburg, which stands high, and close to an extensive forest. The old fashioned furniture within the house, and the distant views from the park into the Hartz mountains, produced immediately a peculiar impression. All the young peasants had assembled at the castle to celebrate the birthday of their beloved young Duke; climbing-poles, from which fluttered handkerchiefs and ribbons, were erected; fiddles sounded, and people danced merrily under the branches of the large and flowering limetrees. Sabbath splendor, contentment and happiness were diffused over the whole.

The young and but new married princely pair seemed to be united by true heartfelt sentiment. The heart must be able to forget the star on the breast under which it beats, if its possessor wish to remain long free and happy in a court; and such a heart, certainly one of the noblest and best which beats, is possessed by Karl Alexander of Saxe-Weimar. I had the happiness of a sufficient length of time to establish this belief. During this, my first residence here, I came several times to the happy Ettersburg. The young Duke showed me the garden and the tree on the trunk of which Goethe, Schiller, and Wieland had cut their names; nay even Jupiter himself had wished to add his to theirs, for his thunder-bolt had splintered it in one of the branches.

The intellectual Mrs. von Gross (Amalia Winter), Chancellor von M ller, who was able livingly to unroll the times of Goethe and to explain his Faust, and the soundly honest and child-like minded Eckermann belonged to the circle at Ettersburg. The evenings passed like a spiritual dream; alternately some one read aloud; even I ventured, for the first time in a foreign language to me, to read one of my own tales — the Constant Tin Soldier.

Chancellor von M ller accompanied me to the princely burial-place, where Karl August sleeps with his glorious wife, not between Schiller and Goethe, as I believed when I wrote — "the prince has made for himself a rainbow glory, whilst he stands between the sun and the rushing waterfall." Close beside the princely pair, who understood and valued that which was great, repose these their immortal friends. Withered laurel garlands lay upon the simple brown coffins, of which the whole magnificence consists in the immortal names of Goethe and Schiller. In life the prince and the poet walked side by side, in death they slumber under the same vault. Such a place as this is never effaced from the mind; in such a spot those quiet prayers are offered, which God alone hears.

I remained above eight days in Weimar; it seemed to me as if I had formerly lived in this city; as if it were a beloved home which I must now leave. As I drove out of the city, over the bridge and past the mill, and for the last time looked back to the city and the castle, a deep melancholy took hold on my soul, and it was to me as if a beautiful portion of my life here had its close; I thought

153

that the journey, after I had left Weimar, could afford me no more pleasure. How often since that time has the carrier pigeon, and still more frequently, the mind, flown over to this place! Sunshine has streamed forth from Weimar upon my poet-life.

From Weimar I went to Leipzig where a truly poetical evening awaited me with Robert Schumann. This great composer had a year before surprised me by the honor of dedicating to me the music which he had composed to four of my songs; the lady of Dr. Frege whose singing, so full of soul, has pleased and enchanted so many thousands, accompanied Clara Schumann, and the composer and the poet were alone the audience: a little festive supper and a mutual interchange of ideas shortened the evening only too much. I met with the old, cordial reception at the house of Mr. Brockhaus, to which from former visits I had almost accustomed myself. The circle of my friends increased in the German cities; but the first heart is still that to which we most gladly turn again.

I found in Dresden old friends with youthful feelings; my gifted half-countryman Dahl, the Norwegian, who knows how upon canvas to make the waterfall rush foaming down, and the birch-tree to grow as in the valleys of Norway, and Vogel von Vogelstein, who did me the honor of painting my portrait, which was included in the royal collection of portraits. The theatre intendant, Herr von L ttichau, provided me every evening with a seat in the manager's box; and one of the noblest ladies, in the first circles of Dresden, the worthy Baroness von Decken, received me as a mother would receive her son. In this character I was ever afterwards received in her family and in the amiable circle of her friends.

How bright and beautiful is the world! How good are human beings! That it is a pleasure to live becomes ever more and more clear to me.

Beaulieu's younger brother Edmund, who is an officer in the army, came one day from Tharand, where he had spent the summer months. I accompanied him to various places, spent some happy days among the pleasant scenery of the hills, and was received at the same time into various families.

I visited with the Baroness Decken, for the first time, the celebrated and clever painter Retsch, who has published the bold outlines of Goethe, Shakspeare, &c. He lives a sort of Arcadian life among lowly vineyards on the way to Meissen. Every year he makes a present to his wife, on her birthday, of a new drawing, and always one of his best; the collection has grown through a course of years to a valuable album, which she, if he die before her, is to publish. Among the many glorious ideas there, one struck me as peculiar; the Flight into Egypt. It is night; every one sleeps in the picture, — Mary, Joseph, the flowers and the shrubs, nay even the ass which carries her — all, except the child Jesus, who, with open round countenance, watches over and illumines all. I related one of my stories to him, and for this I received a lovely drawing, — a beautiful young girl hiding herself behind the mask of an old woman; thus should the eternally youthful soul, with its blooming loveliness, peep forth from behind the old mask of the fairy-tale. Retsch's pictures are rich in thought, full of beauty, and a genial spirit.

I enjoyed the country-life of Germany with Major Serre and his amiable wife at their splendid residence of Maren; it is not possible for any one to exercise greater hospitality than is done by these two kind-hearted people. A circle of intelligent, interesting individuals, were here assembled; I remained among them above eight days, and there became acquainted with Kohl the traveller, and the clever authoress, the Countess Hahn-Hahn, in whom I discerned a woman by disposition and individual character in whom confidence may be placed. Where one is well received there one gladly lingers. I found myself unspeakably happy on this little journey in Germany, and became convinced that I was there no stranger. It was heart and truth to nature which people valued in my writings; and, however excellent and praiseworthy the exterior beauty may be, however imposing the maxims of this world's wisdom, still it is heart and nature which have least changed by time, and which everybody is best able to understand.

I returned home by way of Berlin, where I had not been for several years; but the dearest of my friends there — Chamisso, was dead.

The fair wild swan which flew far o'er the earth, And laid its head upon a wild-swan's breast,

was now flown to a more glorious hemisphere; I saw his children, who were now fatherless and motherless. From the young who here surround me, I discover that I am grown older; I feel it not in myself. Chamisso's sons, whom I saw the last time playing here in the little garden with bare necks, came now to meet me with helmet and sword: they were officers in the Prussian service. I felt in a moment how the years had rolled on, how everything was changed and how one loses so many.

Yet is it not so hard as people deem, To see their soul's beloved from them riven; God has their dear ones, and in death they seem To form a bridge which leads them up to heaven.

I met with the most cordial reception, and have since then always met with the same, in the house of the Minister Savigny, where I became acquainted with the clever, singularly gifted Bettina and her lovely spiritual-minded daughter. One hour's conversation with Bettina during which she was the chief speaker, was so rich and full of interest, that I was almost rendered dumb by all this eloquence, this firework of wit. The world knows her writings, but another talent which she is possessed of, is less generally known, namely her talent for drawing. Here again it is the ideas which astonish us. It was thus, I observed, she had treated in a sketch an accident which had occurred just before, a young man being killed by the fumes of wine. You saw him descending half-naked into the cellar, round which lay the wine casks like monsters: Bacchanals and Bacchantes danced towards him, seized their victim and destroyed him! I know that Thorwaldsen, to whom she once showed all her drawings, was in the highest degree astonished by the ideas they contained.

It does the heart such good when abroad to find a house, where, when immediately you enter, eyes flash like festal lamps, a house where you can take peeps into a quiet, happy domestic life — such a house is that of Professor Weiss. Yet how many new acquaintance which were found, and old acquaintance which were renewed, ought I not to mention! I met Cornelius from Rome, Schelling from Munich, my countryman I might almost call him; Steffens, the Norwegian, and once again Tieck, whom I had not seen since my first visit to Germany. He was very much altered, yet his gentle, wise eyes were the same, the shake of his hand was the same. I felt that he loved me and wished me well. I must visit him in Potsdam, where he lived in ease and comfort. At dinner I became acquainted with his brother the sculptor.

From Tieck I learnt how kindly the King and Queen of Prussia were disposed towards me; that they had read my romance of Only a Fiddler, and inquired from Tieck about me. Meantime their Majesties were absent from Berlin. I had arrived the evening before their departure, when that abominable attempt was made upon their lives.

I returned to Copenhagen by Stettin in stormy weather, full of the joy of life, and again saw my dear friends, and in a few days set off to Count Moltke's in Funen, there to spend a few lovely summer days. I here received a letter from the Minister Count Rantzau-Breitenburg, who was with the King and Queen of Denmark at the watering-place of Fhr. He wrote, saying that he had the pleasure of announcing to me the most gracious invitation of their Majesties to Fhr. This island, as is well known, lies in the North Sea, not far from the coast of Sleswick, in the neighborhood of the interesting Halligs, those little islands which Biernatzky described so charmingly in his novels. Thus, in a manner wholly unexpected by me, I should see scenery of a very peculiar character even in Denmark.

The favor of my king and Queen made me happy, and I rejoiced to be once more in close intimacy with Rantzau. Alas, it was for the last time!

It was just now five and twenty years since I, a poor lad, travelled alone and helpless to Copenhagen. Exactly the five and twentieth anniversary would be celebrated by my being with my king and queen, to whom I was faithfully attached, and whom I at that very time learned to love with my whole soul. Everything that surrounded me, man and nature, reflected themselves imperishably in my soul. I felt myself, as it were, conducted to a point from which I could look forth more distinctly over the past five and twenty years, with all the good fortune and happiness which they had evolved for me. The reality frequently surpasses the most beautiful dream.

I travelled from Funen to Flensborg, which, lying in its great bay, is picturesque with woods and hills, and then immediately opens out into a solitary heath. Over this I travelled in the bright moonlight. The journey across the heath was tedious; the clouds only passed rapidly. We went on monotonously through the deep sand, and monotonous was the wail of a bird among the shrubby heath. Presently we reached moorlands. Long-continued rain had changed meadows and cornfields into great lakes; the embankments along which we drove were like morasses; the horses sank deeply into them. In many places the light carriage was obliged to be supported by the peasants, that it might not fall upon the cottages below the embankment. Several hours were consumed over each mile (Danish). At length the North Sea with its islands lay before me. The whole coast was an embankment, covered for miles with woven straw, against which the waves broke. I arrived at high tide. The wind was favorable, and in less than an hour I reached Fhr, which, after my difficult journey, appeared to me like a real fairy land.

The largest city, Wyck, in which are the baths, is exactly built like a Dutch town. The houses are only one story high, with sloping roofs and gables turned to the street. The many strangers there, and the presence of the court, gave a peculiar animation to the principal street. Well-known faces looked out from almost every house; the

Danish flag waved, and music was heard. I was soon established in my quarters, and every day, until the departure of their Majesties, had I the honor of an invitation from them to dinner, as well as to pass the evening in their circle. On several evenings I read aloud my little stories (M rchen) to the king and queen, and both of them were gracious and affectionate towards me. It is so good when a noble human nature will reveal itself where otherwise only the king's crown and the purple mantle might be discovered. Few people can be more amiable in private life than their present Majesties of Denmark. May God bless them and give them joy, even as they filled my breast with happiness and sunshine!

I sailed in their train to the largest of the Halligs, those grassy runes in the ocean, which bear testimony to a sunken country. The violence of the sea has changed the mainland into islands, has riven these again, and buried men and villages. Year after year are new portions rent away, and, in half a century's time, there will be nothing here but sea. The Halligs are now only low islets covered with a dark turf, on which a few flocks graze. When the sea rises these are driven into the garrets of the houses, and the waves roll over this little region, which is miles distant from the shore. Oland, which we visited, contains a little town. The houses stand closely side by side, as if, in their sore need they would all huddle together. They are all erected upon a platform, and have little windows, as in the cabin of a ship. There, in the little room, solitary through half the year, sit the wife and her daughters spinning. There, however, one always finds a little collection of books. I found books in Danish, German, and Frieslandish. The people read and work, and the sea rises round the houses, which lie like a wreck in the ocean. Sometimes, in the night, a ship, having mistaken the lights, drives on here and is stranded.

In the year 1825, a tempestuous tide washed away men and houses. The people sat for days and nights half naked upon the roofs, till these gave way; nor from Fhr nor the mainland could help be sent to them. The church-yard is half washed away; coffins and corpses were frequently exposed to view by the breakers: it is an appalling sight. And yet the inhabitants of the Halligs are attached to their little home. They cannot remain on the mainland, but are driven thence by home sickness.

We found only one man upon the island, and he had only lately arisen from a sick bed. The others were out on long voyages. We were received by girls and women. They had erected before the church a triumphal arch with flowers which they had fetched from Fhr; but it was so small and low, that one was obliged to go round it; nevertheless they showed by it their good will. The queen was deeply affected by their having cut down their only shrub, a rose bush, to lay over a marshy place which she would have to cross. The girls are pretty, and are dressed in a half Oriental fashion. The people trace their descent from Greeks. They wear their faces half concealed, and beneath the strips of linen which lie upon the head is placed a Greek fez, around which the hair is wound in plaits.

On our return, dinner was served on board the royal steamer; and afterwards, as we sailed in a glorious sunset through this archipelago, the deck of the vessel was changed to a dancing room. Young and old danced; servants flew hither and thither with refreshments; sailors stood upon the paddle-boxes and took the soundings, and their deep-toned voices might be heard giving the depth of the water. The moon rose round and large, and the promontory of Amrom assumed the appearance of a snow-covered chain of Alps.

I visited afterwards these desolate sand hills: the king went to shoot rabbits there. Many years ago a ship was wrecked here, on board of which were two rabbits, and from this pair Amrom is now stored with thousands of their descendants. At low tide the sea recedes wholly from between Amrom and Fhr, and then people drive across from one island to another; but still the time must be well observed and the passage accurately known, or else, when the tide comes, he who crosses will be inevitably lost. It requires only a few minutes, and then where dry land was large ships may sail. We saw a whole row of wagons driving from Fhr to Amrom. Seen upon the white sand and against the blue horizon, they seem to be twice as large as they really were. All around were spread out, like a net, the sheets of water, as if they held firmly the extent of sand which belonged to the ocean and which would be soon overflowed by it. This promontory brings to one's memory the mounds of ashes at Vesuvius; for here one sinks at every step, the wiry moor-grass not being able to bind together the loose sand. The sun shone burningly hot between the white sand hills: it was like a journey through the deserts of Africa.

A peculiar kind of rose, and the heath were in flower in the valleys between the hills; in other places there was no vegetation whatever; nothing but the wet sand on which the waves had left their impress; the sea had inscribed on its receding strange hieroglyphics. I gazed from one of the highest points over the North Sea; it was ebb-tide; the sea had retired above a mile; the vessels lay like dead fishes upon the sand, and awaiting the returning tide. A few sailors had clambered down and moved about on the sandy ground like black points. Where the sea itself kept the white level sand in movement, a long bank elevated itself, which, during the time of high-water, is concealed, and upon which occur many wrecks. I saw the lofty wooden tower which is here erected, and in which a cask is always kept filled with water, and a basket supplied with bread and brandy, that the unfortunate human beings, who are here stranded, may be able in this place, amid the swelling sea, to preserve life for a few days until it is possible to rescue them.

To return from such a scene as this to a royal table, a charming court-concert, and a little ball in the bath-saloon, as well as to the promenade by moonlight, thronged with guests, a little Boulevard, had something in it like a fairy tale, — it was a singular contrast.

As I sat on the above-mentioned five-and-twentieth anniversary, on the 5th of September, at the royal dinner-table, the whole of my former life passed in review before my mind. I was obliged to summon all my strength to prevent myself bursting into tears. There are moments of thankfulness in which, as it were, we feel a desire to press God to our hearts. How deeply I felt, at this time, my own nothingness; how all, all, had come from him. Rantzau knew what an interesting day this was to me. After dinner the king and the queen wished me happiness, and that so — *graciously*, is a poor word, — so cordially, so sympathizingly! The king wished me happiness in that which I had endured and won. He asked me about my first entrance into the world, and I related to him some characteristic traits.

In the course of conversation he inquired if I had not some certain yearly income; I named the sum to him.

"That is not much," said the king.

"But I do not require much," replied I, "and my writings procure me something."

The king, in the kindest manner, inquired farther into my circumstances, and closed by saying,

"If I can, in any way, be serviceable to your literary labors, then come to me."

In the evening, during the concert, the conversation was renewed, and some of those who stood near me reproached me for not having made use of my opportunity.

"The king," said they, "put the very words into your mouth."

But I could not, I would not have done it. "If the king," I said, "found that I required something more, he could give it to me of his own will."

And I was not mistaken. In the following year King Christian VIIIincreased my annual stipend, so that with this and that which my writings bring in, I can live honorably and free from care. My king gave it to me out of the pure good-will of his own heart. King Christian is enlightened, clear-sighted, with a mind enlarged by science; the gracious sympathy, therefore, which he has felt in my fate is to me doubly cheering and ennobling.

The 5th of September was to me a festival-day; even the German visitors at the baths honored me by drinking my health in the pump-room.

So many flattering circumstances, some people argue, may easily spoil a man, and make him vain. But, no; they do not spoil him, they make him on the contrary — better; they purify his mind, and he must thereby feel an impulse, a wish, to deserve all that he enjoys. At my parting-audience with the queen, she gave me a valuable ring as a remembrance of our residence at Fhr; and the king again expressed himself full of kindness and noble sympathy. God bless and preserve this exalted pair!

The Duchess of Augustenburg was at this time also at Fhr with her two eldest daughters. I had daily the happiness of being with them, and received repeated invitations to take Augustenburg on my return. For this purpose I went from Fhr to Als, one of the most beautiful islands in the Baltic. That little region resembles a blooming garden; luxuriant corn and clover-fields are enclosed, with hedges of hazels and wild roses; the peasants' houses are surrounded by large apple-orchards, full of fruit. Wood and hill alternate. Now we see the ocean, and now the narrow Lesser Belt, which resembles a river. The Castle of Augustenburg is magnificent, with its garden full of flowers, extending down to the very shores of the serpentine bay. I met with the most cordial reception, and found the most amiable family-life in the ducal circle. I spent fourteen days here, and was present at the birth-day festivities of the duchess, which lasted three days; among these festivities was racing, and the town and the castle were filled with people.

Happy domestic life is like a beautiful summer's evening; the heart is filled with peace; and everything around derives a peculiar glory. The full heart says "it is good to be here;" and this I felt at Augustenburg.

CHAPTER VIII

In the spring of 1844 I had finished a dramatic tale, "The Flower of Fortune." The idea of this was, that it is not the immortal name of the artist, nor the splendor of a crown which can make man happy; but that happiness is to be found where people, satisfied with little, love and are loved again. The scene was perfectly Danish, an idyllian, sunbright life, in whose clear heaven two dark pictures are reflected as in a dream; the unfortunate Danish poet Ewald and Prince Buris, who is tragically sung of in our heroic ballads. I wished to show, in honor of our times, the middle ages to have been dark and miserable, as they were, but which many poets only represent to us in a beautiful light.

Professor Heiberg, who was appointed censor, declared himself against the reception of my piece. During the last years I had met with nothing but hostility from this party; I regarded it as personal ill-will, and this was to me still more painful than the rejection of the pieces. It was painful for me to be placed in a constrained position with regard to a poet whom I respected, and towards whom, according to my own conviction, I had done everything in order to obtain a friendly relationship. A further attempt, however, must be made. I wrote to Heiberg, expressed myself candidly, and, as I thought, cordially, and entreated him to give me explicitly the reasons for his

166

rejection of the piece and for his ill-will towards me. He immediately paid me a visit, which I, not being at home when he called, returned on the following day, and I was received in the most friendly manner. The visit and the conversation belong certainly to the extraordinary, but they occasioned an explanation, and I hope led to a better understanding for the future.

He clearly set before me his views in the rejection of my piece. Seen from his point of sight they were unquestionably correct; but they were not mine, and thus we could not agree. He declared decidedly that he cherished no spite against me, and that he acknowledged my talent. I mentioned his various attacks upon me, for example, in the Intelligence, and that he had denied to me original invention: I imagined, however, that I had shown this in my novels; "But of these," said I, "you have read none; you, yourself have told me so."

"Yes, that is the truth," replied he; "I have not yet read them, but I will do so."

"Since then," continued I, "you have turned me and my Bazaar to ridicule in your poem called Denmark, and spoken about my fanaticism for the beautiful Dardanelles; and yet I have, precisely in that book, described the Dardanelles as not beautiful; it is the Bosphorus which I thought beautiful; you seem not to be aware of that; perhaps you have not read The Bazaar either?"

"Was it the Bosphorus?" said he, with his own peculiar smile; "yes, I had quite forgotten that, and, you see, people do not remember it either; the object in this case was only to give you a stab."

This confession sounded so natural, so like him, that I was obliged to smile. I looked into his clever eyes, thought how many beautiful things he had written, and I could not be angry with him. The conversation became more lively, more free, and he said many kind things to me; for example, he esteemed my stories very highly, and entreated me frequently to visit him. I have become more and more acquainted with his poetical temperament, and I fancy that he too will understand mine. We are very dissimilar, but we both strive after the same object. Before we separated he conducted me to his little observatory; now his dearest world. He seems now to live for poetry and now for philosophy, andufor which I fancy he is least of all calculated — for astronomy. I could almost sigh and sing,

Thou wast erewhile the star at which them gazest now!

My dramatic story came at length on the stage, and in the course of the season was performed seven times.

As people grow older, however much they may be tossed about in the world, some one place must be the true home; even the bird of passage has one fixed spot to which it hastens; mine was and is the house of my friend Collin. Treated as a son, almost grown up with the children, I have become a member of the family; a more heartfelt connection, a better home have I never known: a link broke in this chain, and precisely in the hour of bereavement, did I feel how firmly I have been engrafted here, so that I was regarded as one of the children.

If I were to give the picture of the mistress of a family who wholly loses her own individual *I* in her husband and children, I must name the wife of Collin; with the sympathy of a mother, she also followed me in sorrow

168

and in gladness. In the latter years of her life she became very deaf, and besides this she had the misfortune of being nearly blind. An operation was performed on her sight, which succeeded so well, that in the course of the winter she was able to read a letter, and this was a cause of grateful joy to her. She longed in an extraordinary manner for the first green of spring, and this she saw in her little garden.

I parted from her one Sunday evening in health and joy; in the night I was awoke; a servant brought me a letter. Collin wrote, "My wife is very ill; the children are all assembled here!" I understood it, and hastened thither. She slept quietly and without pain; it was the sleep of the just; it was death which was approaching so kindly and calmly. On the third day she yet lay in that peaceful slumber: then her countenance grew pale — and she was dead!

Thou didst but close thine eyes to gather in The large amount of all thy spiritual bliss; We saw thy slumbers like a little child's. O death! thou art all brightness and not shadow.

Never had I imagined that the departure from this world could be so painless, so blessed. A devotion arose in my soul; a conviction of God and eternity, which this moment elevated to an epoch in my life. It was the first death-bed at which I had been present since my childhood. Children, and children's children were assembled. In such moments all is holy around us. Her soul was love; she went to love and to God!

At the end of July, the monument of King Frederick VI. was to be uncovered at Skanderburg, in the middle of Jutland. I had, by solicitation, written the cantata for the festival, to which Hartmann had furnished the music, and this was to be sung by Danish students. I had been invited to the festival, which thus was to form the object of my summer excursion.

Skanderburg lies in one of the most beautiful districts of Denmark. Agreeable hills rise covered with vast beech-woods, and a large inland lake of a pleasing form extends among them. On the outside of the city, close by the church, which is built upon the ruins of an old castle, now stands the monument, a work of Thorwaldsen's. The most beautiful moment to me at this festival was in the evening, after the unveiling of the monument; torches were lighted around it, and threw their unsteady flame over the lake; within the woods blazed thousands of lights, and music for the dance resounded from the tents. Round about upon the hills, between the woods, and high above them, bonfires were lighted at one and the same moment, which burned in the night like red stars. There was spread over lake and land a pure, a summer fragrance which is peculiar to the north, in its beautiful summer nights. The shadows of those who passed between the monument and the church, glided gigantically along its red walls, as if they were spirits who were taking part in the festival.

I returned home. In this year my novel of the Improvisatore was translated into English, by the well-known authoress, Mary Howitt, and was received by her countrymen with great applause. O. T. and the Fiddler soon followed, and met with, as it seemed, the same reception. After that appeared a Dutch, and lastly a Russian translation of the Improvisatore. That which should never have ventured to have dreamed of was accomplished; my writings seem to come forth under a lucky star; they fly over all lands. There is something elevating, but at the same time, a something terrific in seeing one's thoughts spread so far, and among so many people; it is indeed, almost a fearful thing to belong to so many. The noble and the good in us becomes a blessing; but the bad, one's errors, shoot forth also, and involuntarily the thought forces itself from us: God! let me never write down a word of which I shall not be able to give an account to thee. A peculiar feeling, a mixture of joy and anxiety, fills my heart every time my good genius conveys my fictions to a foreign people.

Travelling operates like an invigorating bath to the mind; like a Medea-draft which always makes young again. I feel once more an impulse for it — not in order to seek up material, as a critic fancied and said, in speaking of my Bazaar; there exists a treasury of material in my own inner self, and this life is too short to mature this young existence; but there needs refreshment of spirit in order to convey it vigorously and maturely to paper, and travelling is to me, as I have said, this invigorating bath, from which I return as it were younger and stronger.

By prudent economy, and the proceeds of my writings, I was in a condition to undertake several journeys during the last year. That which for me is the most sunbright, is the one in which these pages were written. Esteem, perhaps over-estimation, but especially kindness, in short, happiness and pleasure have flowed towards me in abundant measure.

I wished to visit Italy for the third time, there to spend a summer, that I might become acquainted with the south in its warm season, and probably return thence by Spain and France. At the end of October, 1845, I left Copenhagen. Formerly I had thought when I set out on a journey, God! what wilt thou permit to happen to me on

171

this journey! This time my thoughts were, God, what will happen to my friends at home during this long time! And I felt a real anxiety. In one year the hearse may drive up to the door many times, and whose name may shine upon the coffin! The proverb says, when one suddenly feels a cold shudder, "now death passes over my grave." The shudder is still colder when the thoughts pass over the graves of our best friends.

I spent a few days at Count Moltke's, at Glorup; strolling players were acting some of my dramatic works at one of the nearest provincial towns. I did not see them; country life firmly withheld me. There is something in the late autumn poetically beautiful; when the leaf is fallen from the tree, and the sun shines still upon the green grass, and the bird twitters, one may often fancy that it is a spring-day; thus certainly also has the old man moments in his autumn in which his heart dreams of spring.

I passed only one day in Odense — I feel myself there more of a stranger than in the great cities of Germany. As a child I was solitary, and had therefore no youthful friend; most of the families whom I knew have died out; a new generation passes along the streets; and the streets even are altered. The later buried have concealed the miserable graves of my parents. Everything is changed. I took one of my childhood's rambles to the Marian-heights which had belonged to the Iversen family; but this family is dispersed; unknown faces looked out from the windows. How many youthful thoughts have been here exchanged!

One of the young girls who at that time sat quietly there with beaming eyes and listened to my first poem, when I came here in the summer time as a scholar from Slagelse, sits now far quieter in noisy Copenhagen, and has thence sent out her first writings into the world. Her German publisher thought that some introductory words from me might be useful to them, and I, the stranger, but the almost too kindly received, have introduced the works of this clever girl into Germany.

It is Henriette Hanck of whom I speak, the authoress of "Aunt Anna," and "An Author's Daughter." [Footnote: Since these pages were written, I have received from home the news of her death, in July, 1846. She was an affectionate daughter to her parents, and was, besides this, possessed of a deeply poetical mind. In her I have lost a true friend from the years of childhood, one who had felt an interest and a sisterly regard for me, both in my good and my evil days.] I visited her birth-place when the first little circle paid me homage and gave me joy. But all was strange there, I myself a stranger.

The ducal family of Augustenburg was now at Castle Gravenstein; they were informed of my arrival, and all the favor and the kindness which was shown to me on the former occasion at Augustenburg, was here renewed in rich abundance. I remained here fourteen days, and it was as if these were an announcement of all the happiness which should meet me when I arrived in Germany. The country around here is of the most picturesque description; vast woods, cultivated uplands in perpetual variety, with the winding shore of the bay and the many quiet inland lakes. Even the floating mists of autumn lent to the landscape a some what picturesque, something strange to the islander. Everything here is on a larger scale than on the island. Beautiful was it without, glorious was it within. I wrote here a new little story. The Girl with the Brimstone-matches; the only thing which I wrote upon this journey. Receiving the invitation to come often to Gravenstein and Augustenburg, I left, with a grateful heart, a place where I had spent such beautiful and such happy days.

Now, no longer the traveller goes at a snail's pace through the deep sand over the heath; the railroad conveys him in a few hours to Altona and Hamburg. The circle of my friends there is increased within the last years. The greater part of my time I spent with my oldest friends Count Hoik, and the resident Minister Bille, and with Zeise, the excellent translator of my stories. Otto Speckter, who is full of genius, surprised me by his bold, glorious drawings for my stories; he had made a whole collection of them, six only of which were known to me. The same natural freshness which shows itself in every one of his works, and makes them all little works of art, exhibits itself in his whole character. He appears to possess a patriarchal family, an affectionate old father, and gifted sisters, who love him with their whole souls. I wished one evening to go to the theatre; it was scarcely a quarter of an hour before the commencement of the opera: Speckter accompanied me, and on our way we came up to an elegant house.

"We must first go in here, dear friend," said he; "a wealthy family lives here, friends of mine, and friends of your stories; the children will be happy."

"But the opera," said I.

"Only for two minutes," returned he; and drew me into the house, mentioned my name, and the circle of children collected around me.

"And now tell us a tale," said he; "only one."

I told one, and then hastened away to the theatre.

"That was an extraordinary visit," said I.

"An excellent one; one entirely out of the common way; one entirely out of the common way!" said he exultingly; "only think; the children are full of Andersen and his stories; he suddenly makes his appearance amongst them, tells one of them himself, and then is gone! vanished! That is of itself like a fairy-tale to the children, that will remain vividly in their remembrance."

I myself was amused by it.

In Oldenburg my own little room, home-like and comfortable, was awaiting me. Hofrath von Eisendecker and his well-informed lady, whom, among all my foreign friends I may consider as my most sympathizing, expected me. I had promised to remain with them a fortnight, but I stayed much longer. A house where the best and the most intellectual people of a city meet, is an agreeable place of residence, and such a one had I here. A deal of social intercourse prevailed in the little city, and the theatre, in which certainly either opera or ballet was given, is one of the most excellent in Germany. The ability of Gall, the director, is sufficiently known, and unquestionably the nominationof the poet Mosen has a great and good influence. I have to thank him for enabling me to see one of the classic pieces of Germany, "Nathan the Wise," the principal part in which was played by Kaiser, who is as remarkable for his deeply studied and excellent tragic acting, as for his readings.

Moses, who somewhat resembles Alexander Dumas, with his half African countenance, and brown sparkling eyes, although he was suffering in body, was full of life and soul, and we soon understood one another. A trait of his little son affected me. He had listened to me with great devotion, as I read one of my stories; and when on the last day I was there, I took leave, the mother said that he must give me his hand, adding, that probably a long time must pass before he would see me again, the boy burst into tears. In the evening, when Mosen came into the theatre, he said to me, "My little Erick has two tin soldiers; one of them he has given me for you, that you may take him with you on your journey."

The tin soldier has faithfully accompanied me; he is a Turk: probably some day he may relate his travels.

Mosen wrote in the dedication of his "John of Austria," the following lines to me: —

Once a little bird flew over From the north sea's dreary strand; Singing, flew unto me over, Singing M rchen through the land. Farewell! yet again bring hither Thy warm heart and song together.

Here I again met with Mayer, who has described Naples and the Neapolitans so charmingly. My little stories interested him so much that he had written a little treaties on them for Germany, Kapellmeister Pott, and my countryman Jerndorff, belong to my earlier friends. I made every day new acquaintance, because all houses were open to me through the family with whom I was staying. Even the Grand Duke was so generous as to have me invited to a concert at the palace the day after my arrival, and later I had the honor of being asked to dinner. I received in this foreign court, especially, many unlooked-for favors. At the Eisendeckers and at the house of the parents of my friend Beaulieu — the Privy-Counsellor Beaulieu, at Oldenburg, I heard several times my little stones read in German.

I can read Danish very well, as it ought to be read, and I can give to it perfectly the expression which ought to be given in reading; there is in the Danish language a power which cannot be transfused into a translation; the Danish language is peculiarly excellent for this species of fiction. The stories have a something strange to me in German; it is difficult for me in reading it to put my Danish soul into it; my pronunciation of the German also is feeble, and with particular words I must, as it were, use an effort to bring them out — and yet people everywhere in Germany have had great interest in hearing me read them aloud. I can very well believe that the foreign pronunciation in the reading of these tales may be easily permitted, because this foreign manner approaches, in this instance, to the childlike; it gives a natural coloring to the reading. I saw everywhere that the most distinguished men and women of the most highly cultivated minds, listened to me with interest; people entreated me to read, and I did so willingly. I read for the first time my stories in a foreign tongue, and at a foreign court, before the Grand Duke of Oldenburg and a little select circle.

The winter soon came on; the meadows which lay under water, and which formed large lakes around the city, were already covered with thick ice; the skaters flew over it, and I yet remained in Oldenburg among my hospitable friends. Days and evenings slid rapidly away; Christmas approached, and this season I wished to spend in Berlin. But what are distances in our days? — the steam-carriage goes from Hanover to Berlin in one day! I must away from the beloved ones, from children and old people, who were near, as it were, to my heart.

I was astonished in the highest degree on taking leave of the Grand Duke, to receive from him, as a mark of his favor and as a keepsake, a valuable ring. I shall always preserve it, like every other remembrance of this country, where I have found and where I possess true friends.

When I was in Berlin on the former occasion, I was invited, as the author of the Improvisatore, to the Italian Society, into which only those who have visited Italy can be admitted. Here I saw Rauch for the first time, who with his white hair and his powerful, manly figure, is not unlike Thorwaldsen. Nobody introduced me to him, and I did not venture to present myself, and therefore walked alone about his studio, like the other strangers. Afterwards I became personally acquainted with him at the house of the Prussian Ambassador, in Copenhagen; I now hastened to him.

He was in the highest degree captivated by my little stories, pressed me to his breast, and expressed the highest praise, but which was honestly meant. Such a momentary estimation or over-estimation from a man of genius erases many a dark shadow from the mind. I received from Rauch my first welcome in Berlin: he told me what a large circle of friends I had in the capital of Prussia. I must acknowledge that it was so. They were of the noblest in mind as well as the first in rank, in art, and in science. Alexander von Humboldt, Prince Radziwil, Savigny, and many others never to be forgotten.

I had already, on the former occasion, visited the brothers Grimm, but I had not at that time made much progress with the acquaintance. I had not brought any letters of introduction to them with me, because people had told me, and I myself believed it, that if I were known by any body in Berlin, it must be the brothers Grimm. I therefore sought out their residence. The servant-maid asked me with which of the brothers I wished to speak.

"With the one who has written the most," said I, because I did not know, at that time, which of them had most interested himself in the M rchen.

"Jacob is the most learned," said the maidservant.

"Well, then, take me to him."

I entered the room, and Jacob Grimm, with his knowing and strongly-marked countenance, stood before me.

"I come to you," said I, "without letters of introduction, because I hope that my name is not wholly unknown to you."

"Who are you?" asked he.

I told him, and Jacob Grimm said, in a half-embarrassed voice, "I do not remember to have heard this name; what have you written?"

It was now my turn to be embarrassed in a high degree: but I now mentioned my little stories.

"I do not know them," said he; "but mention to me some other of your writings, because I certainly must have heard them spoken of."

I named the titles of several; but he shook his head. I felt myself quite unlucky.

"But what must you think of me," said I, "that I come to you as a total stranger, and enumerate myself what I have written: you must know me! There has been published in Denmark a collection of the M rchen of all nations, which is dedicated to you, and in it there is at least one story of mine."

"No," said he good-humoredly, but as much embarrassed as myself; "I have not read even that, but it delights me to make your acquaintance; allow me to conduct you to my brother Wilhelm?"

"No, I thank you," said I, only wishing now to get away; I had fared badly enough with one brother. I pressed his hand and hurried from the house.

That same month Jacob Grimm went to Copenhagen; immediately on his arrival, and while yet in his travelling dress, did the amiable kind man hasten up to me. He now knew me, and he came to me with cordiality. I was just then standing and packing my clothes in a trunk for a journey to the country; I had only a few minutes time: by this means my reception of him was just as laconic as had been his of me in Berlin.

Now, however, we met in Berlin as old acquaintance. Jacob Grimm is one of those characters whom one must love and attach oneself to.

One evening, as I was reading one of my little stories at the Countess Bismark-Bohlen's, there in the little circle one person in particular who listened with evident fellowship of feeling, and who expressed himself in a peculiar and sensible manner on the subject, — this was Jacob's brother, Wilhelm Grimm.

"I should have known you very well, if you had come to me," said he, "the last time you were here."

I saw these two highly-gifted and amiable brothers almost daily; the circles into which I was invited seemed also to be theirs, and it was my desire and pleasure that they should listen to my little stories, that they should participate in them, they whose names will be always spoken as long as the German *Volks M rchen* are read.

The fact of my not being known to Jacob Grimm on my first visit to Berlin, had so disconcerted me, that when any one asked me whether I had been well received in this city, I shook my head doubtfully and said, "but Grimm did not know me."

I was told that Tieck was ill — could see no one; I therefore only sent in my card. Some days afterwards I met at a friend's house, where Rauch's birth-day was being celebrated, Tieck, the sculptor, who told me that his brother had lately waited two hours for me at dinner. I went to him and discovered that he had sent me an invitation, which, however, had been taken to a wrong inn. A fresh invitation was given, and I passed some delightfully cheerful hours with Raumer the historian, and with the widow and daughter of Steffens. There is a music in Tieck's voice, a spirituality in his intelligent eyes, which age cannot lessen, but, on the contrary, must increase. The Elves, perhaps the most beautiful story which has been conceived in our time, would alone be sufficient, had Tieck written nothing else, to make his name immortal. As the author of *M rchen*, I bow myself before him, the elder and The master, and who was the first German poet, who many years before pressed me to his breast, as if it were to consecrate me, to walk in the same path with himself.

The old friends had all to be visited; but the number of new ones grew with each day. One invitation followed another. It required considerable physical power to support so much good-will. I remained in Berlin about three weeks, and the time seemed to pass more rapidly with each succeeding day. I was, as it were, overcome by kindness. I, at length, had no other prospect for repose than to seat myself in a railway-carriage, and fly away out of the country.

And yet amid these social festivities, with all the amiable zeal and interest that then was felt for me, I had one disengaged evening; one evening on which I suddenly felt solitude in its most oppressive form; Christmas-eve, that very evening of all others on which I would most willingly witness something festal, willingly stand beside a Christmas-tree, gladdening myself with the joy of children, and seeing the parents joyfully become children again. Every one of the many families in which I in truth felt that I was received as a relation, had fancied, as I afterwards discovered, that I must be invited out; but I sat quite alone in my room at the inn, and thought on home. I seated myself at the open window, and gazed up to the starry heavens, which was the Christmas-tree that was lighted for me.

"Father in Heaven," I prayed, as the children do, "what dost thou give to me!"

When the friends heard of my solitary Christmas night, there were on the following evening many Christmas-trees lighted, and on the last evening in the year, there was planted for me alone, a little tree with its lights, and its beautiful presents — and that was by Jenny Lind. The whole company consisted of herself, her attendant, and me; we three children from the north were together on

Sylvester-eve, and I was the child for which the Christmas-tree was lighted. She rejoiced with the feeling of a sister in my good fortune in Berlin; and I felt almost pride in the sympathy of such a pure, noble, and womanly being. Everywhere her praise resounded, not merely as a singer, but also as a woman; the two combined awoke a real enthusiasm for her.

It does one good both in mind and heart to see that which is glorious understood and beloved. In one little anecdote contributing to her triumph I was myself made the confidant.

One morning as I looked out of my window *unter den Linden*, I saw a man under one of the trees, half hidden, and shabbily dressed, who took a comb out of his pocket, smoothed his hair, set his neckerchief straight, and brushed his coat with his hand; I understood that bashful poverty which feels depressed by its shabby dress. A moment after this, there was a knock at my door, and this same man entered. It was W —— , the poet of nature, who is only a poor tailor, but who has a truly poetical mind. Rellstab and others in Berlin have mentioned him with honor; there is something healthy in his poems, among which several of a sincerely religious character may be found. He had read that I was in Berlin, and wished now to visit me. We sat together on the sofa and conversed: there was such an amiable contentedness, such an unspoiled and good tone of mind about him, that I was sorry not to be rich in order that I might do something for him. I was ashamed of offering him the little that I could give; in any case I wished to put it in as agreeable a form as I could. I asked him whether I might invite him to hear Jenny Lind.

"I have already heard her," said he smiling; "I had, it is true, no money to buy a ticket; but I went to the leader of the supernumeraries, and asked whether I might not act as a supernumerary for one evening in Norma: I was accepted and habited as a Roman soldier, with a long sword by my side, and thus got to the theatre, where I could hear her better than any body else, for I stood close to her. Ah, how she sung, how she played! I could not help crying; but they were angry at that: the leader forbade and would not let me again make my appearance, because no one must weep on the stage."

With the exception of the theatre, I had very little time to visit collections of any kind or institutions of art. The able and amiable Olfers, however, the Director of the Museum, enabled me to pay a rapid but extremely interesting visit to that institution. Olfers himself was my conductor; we delayed our steps only for the most interesting objects, and there are here not a few of these; his remarks threw light upon my mind, — for this therefore I am infinitely obliged to him.

I had the happiness of visiting the Princess of Prussia many times; the wing of the castle in which she resided was so comfortable, and yet like a fairy palace. The blooming winter-garden, where the fountain splashed among the moss at the foot of the statue, was close beside the room in which the kind-hearted children smiled with their soft blue eyes. On taking leave she honored me with a richly bound album, in which, beneath the picture of the palace, she wrote her name. I shall guard this volume as a treasure of the soul; it is not the gift which has a value only, but also the manner in which it is given. One forenoon I read to her several of my little stories, and her noble husband listened kindly: Prince P ckler-Muskau also was present.

184

A few days after my arrival in Berlin, I had the honor to be invited to the royal table. As I was better acquainted with Humboldt than any one there, and he it was who had particularly interested himself about me, I took my place at his side. Not only on account of his high intellectual character, and his amiable and polite behavior, but also from his infinite kindness towards me, during the whole of my residence in Berlin, is he become unchangeably dear to me.

The King received me most graciously, and said that during his stay in Copenhagen he had inquired after me, and had heard that I was travelling. He expressed a great interest in my novel of Only a Fiddler; her Majesty the Queen also showed herself graciously and kindly disposed towards me. I had afterwards the happiness of being invited to spend an evening at the palace at Potsdam; an evening which is full of rich remembrance and never to be forgotten! Besides the ladies and gentlemen in waiting, Humboldt and myself were only invited. A seat was assigned to me at the table of their Majesties, exactly the place, said the Queen, where Oehlenschl ger had sat and read his tragedy of Dina. I read four little stories, the Fir-Tree, the Ugly Duckling, the Ball and the Top, and The Swineherd. The King listened with great interest, and expressed himself most wittily on the subject. He said, how beautiful he thought the natural scenery of Denmark, and how excellently he had seen one of Holberg's comedies performed.

It was so deliciously pleasant in the royal apartment, — gentle eyes were gazing at me, and I felt that they all wished me well. When at night I was alone in my chamber, my thoughts were so occupied with this evening, and my mind in such a state of excitement, that I

185

could not sleep. Everything seemed to me like a fairy tale. Through the whole night the chimes sounded in the tower, and the aerial music mingled itself with my thoughts.

I received still one more proof of the favor and kindness of the King of Prussia towards me, on the evening before my departure from the city. The order of the Red Eagle, of the third class, was conferred upon me. Such a mark of honor delights certainly every one who receives it. I confess candidly that I felt myself honored in a high degree. I discerned in it an evident token of the kindness of the noble, enlightened King towards me: my heart is filled with gratitude. I received this mark of honor exactly on the birth-day of my benefactor Collin, the 6th of January; this day has now a twofold festal significance for me. May God fill with gladness the mind of the royal donor who wished to give me pleasure!

The last evening was spent in a warm-hearted circle, for the greater part, of young people. My health was drunk; a poem, Der M rchenknig, declaimed. It was not until late in the night that I reached home, that I might set off early in the morning by railroad.

I have here given in part a proof of the favor and kindness which was shown to me in Berlin: I feel like some one who has received a considerable sum for a certain object from a large assembly, and now would give an account thereof. I might still add many other names, as well from the learned world, as Theodor, M gge, Geibel, H ring, etc., as from the social circle; — the reckoning is too large. God give me strength for that which I now have to perform, after I have, as an earnest of good will, received such a richly abundant sum.

186

After a journey of a day and night I was once more in Weimar, with my noble Hereditary Grand Duke. What a cordial reception! A heart rich in goodness, and a mind full of noble endeavors, live in this young prince. I have no words for the infinite favor, which, during my residence here, I received daily from the family of the Grand Duke, but my whole heart is full of devotion. At the court festival, as well as in the familiar family circle, I had many evidences of the esteem in which I was held. Beaulieu cared for me with the tenderness of a brother. It was to me a month-long Sabbath festival. Never shall I forget the quiet evenings spent with him, when friend spoke freely to friend.

My old friends were also unchanged; the wise and able Schll, as well as Schober, joined them also. Jenny Lind came to Weimar; I heard her at the court concerts and at the theatre; I visited with her the places which are become sacred through Goethe and Schiller: we stood together beside their coffins, where Chancellor von M ller led us. The Austrian poet, Rollet, who met us here for the first time, wrote on this subject a sweet poem, which will serve me as a visible remembrance of this hour and this place. People lay lovely flowers in their books, and as such, I lay in here this verse of his: —

Weimar, 29th January, 1846.

M rchen rose, which has so often Charmed me with thy fragrant breath; Where the prince, the poets slumber, Thou hast wreathed the hall of death.

And with thee beside each coffin, In the death-hushed chamber pale, I beheld a grief-enchanted, Sweetly dreaming nightingale.

I rejoiced amid the stillness; Gladness through my bosom past, That the gloomy poets' coffins Such a magic crowned at last.

And thy rose's summer fragrance Floated round that chamber pale, With the gentle melancholy Of the grief-hushed nightingale.

It was in the evening circle of the intellectual Froriep that I met, for the first time, with Auerbach, who then chanced to be staying in Weimar. His "Village Tales" interested me in the highest degree; I regard them as the most poetical, most healthy, and joyous production of the young German literature. He himself made the same agreeable impression upon me; there is something so frank and straightforward, and yet so sagacious, in his whole appearance, I might almost say, that he looks himself like a village tale, healthy to the core, body and soul, and his eyes beaming with honesty. We soon became friends — and I hope forever.

My stay in Weimar was prolonged; it became ever more difficult to tear myself away. The Grand Duke's birth-day occurred at this time, and after attending all the festivities to which I was invited, I departed. I would and must be in Rome at Easter. Once more in the early morning, I saw the Hereditary Grand Duke, and, with a heart full of emotion, bade him farewell. Never, in presence of the world, will I forget the high position which his birth gives him, but I may say, as the very poorest subject may say of a prince, I love him as one who is dearest to my heart. God give him joy and bless him in his noble endeavors! A generous heart beats beneath the princely star.

Beaulieu accompanied me to Jena. Here a hospitable home awaited me, and filled with beautiful memories from the time of Goethe, the house of the publisher Frommann. It was his kind, warm-hearted sister, who had shown me such sympathy in Berlin; the brother was not here less kind.

The Holstener Michelsen, who has a professorship at Jena, assembled a number of friends one evening, and in a graceful and cordial toast for me, expressed his sense of the importance of Danish literature, and the healthy and natural spirit which flourished in it.

In Michelsen's house I also became acquainted with Professor Hase, who, one evening having heard some of my little stories, seemed filled with great kindness towards me. What he wrote in this moment of interest on an album leaf expresses this sentiment:

"Schelling — not he who now lives in Berlin, but he who lives an immortal hero in the world of mind — once said: 'Nature is the visible spirit.' This spirit, this unseen nature, last evening was again rendered visible to me through your little tales. If on the one hand you penetrate deeply into the mysteries of nature; know and understand the language of birds, and what are the feelings of a fir-tree or a daisy, so that each seems to be there on its own account, and we and our children sympathize with them in their joys and sorrows; yet, on the other hand, all is but the image of mind; and the human heart in its infinity, trembles and throbs throughout. May this fountain in the poet's heart, which God has lent you, still for a time pour forth this refreshingly, and may these stories in the memories of the Germanic nations, become the legends of the people!" That object, for which as a writer of

189

poetical fictions, I must strive after, is contained in these last lines.

It is also to Hase and the gifted improvisatore, Professor Wolff of Jena, to whom I am most indebted for the appearance of a uniform German edition of my writings.

This was all arranged on my arrival at Leipzig: several hours of business were added to my traveller's mode of life. The city of bookselling presented me with her bouquet, a sum of money; but she presented me with even more. I met again with Brockhaus, and passed happy hours with Mendelssohn, that glorious man of genius. I heard him play again and again; it seemed to me that his eyes, full of soul, looked into the very depths of my being. Few men have more the stamp of the inward fire than he. A gentle, friendly wife, and beautiful children, make his rich, well-appointed house, blessed and pleasant. When he rallied me about the Stork, and its frequent appearance in my writings, there was something so childlike and amiable revealed in this great artist!

I also met again my excellent countryman Gade, whose compositions have been so well received in Germany. I took him the text for a new opera which I had written, and which I hope to see brought out on the German stage. Gade had written the music to my drama of Agnete and the Merman, compositions which were very successful. Auerbach, whom I again found here, introduced me to many agreeable circles. I met with the composer Kalliwoda, and with K hne, whose charming little son immediately won my heart.

On my arrival at Dresden I instantly hastened to my motherly friend, the Baroness von Decken. That was a joyous hearty welcome! One equally cordial I met with from Dahl. I saw once more my Roman friend, the poet with word and color, Reineck, and met the kind-hearted Bendemann. Professor Grahl painted me. I missed, however, one among my olden friends, the poet Brunnow. With life and cordiality he received me the last time in his room, where stood lovely flowers; now these grew over his grave. It awakens a peculiar feeling, thus for once to meet on the journey of life, to understand and love each other, and then to part — until the journey for both is ended.

I spent, to me, a highly interesting evening, with the royal family, who received me with extraordinary favor. Here also the most happy domestic life appeared to reign — a number of amiable children, all belonging to Prince Johann, were present. The least of the Princesses, a little girl, who knew that I had written the history of the Fir-tree, began very confidentially with — "Last Christmas we also had a Fir-tree, and it stood here in this room!" Afterwards, when she was led out before the other children, and had bade her parents and the King and Queen good night, she turned round at the half-closed door, and nodding to me in a friendly and familiar manner, said I was her Fairy-tale Prince.

My story of Holger Danske led the conversation to the rich stores of legends which the north possesses. I related several, and explained the peculiar spirit of the fine scenery of Denmark. Neither in this royal palace did I feel the weight of ceremony; soft, gentle eyes shone upon me. My last morning in Dresden was spent with the Minister von Knneritz, where I equally met with the most friendly reception.

The sun shone warm: it was spring who was celebrating her arrival, as I rolled out of the dear city. Thought assembled in one amount all the many who had rendered my visits so rich and happy: it was spring around me, and spring in my heart.

In Prague I had only one acquaintance, Professor Wiesenfeldt. But a letter from Dr. Carus in Dresden opened to me the hospitable house of Count Thun. The Archduke Stephan received me also in the most gracious manner; I found in him a young man full of intellect and heart. Besides it was a very interesting point of time when I left Prague. The military, who had been stationed there a number of years, were hastening to the railway, to leave for Poland, where disturbances had broken out. The whole city seemed in movement to take leave of its military friends; it was difficult to get through the streets which led to the railway. Many thousand soldiers were to be accommodated; at length the train was set in motion. All around the whole hill-side was covered with people; it looked like the richest Turkey carpet woven of men, women and children, all pressed together, head to head, and waving hats and handkerchiefs. Such a mass of human beings I never saw before, or at least, never at one moment surveyed them: such a spectacle could not be painted.

We travelled the whole night through wide Bohemia: at every town stood groups of people; it was as though all the inhabitants had assembled themselves. Their brown faces, their ragged clothes, the light of their torches, their, to me, unintelligible language, gave to the whole a stamp of singularity. We flew through tunnel and over viaduct; the windows rattled, the signal whistle sounded, the steam horses snorted — I laid back my head at last in the carriage, and fell asleep under the protection of the god Morpheus.

At Olm tz, where we had fresh carnages, a voice spoke my name — it was Walter Goethe! We had travelled together the whole night without knowing it. In Vienna we met often. Noble powers, true genius, live in Goethe's grandsons, in the composer as well as in the poet; but it is as if the greatness of their grandfather pressed upon them. Liszt was in Vienna, and invited me to his concert, in which otherwise it would have been impossible to find a place. I again heard his improvising of Robert! I again heard him, like a spirit of the storm, play with the chords: he is an enchanter of sounds who fills the imagination with astonishment. Ernst also was here; when I visited him he seized the violin, and this sang in tears the secret of a human heart.

I saw the amiable Grillparzer again, and was frequently with the kindly Castelli, who just at this time had been made by the King of Denmark Knight of the Danebrog Order. He was full of joy at this, and begged me to tell my countrymen that every Dane should receive a hearty welcome from him. Some future summer he invited me to visit his grand country seat. There is something in Castelli so open and honorable, mingled with such good-natured humor, that one must like him: he appears to me the picture of a thorough Viennese. Under his portrait, which he gave me, he wrote the following little improvised verse in the style so peculiarly his own:

This portrait shall ever with loving eyes greet thee, From far shall recall the smile of thy friend; For thou, dearest Dane, 'tis a pleasure to meet thee, Thou art one to be loved and esteemed to the end.

Castelli introduced me to Seidl and Bauernfeld. At the Danisti ambassador's, Baron von Lwenstern, I met Zedlitz. Most of the shining stars of Austrian literature I

193

saw glide past me, as people on a railway see church towers; you can still say you have seen them; and still retaining the simile of the stars, I can say, that in the Concordia Society I saw the entire galaxy. Here was a host of young growing intellects, and here were men of importance. At the house of Count Szechenye, who hospitably invited me, I saw his brother from Pest, whose noble activity in Hungary is known. This short meeting I account one of the most interesting events of my stay in Vienna; the man revealed himself in all his individuality, and his eye said that you must feel confidence in him.

At my departure from Dresden her Majesty the Queen of Saxony had asked me whether I had introductions to any one at the Court of Vienna, and when I told her that I had not, the Queen was so gracious as to write a letter to her sister, the Archduchess Sophia of Austria. Her imperial Highness summoned me one evening, and received me in the most gracious manner. The dowager Empress, the widow of the Emperor Francis I., was present, and full of kindness and friendship towards me; also Prince Wasa, and the hereditary Archduchess of Hesse-Darmstadt. The remembrance of this evening will always remain dear and interesting to me. I read several of my little stories aloud — when I wrote them, I thought least of all that I should some day read them aloud in the imperial palace.

Before my departure I had still another visit to make, and this was to the intellectual authoress, Frau von Weissenthurn. She had just left a bed of sickness and was still suffering, but wished to see me. As though she were already standing on the threshold of the realm of shades, she pressed my hand and said this was the last time we should ever see each other. With a soft motherly gaze she looked at me, and at parting her penetrating eye followed me to the door.

With railway and diligence my route now led towards Triest. With steam the long train of carriages flies along the narrow rocky way, following all the windings of the river. One wonders that with all these abrupt turnings one is not dashed against the rock, or flung down into the roaring stream, and is glad when the journey is happily accomplished. But in the slow diligence one wishes its more rapid journey might recommence, and praise the powers of the age.

At length Triest and the Adriatic sea lay before us; the Italian language sounded in our ears, but yet for me it was not Italy, the land of my desire. Meanwhile I was only a stranger here for a few hours; our Danish consul, as well as the consuls of Prussia and Oldenburg, to whom I was recommended, received me in the best possible manner. Several interesting acquaintances were made, especially with the Counts O'Donnell and Waldstein, the latter for me as a Dane having a peculiar interest, as being the descendant of that unfortunate Confitz Ulfeld and the daughter of Christian IV., Eleanore, the noblest of all Danish women. Their portraits hung in his room, and Danish memorials of that period were shown me. It was the first time I had ever seen Eleanore Ulfeld's portrait, and the melancholy smile on her lips seemed to say, "Poet, sing and free from chains which a hard age had cast upon him, for whom to live and to suffer was my happiness!" Before Oehlenschl ger wrote his Dina, which treats of an episode in Ulfeld's life, I was at work on this subject, and wished to bring it on the stage, but it was then feared this would not be allowed, and I gave it up — since then I have only written four lines on Ulfeld: —

195

Thy virtue was concealed, not so thy failings, Thus did the world thy greatness never know, Yet still love's glorious monument proclaims it, That the best wife from thee would never go.

On the Adriatic sea I, in thought, was carried back to Ulfeld's time and the Danish islands. This meeting with Count Waldstein and his ancestor's portrait brought me back to my poet's world, and I almost forgot that the following day I could be in the middle of Italy. In beautiful mild weather I went with the steam-boat to Ancona.

It was a quiet starlight night, too beautiful to be spent in sleep. In the early morning the coast of Italy lay before us, the beautiful blue mountains with glittering snow. The sun shone warmly, the grass and the trees were so splendidly green. Last evening in Trieste, now in Ancona, in a city of the papal states, — that was almost like enchantment! Italy in all its picturesque splendor lay once more before me; spring had ripened all the fruit trees so that they had burst forth into blossom; every blade of grass in the field was filled with sunshine, the elm trees stood like caryatides enwreathed with vines, which shot forth green leaves, and above the luxuriance of foliage rose the wavelike blue mountains with their snow covering. In company with Count Paar from Vienna, the most excellent travelling companion, and a young nobleman from Hungary, I now travelled on with a vetturino for five days: solitary, and more picturesque than habitable inns among the Apennines were our night's quarters. At length the Campagna, with its thought-awakening desolation, lay before us.

It was the 31st of March, 1846, when I again saw Rome, and for the third time in my life should reach this city of

196

the world. I felt so happy, so penetrated with thankfulness and joy; how much more God had given me than a thousand others — nay, than to many thousands! And even in this very feeling there is a blessing — where joy is very great, as in the deepest grief, there is only God on whom one can lean! The first impression was — I can find no other word for it — adoration. When day unrolled for me my beloved Rome, I felt what I cannot express more briefly or better than I did in a letter to a friend: "I am growing here into the very ruins, I live with the petrified gods, and the roses are always blooming, and the church bells ringing — and yet Rome is not the Rome it was thirteen years ago when I first was here. It is as if everything were modernized, the ruins even, grass and bushes are cleared away. Everything is made so neat; the very life of the people seems to have retired; I no longer hear the tamborines in the streets, no longer see the young girls dancing their Saltarella, even in the Campagna intelligence has entered by invisible railroads; the peasant no longer believes as he used to do. At the Easter festival I saw great numbers of the people from the Campagna standing before St. Peters whilst the Pope distributed his blessing, just as though they had been Protestant strangers. This was repulsive to my feelings, I felt an impulse to kneel before the invisible saint. When I was here thirteen years ago, all knelt; now reason had conquered faith. Ten years later, when the railways will have brought cities still nearer to each other, Rome will be yet more changed. But in all that happens, everything is for the best; one always must love Rome; it is like a story book, one is always discovering new wonders, and one lives in imagination and reality."

The first time I travelled to Italy I had no eyes for sculpture; in Paris the rich pictures drew me away from the statues; for the first time when I came to Florence and stood before the Venus de Medicis, I felt as Thorwaldsen expressed, "the snow melted away from my eyes;" and a new world of art rose before me. And now at my third sojourn in Rome, after repeated wanderings through the Vatican, I prize the statues far higher than the paintings. But at what other places as at Rome, and to some degree in Naples, does this art step forth so grandly into life! One is carried away by it, one learns to admire nature in the work of art, the beauty of form becomes spiritual.

Among the many clever and beautiful things which I saw exhibited in the studios of the young artists, two pieces of sculpture were what most deeply impressed themselves on my memory; and these were in the studio of my countryman Jerichau. I saw his group of Hercules and Hebe, which had been spoken of with such enthusiasm in the Allgemeine Zeitung and other German papers, and which, through its antique repose, and its glorious beauty, powerfully seized upon me. My imagination was filled by it, and yet I must place Jerichau's later group, the Fighting Hunter, still higher. It is formed after the model, as though it had sprung from nature. There lies in it a truth, a beauty, and a grandeur which I am convinced will make his name resound through many lands!

I have known him from the time when he was almost a boy. We were both of us born on the same island: he is from the little town of Assens. We met in Copenhagen. No one, not even he himself, knew what lay within him; and half in jest, half in earnest, he spoke of the combat with himself whether he should go to America and become a savage, or to Rome and become an artist — painter or sculptor; that he did not yet know. His pencil was meanwhile thrown away: he modelled in clay, and my bust was the first which he made. He received no travelling stipendium from the Academy. As far as I

198

know, it was a noble-minded woman, an artist herself, unprovided with means, who, from the interest she felt for the spark of genius she observed in him, assisted him so far that he reached Italy by means of a trading vessel. In the beginning he worked in Thorwaldsen's atelier. During a journey of several years, he has doubtless experienced the struggles of genius and the galling fetters of want; but now the star of fortune shines upon him. When I came to Rome, I found him physically suffering and melancholy. He was unable to bear the warm summers of Italy; and many people said he could not recover unless he visited the north, breathed the cooler air, and took sea-baths. His praises resounded through the papers, glorious works stood in his atelier; but man does not live on heavenly bread alone. There came one day a Russian Prince, I believe, and he gave a commission for the Hunter. Two other commissions followed on the same day. Jerichau came full of rejoicing and told this to me. A few days after he travelled with his wife, a highly gifted painter, to Denmark, from whence, strengthened body and soul, he returned, with the winter, to Rome, where the strokes of his chisel will resound so that, I hope, the world will hear them. My heart will beat joyfully with them!

I also met in Rome, Kolberg, another Danish sculptor, until now only known in Denmark, but there very highly thought of, a scholar of Thorwaldsen's and a favorite of that great master. He honored me by making my bust. I also sat once more with the kindly K chler, and saw the forms fresh as nature spread themselves over the canvas.

I sat once again with the Roman people in the amusing puppet theatre, and heard the children's merriment. Among the German artists, as well as among the Swedes and my own countrymen, I met with a hearty reception.

199

My birth-day was joyfully celebrated. Frau von Goethe, who was in Rome, and who chanced to be living in the very house where I brought my Improvisatore into the world, and made him spend his first years of childhood, sent me from thence a large, true Roman bouquet, a fragrant mosaic. The Swedish painter, Sdermark, proposed my health to the company whom the Danes, Swedes, and Norwegians had invited me to meet. From my friends I received some pretty pictures and friendly keepsakes.

The Hanoverian minister, K stner, to whose friendship I am indebted for many pleasant hours, is an extremely agreeable man, possessed of no small talent for poetry, music, and painting. At his house I really saw for the first time flower-painting elevated by a poetical idea. In one of his rooms he has introduced an arabesque of flowers which presents us with the flora of the whole year. It commences with the first spring flowers, the crocus, the snow drop, and so on; then come the summer flowers, then the autumn, and at length the garland ends with the red berries and yellow-brown leaves of December.

Constantly in motion, always striving to employ every moment and to see everything, I felt myself at last very much affected by the unceasing sirocco. The Roman air did not agree with me, and I hastened, therefore, as soon as I had seen the illumination of the dome and the *girandola*, immediately after the Easter festival, through Terracina to Naples. Count Paar travelled with me. We entered St. Lucia: the sea lay before us; Vesuvius blazed. Those were glorious evenings! moonlight nights! It was as if the heavens had elevated themselves above and the stars were withdrawn. What effect of light! In the north the moon scatters silver over the water: here it was gold. The circulating lanterns of the lighthouse now exhibited their dazzling light, now were totally extinguished. The torches of the fishing-boats threw their obelisk-formed blaze along the surface of the water, or else the boat concealed them like a black shadow, below which the surface of the water was illuminated. One fancied one could see to the bottom, where fishes and plants were in motion. Along the street itself thousands of lights were burning in the shops of the dealers in fruit and fish. Now came a troop of children with lights, and went in procession to the church of St. Lucia. Many fell down with their lights; but above the whole stood, like the hero of this great drama of light, Vesuvius with his blood-red flame and his illumined cloud of smoke.

I visited the islands of Capri and Ischia once more; and, as the heat of the sun and the strong sirocco made a longer residence in Naples oppressive to me, I went to Sarrento, Tasso's city, where the foliage of the vine cast a shade, and where the air appears to me lighter. Here I wrote these pages. In Rome, by the bay of Naples and amid the Pyrenees, I put on paper the story of my life.

The well-known festival of the Madonna dell' Arco called me again to Naples, where I took up my quarters at an hotel in the middle of the city, near the Toledo Street, and found an excellent host and hostess. I had already resided here, but only in the winter. I had now to see Naples in its summer heat and with all its wild tumult, but in what degree I had never imagined. The sun shone down with its burning heat into the narrow streets, in at the balcony door. It was necessary to shut up every place: not a breath of air stirred. Every little corner, every spot in the street on which a shadow fell was crowded with working handicraftsmen, who chattered loudly and merrily; the carriages rolled past; the drivers screamed; the tumult of the people roared like a sea in the other streets;

the church bells sounded every minute; my opposite neighbor, God knows who he was, played the musical scale from morning till evening. It was enough to make one lose one's senses!

The sirocco blew its boiling-hot breath and I was perfectly overcome. There was not another room to be had at St. Lucia, and the sea-bathing seemed rather to weaken than to invigorate me. I went therefore again into the country; but the sun burned there with the same beams; yet still the air there was more elastic, yet for all that it was to me like the poisoned mantle of Hercules, which, as it were, drew out of me strength and spirit. I, who had fancied that I must be precisely a child of the sun, so firmly did my heart always cling to the south, was forced to acknowledge that the snow of the north was in my body, that the snow melted, and that I was more and more miserable.

Most strangers felt as I myself did in this, as the Neapolitans themselves said, unusually hot summer; the greater number went away. I also would have done the same, but I was obliged to wait several days for a letter of credit; it had arrived at the right time, but lay forgotten in the hands of my banker. Yet there was a deal for me to see in Naples; many houses were open to me. I tried whether the will were not stronger than the Neapolitan heat, but I fell into such a nervous state in consequence, that till the time of my departure I was obliged to lie quietly in my hot room, where the night brought no coolness. From the morning twilight to midnight roared the noise of bells, the cry of the people, the trampling of horses on the stone pavement, and the before-mentioned practiser of the scale — it was like being on the rack; and this caused me to give up my journey to Spain, especially as I was assured, for my consolation, that I should find it just as warm there as here. The physician said that, at this season of the year, I could not sustain the journey.

I took a berth in the steam-boat Castor for Marseilles; the vessel was full to overflowing with passengers; the whole quarter-deck, even the best place, was occupied by travelling carriages; under one of these I had my bed laid; many people followed my example, and the quarter-deck was soon covered with mattresses and carpets. It blew strongly; the wind increased, and in the second and third night raged to a perfect storm; the ship rolled from side to side like a cask in the open sea; the waves dashed on the ship's side and lifted up their broad heads above the bulwarks as if they would look in upon us. It was as if the carriages under which we lay would crush us to pieces, or else would be washed away by the sea. There was a lamentation, but I lay quiet, looked up at the driving clouds, and thought upon God and my beloved. When at length we reached Genoa most of the passengers went on land: I should have been willing enough to have followed their example, that I might go by Milan to Switzerland, but my letter of credit was drawn upon Marseilles and some Spanish sea-ports. I was obliged to go again on board. The sea was calm; the air fresh; it was the most glorious voyage along the charming Sardinian coast. Full of strength and new life I arrived at Marseilles, and, as I here breathed more easily, my longing to see Spain was again renewed. I had laid the plan of seeing this country last, as the bouquet of my journey. In the suffering state in which I had been I was obliged to give it up, but I was now better. I regarded it therefore as a pointing of the finger of heaven that I should be compelled to go to Marseilles, and determined to venture upon the journey. The steam-vessel to Barcelona had, in the meantime, just sailed, and several days must pass before another set out. I determined therefore to travel by short days' journeys through the south of France across the Pyrenees.

Before leaving Marseilles, chance favored me with a short meeting with one of my friends from the North, and this was Ole Bull! He came from America, and was received in France with jubilees and serenades, of which I was myself a witness. At the *table d'h te* in the *H tel des Empereurs*, where we both lodged, we flew towards each other. He told me what I should have expected least of all, that my works had also many friends in America, that people had inquired from him about me with the greatest interest, and that the English translations of my romances had been reprinted, and spread through the whole country in cheap editions. My name flown over the great ocean! I felt myself at this thought quite insignificant, but yet glad and happy; wherefore should I, in preference to so many thousand others, receive such happiness?

I had and still have a feeling as though I were a poor peasant lad over whom a royal mantle is thrown. Yet I was and am made happy by all this! Is *this* vanity, or does it show itself in these expressions of my joy?

Ole Bull went to Algiers, I towards the Pyrenees. Through Provence, which looked to me quite Danish, I reached Nismes, where the grandeur of the splendid Roman amphitheatre at once carried me back to Italy. The memorials of antiquity in the south of France I have never heard praised as their greatness and number deserve; the so-called *Maison Quar e* is still standing in all its splendor, like the Theseus Temple at Athens: Rome has nothing so well preserved.

In Nismes dwells the baker Reboul, who writes the most charming poems: whoever may not chance to know him from these is, however, well acquainted with him through Lamartine's Journey to the East. I found him at the house, stepped into the bakehouse, and addressed myself to a man in shirt sleeves who was putting bread into the oven; it was Reboul himself! A noble countenance which expressed a manly character greeted me. When I mentioned my name, he was courteous enough to say he was acquainted with it through the Revue de Paris, and begged me to visit him in the afternoon, when he should be able to entertain me better. When I came again I found him in a little room which might be called almost elegant, adorned with pictures, casts and books, not alone French literature, but translations of the Greek classics. A picture on the wall represented his most celebrated poem, "The Dying Child," from Marmier's *Chansons du Nord*. He knew I had treated the same subject, and I told him that this was written in my school days. If in the morning I had found him the industrious baker, he now was the poet completely; he spoke with animation of the literature of his country, and expressed a wish to see the north, the scenery and intellectual life of which seemed to interest him. With great respect I took leave of a man whom the Muses have not meanly endowed, and who yet has good sense enough, spite of all the homage paid him, to remain steadfast to his honest business, and prefer being the most remarkable baker of Nismes to losing himself in Paris, after a short triumph, among hundreds of other poets.

By railway I now travelled by way of Montpelier to Cette, with that rapidity which a train possesses in France; you fly there as though for a wager with the wild huntsman. I involuntarily remembered that at Basle, at the corner of a street where formerly the celebrated Dance of Death was painted, there is written up in large letters "Dance of Death," and on the opposite corner "Way to the

205

Railroad." This singular juxtaposition just at the frontiers of France, gives play to the fancy; in this rushing flight it came into my thoughts; it seemed as though the steam whistle gave the signal to the dance. On German railways one does not have such wild fancies.

The islander loves the sea as the mountaineer loves his mountains!

Every sea-port town, however small it may be, receives in my eyes a peculiar charm from the sea. Was it the sea, in connexion perhaps with the Danish tongue, which sounded in my ears in two houses in Cette, that made this town so homelike to me? I know not, but I felt more in Denmark than in the south of France. When far from your country you enter a house where all, from the master and mistress to the servants, speak your own language, as was here the case, these home tones have a real power of enchantment: like the mantle of Faust, in a moment they transport you, house and all, into your own land. Here, however, there was no northern summer, but the hot sun of Naples; it might even have burnt Faust's cap. The sun's rays destroyed all strength. For many years there had not been such a summer, even here; and from the country round about arrived accounts of people who had died from the heat: the very nights were hot. I was told beforehand I should be unable to bear the journey in Spain. I felt this myself, but then Spain was to be the bouquet of my journey. I already saw the Pyrenees; the blue mountains enticed me — and one morning early I found myself on the steam-boat. The sun rose higher; it burnt above, it burnt from the expanse of waters, myriads of jelly-like medusas filled the river; it was as though the sun's rays had changed the whole sea into a heaving world of animal life; I had never before seen anything like it. In the Languedoc canal we had all to get into a large boat which had been constructed more for goods than for passengers. The deck was coveted with boxes and trunks, and these again occupied by people who sought shade under umbrellas. It was impossible to move; no railing surrounded this pile of boxes and people, which was drawn along by three or four horses attached by long ropes. Beneath in the cabins it was as crowded; people sat close to each other, like flies in a cup of sugar. A lady who had fainted from the heat and tobacco smoke, was carried in and laid upon the only unoccupied spot on the floor; she was brought here for air, but here there was none, spite of the number of fans in motion; there were no refreshments to be had, not even a drink of water, except the warm, yellow water which the canal afforded. Over the cabin windows hung booted legs, which at the same time that they deprived the cabin of light, seemed to give a substance to the oppressive air. Shut up in this place one had also the torment of being forced to listen to a man who was always trying to say something witty; the stream of words played about his lips as the canal water about the boat. I made myself a way through boxes, people, and umbrellas, and stood in a boiling hot air; on either side the prospect was eternally the same, green grass, a green tree, flood-gates — green grass, a green tree, flood-gates — and then again the same; it was enough to drive one insane.

At the distance of a half-hour's journey from Beziers we were put on land; I felt almost ready to faint, and there was no carriage here, for the omnibus had not expected us so early; the sun burnt infernally. People say the south of France is a portion of Paradise; under the present circumstances it seemed to me a portion of hell with all its heat. In Beziers the diligence was waiting, but all the best places were already taken; and I here for the first, and I hope for the last time, got into the hinder part of such a conveyance. An ugly woman in slippers, and with a head-dress a yard high, which she hung up, took her seat beside me; and now came a singing sailor who had certainly drunk too many healths; then a couple of dirty fellows, whose first manoeuvre was to pull off their boots and coats and sit upon them, hot and dirty, whilst the thick clouds of dust whirled into the vehicle, and the sun burnt and blinded me. It was impossible to endure this farther than Narbonne; sick and suffering, I sought rest, but then came gensdarmes and demanded my passport, and then just as night began, a fire must needs break out in the neighboring village; the fire alarm resounded, the fire-engines rolled along, it was just as though all manner of tormenting spirits were let loose. From here as far as the Pyrenees there followed repeated demands for your passport, so wearisome that you know nothing like it even in Italy: they gave you as a reason, the nearness to the Spanish frontiers, the number of fugitives from thence, and several murders which had taken place in the neighborhood: all conduced to make the journey in my then state of health a real torment.

I reached Perpignan. The sun had here also swept the streets of people, it was only when night came that they came forth, but then it was like a roaring stream, as though a real tumult were about to destroy the town. The human crowd moved in waves beneath my windows, a loud shout resounded; it pierced through my sick frame. What was that? — what did it mean? "Good evening, Mr. Arago!" resounded from the strongest voices, thousands repeated it, and music sounded; it was the celebrated Arago, who was staying in the room next to mine: the people gave him a serenade. Now this was the third I had witnessed on my journey. Arago addressed them from the balcony, the shouts of the people filled the streets. There are few evenings in my life when I have felt

208

so ill as on this one, the tumult went through my nerves; the beautiful singing which followed could not refresh me. Ill as I was, I gave up every thought of travelling into Spain; I felt it would be impossible for me. Ah, if I could only recover strength enough to reach Switzerland! I was filled with horror at the idea of the journey back. I was advised to hasten as quickly as possible to the Pyrenees, and there breathe the strengthening mountain air: the baths of Vernet were recommended as cool and excellent, and I had a letter of introduction to the head of the establishment there. After an exhausting journey of a night and some hours in the morning, I have reached this place, from whence I sent these last sheets. The air is so cool, so strengthening, such as I have not breathed for months. A few days here have entirely restored me, my pen flies again over the paper, and my thoughts towards that wonderful Spain. I stand like Moses and see the land before me, yet may not tread upon it. But if God so wills it, I will at some future time in the winter fly from the north hither into this rich beautiful land, from which the sun with his sword of flame now holds me back.

Vernet as yet is not one of the well-known bathing places, although it possesses the peculiarity of being visited all the year round. The most celebrated visitor last winter was Ibrahim Pacha; his name still lives on the lips of the hostess and waiter as the greatest glory of the establishment; his rooms were shown first as a curiosity. Among the anecdotes current about him is the story of his two French words, *merci* and *très bien*, which he pronounced in a perfectly wrong manner.

In every respect, Vernet among baths is as yet in a state of innocence; it is only in point of great bills that the Commandant has been able to raise it on a level with the first in Europe. As for the rest, you live here in a solitude, and separated from the world as in no other bathing place: for the amusement of the guests nothing in the least has been done; this must be sought in wanderings on foot or on donkey-back among the mountains; but here all is so peculiar and full of variety, that the want of artificial pleasures is the less felt. It is here as though the most opposite natural productions had been mingled together, — northern and southern, mountain and valley vegetation. From one point you will look over vineyards, and up to a mountain which appears a sample card of corn fields and green meadows, where the hay stands in cocks; from another you will only see the naked, metallic rocks with strange crags jutting forth from them, long and narrow as though they were broken statues or pillars; now you walk under poplar trees, through small meadows, where the balm-mint grows, as thoroughly Danish a production as though it were cut out of Zealand; now you stand under shelter of the rock, where cypresses and figs spring forth among vine leaves, and see a piece of Italy. But the soul of the whole, the pulses which beat audibly in millions through the mountain chain, are the springs. There is a life, a babbling in the ever-rushing waters! It springs forth everywhere, murmurs in the moss, rushes over the great stones. There is a movement, a life which it is impossible for words to give; you hear a constant rushing chorus of a million strings; above and below you, and all around, you hear the babbling of the river nymphs.

High on the cliff, at the edge of a steep precipice, lie the remains of a Moorish castle; the clouds hang where hung the balcony; the path along which the ass now goes, leads through the hall. From here you can enjoy the view over the whole valley, which, long and narrow, seems like a river of trees, which winds among the red scorched rocks; and in the middle of this green valley rises terrace-like on a hill, the little town of Vernet, which only wants minarets to look like a Bulgarian town. A miserable church with two long holes as windows, and close to it a ruined tower, form the upper portion, then come the dark brown roofs, and the dirty grey houses with opened shutters instead of windows — but picturesque it certainly is.

But if you enter the town itself — where the apothecary's shop is, is also the bookseller's — poverty is the only impression. Almost all the houses are built of unhewn stones, piled one upon another, and two or three gloomy holes form door and windows through which the swallows fly out and in. Wherever I entered, I saw through the worn floor of the first story down into a chaotic gloom beneath. On the wall hangs generally a bit of fat meat with the hairy skin attached; it was explained to me that this was used to rub their shoes with. The sleeping-room is painted in the most glaring manner with saints, angels, garlands, and crowns *al fresco*, as if done when the art of painting was in its greatest state of imperfection.

The people are unusually ugly; the very children are real gnomes; the expression of childhood does not soften the clumsy features. But a few hours' journey on the other side of the mountains, on the Spanish side, there blooms beauty, there flash merry brown eyes. The only poetical picture I retain of Vernet was this. In the market-place, under a splendidly large tree, a wandering pedlar had spread out all his wares, — handkerchiefs, books and pictures, — a whole bazaar, but the earth was his table; all the ugly children of the town, burnt through by the sun, stood assembled round these splendid things; several old women looked out from their open shops; on horses and asses the visitors to the bath, ladies and gentlemen,

211

rode by in long procession, whilst two little children, half hid behind a heap of planks; played at being cocks, and shouted all the time, "kekkeriki!"

Far more of a town, habitable and well-appointed, is the garrison town of Villefranche, with its castle of the age of Louis XIV., which lies a few hours' journey from this place. The road by Olette to Spain passes through it, and there is also some business; many houses attract your eye by their beautiful Moorish windows carved in marble. The church is built half in the Moorish style, the altars are such as are seen in Spanish churches, and the Virgin stands there with the Child, all dressed in gold and silver. I visited Villefranche one of the first days of my sojourn here; all the visitors made the excursion with me, to which end all the horses and asses far and near were brought together; horses were put into the Commandant's venerable coach, and it was occupied by people within and without, just as though it had been a French public vehicle. A most amiable Holsteiner, the best rider of the company, the well-known painter Dauzats, a friend of Alexander Dumas's, led the train. The forts, the barracks, and the caves were seen; the little town of Cornelia also, with its interesting church, was not passed over. Everywhere were found traces of the power and art of the Moors; everything in this neighborhood speaks more of Spain than France, the very language wavers between the two.

And here in this fresh mountain nature, on the frontiers of a land whose beauty and defects I am not yet to become acquainted with, I will close these pages, which will make in my life a frontier to coming years, with their beauty and defects. Before I leave the Pyrenees these written pages will fly to Germany, a great section of my life; I myself shall follow, and a new and unknown section will begin. — What may it unfold? — I know not, but thankfully, hopefully, I look forward. My whole life, the bright as well as the gloomy days, led to the best. It is like a voyage to some known point, — I stand at the rudder, I have chosen my path, — but God rules the storm and the sea. He may direct it otherwise; and then, happen what may, it will be the best for me. This faith is firmly planted in my breast, and makes me happy.

The story of my life, up to the present hour, lies unrolled before me, so rich and beautiful that I could not have invented it. I feel that I am a child of good fortune; almost every one meets me full of love and candor, and seldom has my confidence in human nature been deceived. From the prince to the poorest peasant I have felt the noble human heart beat. It is a joy to live and to believe in God and man. Openly and full of confidence, as if I sat among dear friends, I have here related the story of my life, have spoken both of my sorrows and joys, and have expressed my pleasure at each mark of applause and recognition, as I believe I might even express it before God himself. But then, whether this may be vanity? I know not: my heart was affected and humble at the same time, my thought was gratitude to God. That I have related it is not alone because such a biographical sketch as this was desired from me for the collected edition of my works, but because, as has been already said, the history of my life will be the best commentary to all my works.

In a few days I shall say farewell to the Pyrenees, and return through Switzerland to dear, kind Germany, where so much joy has flowed into my life, where I possess so many sympathizing friends, where my writings have been so kindly and encouragingly received, and where also these sheets will be gently criticized, When the

Christmas-tree is lighted, — when, as people say, the white bees swarm, — I shall be, God willing, again in Denmark with my dear ones, my heart filled with the flowers of travel, and strengthened both in body and mind: then will new works grow upon paper; may God lay his blessing upon them! He will do so. A star of good fortune shines upon me; there are thousands who deserve it far more than I; I often myself cannot conceive why I, in preference to numberless others, should receive so much joy: may it continue to shine! But should it set, perhaps whilst I conclude these lines, still it has shone, I have received my rich portion; let it set! From this also the best will spring. To God and men my thanks, my love!

Vernet (Department of the East Pyrenees), July, 1846.

H. C. ANDERSEN.

TALES

THE SNOW QUEEN

A TALE IN SEVEN STORIES

FIRST STORY

WHICH DEALS WITH A MIRROR AND ITS FRAGMENTS

Now we are about to begin, and you must attend; and when we get to the end of the story, you will know more than you do now about a very wicked hobgoblin. He was one of the worst kind; in fact he was a real demon. One day he was in a high state of delight because he had invented a mirror with this peculiarity, that every good and pretty thing reflected in it shrank away to almost nothing. On the other hand, every bad and good-for-nothing thing stood out and looked its worst. The most beautiful landscapes reflected in it looked like boiled spinach, and the best people became hideous, or else they were upside down and had no bodies. Their faces were distorted beyond recognition, and if they had even one freckle it appeared to spread all over the nose and mouth. The demon thought this immensely amusing. If a good thought passed through any one's mind, it turned to a grin in the mirror, and this caused real delight to the demon. All the scholars in the demon's school, for he kept a school, reported that a miracle had taken place: now for the first time it had become possible to see what the world and mankind were really like. They ran about all over with the mirror, till at last there was not a country or a person which had not been seen in this distorting mirror. They even wanted to fly up to heaven with it to mock the angels; but the higher they flew, the more it grinned, so much so that they could hardly hold it, and at last it slipped out of their hands and fell to the earth, shivered into hundreds of millions and billions of bits. Even then it did more harm than ever. Some of these bits were not as big as a grain of sand, and these flew about all over the world, getting into people's eyes, and, once in, they stuck there, and distorted everything they looked at, or made them see everything that was amiss. Each tiniest grain of glass kept the same power as that possessed by the whole mirror. Some people even got a bit of the glass into their hearts, and that was terrible, for the heart became like a lump of ice. Some of the fragments were so big that they were used for window panes, but it was not advisable to look at one's friends through these panes. Other bits were made into spectacles, and it was a bad business when people put on these spectacles meaning to be just. The bad demon laughed till he split his sides; it tickled him to see the mischief he had done. But some of these fragments were still left floating about the world, and you shall hear what happened to them.

SECOND STORY

ABOUT A LITTLE BOY AND A LITTLE GIRL

In a big town crowded with houses and people, where there is no room for gardens, people have to be content with flowers in pots instead. In one of these towns lived two children who managed to have something bigger than a flower pot for a garden. They were not brother and sister, but they were just as fond of each other as if they had been. Their parents lived opposite each other in two attic rooms. The roof of one house just touched the roof of the next one, with only a rain-water gutter between them. They each had a little dormer window, and one only had to step over the gutter to get from one house to the other. Each of the parents had a large window-box, in which they grew pot herbs and a little rose-tree. There was one in each box, and they both grew splendidly. Then it occurred to the parents to put the boxes across the gutter, from house to house, and they looked just like two banks of flowers. The pea vines hung down over the edges of the boxes, and the roses threw out long creepers which twined round the windows. It was almost like a green triumphal arch. The boxes were high, and the children knew they must not climb up on to them, but they were often allowed to have their little stools out under the rose-trees, and there they had delightful games. Of course in the winter there was an end to these amusements. The windows were often covered with hoar-frost; then they would warm coppers on the stove and stick them on the frozen panes, where they made lovely peep-holes, as round as possible. Then a bright eye would peep through these holes, one from each window. The little boy's name was Kay, and the little girl's Gerda.

In the summer they could reach each other with one bound, but in the winter they had to go down all the stairs in one house and up all the stairs in the other, and outside there were snowdrifts.

'Look! the white bees are swarming,' said the old grandmother.

'Have they a queen bee, too?' asked the little boy, for he knew that there was a queen among the real bees.

'Yes, indeed they have,' said the grandmother. 'She flies where the swarm is thickest. She is biggest of them all, and she never remains on the ground. She always flies up again to the sky. Many a winter's night she flies through the streets and peeps in at the windows, and then the ice freezes on the panes into wonderful patterns like flowers.'

'Oh yes, we have seen that,' said both children, and then they knew it was true.

'Can the Snow Queen come in here?' asked the little girl.

'Just let her come,' said the boy, 'and I will put her on the stove, where she will melt.'

But the grandmother smoothed his hair and told him more stories.

In the evening when little Kay was at home and half undressed, he crept up on to the chair by the window, and peeped out of the little hole. A few snow-flakes were falling, and one of these, the biggest, remained on the edge of the window-box. It grew bigger and bigger, till it became the figure of a woman, dressed in the finest white gauze, which appeared to be made of millions of starry flakes. She was delicately lovely, but all ice, glittering, dazzling ice. Still she was alive, her eyes shone like two bright stars, but there was no rest or peace in them. She nodded to the window and waved her hand. The little boy was frightened and jumped down off the chair, and then he fancied that a big bird flew past the window.

The next day was bright and frosty, and then came the thaw — and after that the spring. The sun shone, green buds began to appear, the swallows built their nests, and people began to open their windows. The little children began to play in their garden on the roof again. The roses were in splendid bloom that summer; the little girl had learnt a hymn, and there was something in it about roses, and that made her think of her own. She sang it to the little boy, and then he sang it with her —

'Where roses deck the flowery vale, There, Infant Jesus, we thee hail!'

The children took each other by the hands, kissed the roses, and rejoiced in God's bright sunshine, and spoke to it as if the Child Jesus were there. What lovely summer days they were, and how delightful it was to sit out under the fresh rose-trees, which seemed never tired of blooming.

Kay and Gerda were looking at a picture book of birds and animals one day — it had just struck five by the church clock — when Kay said, 'Oh, something struck my heart, and I have got something in my eye!'

The little girl put her arms round his neck, he blinked his eye; there was nothing to be seen.

'I believe it is gone,' he said; but it was not gone. It was one of those very grains of glass from the mirror, the magic mirror. You remember that horrid mirror, in which all good and great things reflected in it became small and mean, while the bad things were magnified, and every flaw became very apparent.

Poor Kay! a grain of it had gone straight to his heart, and would soon turn it to a lump of ice. He did not feel it any more, but it was still there.

'Why do you cry?' he asked; 'it makes you look ugly; there's nothing the matter with me. How horrid!' he suddenly cried; 'there's a worm in that rose, and that one is quite crooked; after all, they are nasty roses, and so are the boxes they are growing in!' He kicked the box and broke off two of the roses.

'What are you doing, Kay?' cried the little girl. When he saw her alarm, he broke off another rose, and then ran in by his own window, and left dear little Gerda alone.

When she next got out the picture book he said it was only fit for babies in long clothes. When his grandmother told them stories he always had a but — , and if he could manage it, he liked to get behind her chair, put on her spectacles and imitate her. He did it very well and people laughed at him. He was soon able to imitate every one in the street; he could make fun of all their peculiarities and failings. 'He will turn out a clever fellow,' said people. But it was all that bit of glass in his heart, that bit of glass in his eye, and it made him tease little Gerda who was so devoted to him. He played quite different games now; he seemed to have grown older. One winter's day, when the snow was falling fast, he brought in a big magnifying glass; he held out the tail of his blue coat, and let the snow flakes fall upon it.

'Now look through the glass, Gerda!' he said; every snowflake was magnified, and looked like a lovely flower, or a sharply pointed star.

'Do you see how cleverly they are made?' said Kay. 'Much more interesting than looking at real flowers. And there is not a single flaw in them; they are perfect, if only they would not melt.'

Shortly after, he appeared in his thick gloves, with his sledge on his back. He shouted right into Gerda's ear, 'I have got leave to drive in the big square where the other boys play!' and away he went.

In the big square the bolder boys used to tie their little sledges to the farm carts and go a long way in this fashion. They had no end of fun over it. Just in the middle of their games a big sledge came along; it was painted white, and the occupant wore a white fur coat and cap. The sledge drove twice round the square, and Kay quickly tied his sledge on behind. Then off they went, faster, and faster, into the next street. The driver turned round and nodded to Kay in the most friendly way, just as if they knew each other. Every time Kay wanted to loose his sledge the person nodded again, and

Kay stayed where he was, and they drove right out through the town gates. Then the snow began to fall so heavily that the little boy could not see a hand before him as they rushed along. He undid the cords and tried to get away from the big sledge, but it was no use, his little sledge stuck fast, and on they rushed, faster than the wind. He shouted aloud, but nobody heard him, and the sledge tore on through the snow-drifts. Every now and then it gave a bound, as if they were jumping over hedges and ditches. He was very frightened, and he wanted to say his prayers, but he could only remember the multiplication tables.

The snow-flakes grew bigger and bigger, till at last they looked like big white chickens. All at once they sprang on one side, the big sledge stopped and the person who drove got up, coat and cap smothered in snow. It was a tall and upright lady all shining white, the Snow Queen herself.

'We have come along at a good pace,' she said; 'but it's cold enough to kill one; creep inside my bearskin coat.'

She took him into the sledge by her, wrapped him in her furs, and he felt as if he were sinking into a snowdrift.

'Are you still cold?' she asked, and she kissed him on the forehead. Ugh! it was colder than ice, it went to his very heart, which was already more than half ice; he felt as if he were dying, but only for a moment, and then it seemed to have done him good; he no longer felt the cold.

'My sledge! don't forget my sledge!' He only remembered it now; it was tied to one of the white chickens which flew along behind them. The Snow Queen kissed Kay again, and then he forgot all about little Gerda, Grandmother, and all the others at home.

'Now I mustn't kiss you any more,' she said, 'or I should kiss you to death!'

Kay looked at her, she was so pretty; a cleverer, more beautiful face could hardly be imagined. She did not seem to be made of ice now, as she was outside the window when she waved her hand to him. In his eyes she was quite perfect, and he was not a bit afraid of her; he told her that he could do mental arithmetic, as far as fractions, and that he knew the number of square miles and the number of inhabitants of the country. She always smiled at him, and he then thought that he surely did not know enough, and he looked up into the wide expanse of heaven, into which they rose higher and higher as she flew with him on a dark cloud, while the storm surged around them, the wind ringing in their ears like well-known old songs.

They flew over woods and lakes, over oceans and islands; the cold wind whistled down below them, the wolves howled, the black crows flew screaming over the sparkling snow, but up above, the moon shone bright and clear — and Kay looked at it all the long, long winter nights; in the day he slept at the Snow Queen's feet.

STORY THREE

THE GARDEN OF THE WOMAN LEARNED IN MAGIC

But how was little Gerda getting on all this long time since Kay left her? Where could he be? Nobody knew, nobody could say anything about him. All that the other boys knew was, that they had seen him tie his little sledge to a splendid big one which drove away down the street and out of the town gates. Nobody knew where he was, and many tears were shed; little Gerda cried long and bitterly. At last, people said he was dead; he must have fallen into the river which ran close by the town. Oh, what long, dark, winter days those were!

At last the spring came and the sunshine.

'Kay is dead and gone,' said little Gerda.

'I don't believe it,' said the sunshine.

'He is dead and gone,' she said to the swallows.

'We don't believe it,' said the swallows; and at last little Gerda did not believe it either.

'I will put on my new red shoes,' she said one morning; 'those Kay never saw; and then I will go down to the river and ask it about him!'

It was very early in the morning; she kissed the old grandmother, who was still asleep, put on the red shoes, and went quite alone, out by the gate to the river.

'Is it true that you have taken my little playfellow? I will give you my red shoes if you will bring him back to me again.'

She thought the little ripples nodded in such a curious way, so she took off her red shoes, her most cherished possessions, and threw them both into the river. They fell close by the shore, and were carried straight back to her by the little wavelets; it seemed as if the river would not accept her offering, as it had not taken little Kay.

She only thought she had not thrown them far enough; so she climbed into a boat which lay among the rushes, then she went right out to the further end of it, and threw the shoes into the water again. But the boat was loose, and her movements started it off, and it floated away from the shore: she felt it moving and tried to get out, but before she reached the other end the boat was more than a yard from the shore, and was floating away quite quickly.

Little Gerda was terribly frightened, and began to cry, but nobody heard her except the sparrows, and they could not carry her ashore, but they flew alongside twittering, as if to cheer her, 'We are here, we are here.' The boat floated rapidly away with the current; little Gerda sat quite still with only her stockings on; her little red shoes

227

floated behind, but they could not catch up the boat, which drifted away faster and faster.

The banks on both sides were very pretty with beautiful flowers, fine old trees, and slopes dotted with sheep and cattle, but not a single person.

'Perhaps the river is taking me to little Kay,' thought Gerda, and that cheered her; she sat up and looked at the beautiful green banks for hours.

Then they came to a big cherry garden; there was a little house in it, with curious blue and red windows, it had a thatched roof, and two wooden soldiers stood outside, who presented arms as she sailed past. Gerda called out to them; she thought they were alive, but of course they did not answer; she was quite close to them, for the current drove the boat close to the bank. Gerda called out again, louder than before, and then an old, old woman came out of the house; she was leaning upon a big, hooked stick, and she wore a big sun hat, which was covered with beautiful painted flowers.

'You poor little child,' said the old woman, 'how ever were you driven out on this big, strong river into the wide, wide world alone?' Then she walked right into the water, and caught hold of the boat with her hooked stick; she drew it ashore, and lifted little Gerda out.

Gerda was delighted to be on dry land again, but she was a little bit frightened of the strange old woman.

'Come, tell me who you are, and how you got here,' said she.

When Gerda had told her the whole story and asked her if she had seen Kay, the woman said she had not seen him, but that she expected him. Gerda must not be sad, she was to come and taste her cherries and see her flowers, which were more beautiful than any picture-book; each one had a story to tell. Then she took Gerda by the hand, they went into the little house, and the old woman locked the door.

The windows were very high up, and they were red, blue, and yellow; they threw a very curious light into the room. On the table were quantities of the most delicious cherries, of which Gerda had leave to eat as many as ever she liked. While she was eating, the old woman combed her hair with a golden comb, so that the hair curled, and shone like gold round the pretty little face, which was as sweet as a rose.

'I have long wanted a little girl like you!' said the old woman. 'You will see how well we shall get on together.' While she combed her hair Gerda had forgotten all about Kay, for the old woman was learned in the magic art; but she was not a bad witch, she only cast spells over people for a little amusement, and she wanted to keep Gerda. She therefore went into the garden and waved her hooked stick over all the rose-bushes, and however beautifully they were flowering, all sank down into the rich black earth without leaving a trace behind them. The old woman was afraid that if Gerda saw the roses she would be reminded of Kay, and would want to run away. Then she took Gerda into the flower garden. What a delicious scent there was! and every imaginable flower for every season was in that lovely garden; no picture-book could be brighter or more beautiful. Gerda jumped for joy and played till the sun went down behind the tall cherry trees. Then she was put into a lovely bed with rose-coloured silken coverings stuffed with violets; she slept and dreamt as lovely dreams as any queen on her wedding day.

The next day she played with the flowers in the garden again — and many days passed in the same way. Gerda knew every flower, but however many there were, she always thought there was one missing, but which it was she did not know.

One day she was sitting looking at the old woman's sun hat with its painted flowers, and the very prettiest one of them all was a rose. The old woman had forgotten her hat when she charmed the others away. This is the consequence of being absent-minded.

'What!' said Gerda, 'are there no roses here?' and she sprang in among the flower-beds and sought, but in vain! Her hot tears fell on the very places where the roses used to be; when the warm drops moistened the earth the rose-trees shot up again, just as full of bloom as when they sank. Gerda embraced the roses and kissed them, and then she thought of the lovely roses at home, and this brought the thought of little Kay.

'Oh, how I have been delayed,' said the little girl, 'I ought to have been looking for Kay! Don't you know where he is?' she asked the roses. 'Do you think he is dead and gone?'

'He is not dead,' said the roses. 'For we have been down underground, you know, and all the dead people are there, but Kay is not among them.'

'Oh, thank you!' said little Gerda, and then she went to the other flowers and looked into their cups and said, 'Do you know where Kay is?'

But each flower stood in the sun and dreamt its own dreams. Little Gerda heard many of these, but never anything about Kay.

And what said the Tiger lilies?

'Do you hear the drum? rub-a-dub, it has only two notes, rub-a-dub, always the same. The wailing of women and the cry of the preacher. The Hindu woman in her long red garment stands on the pile, while the flames surround her and her dead husband. But the woman is only thinking of the living man in the circle round, whose eyes burn with a fiercer fire than that of the flames which consume the body. Do the flames of the heart die in the fire?'

'I understand nothing about that,' said little Gerda.

'That is my story,' said the Tiger lily.

'What does the convolvulus say?'

'An old castle is perched high over a narrow mountain path, it is closely covered with ivy, almost hiding the old red walls, and creeping up leaf upon leaf right round the balcony where stands a beautiful maiden. She bends over the balustrade and looks eagerly up the road. No rose on its stem is fresher than she; no apple blossom wafted by the wind moves more lightly. Her silken robes rustle softly as she bends over and says, 'Will he never come?''

'Is it Kay you mean?' asked Gerda.

'I am only talking about my own story, my dream,' answered the convolvulus.

What said the little snowdrop?

'Between two trees a rope with a board is hanging; it is a swing. Two pretty little girls in snowy frocks and green ribbons fluttering on their hats are seated on it. Their brother, who is bigger than they are, stands up behind them; he has his arms round the ropes for supports, and holds in one hand a little bowl and in the other a clay pipe. He is blowing soap-bubbles. As the swing moves the bubbles fly upwards in all their changing colours, the last one still hangs from the pipe swayed by the wind, and the swing goes on. A little black dog runs up, he is almost as light as the bubbles, he stands up on his hind legs and wants to be taken into the swing, but it does not stop. The little dog falls with an angry bark; they jeer at it; the bubble bursts. A swinging plank, a fluttering foam picture — that is my story!'

'I daresay what you tell me is very pretty, but you speak so sadly and you never mention little Kay.'

What says the hyacinth?

'They were three beautiful sisters, all most delicate, and quite transparent. One wore a crimson robe, the other a blue, and the third was pure white. These three danced hand-in-hand, by the edge of the lake in the moonlight. They were human beings, not fairies of the wood. The fragrant air attracted them, and they vanished into the wood; here the fragrance was stronger still. Three coffins glide out of the wood towards the lake, and in them lie the maidens. The fire-flies flutter lightly round them with their little flickering torches. Do these dancing maidens sleep, or are they dead? The scent of the flower says that they are corpses. The evening bell tolls their knell.'

'You make me quite sad,' said little Gerda; 'your perfume is so strong it makes me think of those dead maidens. Oh, is little Kay really dead? The roses have been down underground, and they say no.'

'Ding, dong,' tolled the hyacinth bells; 'we are not tolling for little Kay; we know nothing about him. We sing our song, the only one we know.'

And Gerda went on to the buttercups shining among their dark green leaves.

'You are a bright little sun,' said Gerda. 'Tell me if you know where I shall find my playfellow.'

The buttercup shone brightly and returned Gerda's glance. What song could the buttercup sing? It would not be about Kay.

'God's bright sun shone into a little court on the first day of spring. The sunbeams stole down the neighbouring white wall, close to which bloomed the first yellow flower of the season; it shone like burnished gold in the sun. An old woman had brought her arm-chair out into the sun; her granddaughter, a poor and pretty little maid-servant, had come to pay her a short visit, and she kissed her. There was gold, heart's gold, in the kiss. Gold on the lips, gold on the ground, and gold above, in the early morning beams! Now that is my little story,' said the buttercup.

'Oh, my poor old grandmother!' sighed Gerda. 'She will be longing to see me, and grieving about me, as she did about Kay. But I shall soon go home again and take Kay with me. It is useless for me to ask the flowers about him.

They only know their own stories, and have no information to give me.'

Then she tucked up her little dress, so that she might run the faster; but the narcissus blossoms struck her on the legs as she jumped over them, so she stopped and said, 'Perhaps you can tell me something.'

She stooped down close to the flower and listened. What did it say?

'I can see myself, I can see myself,' said the narcissus. 'Oh, how sweet is my scent. Up there in an attic window stands a little dancing girl half dressed; first she stands on one leg, then on the other, and looks as if she would tread the whole world under her feet. She is only a delusion. She pours some water out of a teapot on to a bit of stuff that she is holding; it is her bodice. "Cleanliness is a good thing," she says. Her white dress hangs on a peg; it has been washed in the teapot, too, and dried on the roof. She puts it on, and wraps a saffron-coloured scarf round her neck, which makes the dress look whiter. See how high she carries her head, and all upon one stem. I see myself, I see myself!'

'I don't care a bit about all that,' said Gerda; 'it's no use telling me such stuff.'

And then she ran to the end of the garden. The door was fastened, but she pressed the rusty latch, and it gave way. The door sprang open, and little Gerda ran out with bare feet into the wide world. She looked back three times, but nobody came after her. At last she could run no further, and she sat down on a big stone. When she looked round she saw that the summer was over; it was quite late autumn. She would never have known it inside the beautiful garden, where the sun always shone, and the flowers of every season were always in bloom.

'Oh, how I have wasted my time,' said little Gerda. 'It is autumn. I must not rest any longer,' and she got up to go on.

Oh, how weary and sore were her little feet, and everything round looked so cold and dreary. The long willow leaves were quite yellow. The damp mist fell off the trees like rain, one leaf dropped after another from the trees, and only the sloe-thorn still bore its fruit; but the sloes were sour and set one's teeth on edge. Oh, how grey and sad it looked, out in the wide world.

FOURTH STORY

PRINCE AND PRINCESS

Gerda was soon obliged to rest again. A big crow hopped on to the snow, just in front of her. It had been sitting looking at her for a long time and wagging its head. Now it said, 'Caw, caw; good-day, good-day,' as well as it could; it meant to be kind to the little girl, and asked her where she was going, alone in the wide world.

Gerda understood the word 'alone' and knew how much there was in it, and she told the crow the whole story of her life and adventures, and asked if it had seen Kay.

The crow nodded its head gravely and said, 'May be I have, may be I have.'

'What, do you really think you have?' cried the little girl, nearly smothering him with her kisses.

'Gently, gently!' said the crow. 'I believe it may have been Kay, but he has forgotten you by this time, I expect, for the Princess.'

'Does he live with a Princess?' asked Gerda.

'Yes, listen,' said the crow; 'but it is so difficult to speak your language. If you understand "crow's language,"[1] I can tell you about it much better.'

'No, I have never learnt it,' said Gerda; 'but grandmother knew it, and used to speak it. If only I had learnt it!'

'It doesn't matter,' said the crow. 'I will tell you as well as I can, although I may do it rather badly.'

Then he told her what he had heard.

'In this kingdom where we are now,' said he, 'there lives a Princess who is very clever. She has read all the newspapers in the world, and forgotten them again, so clever is she. One day she was sitting on her throne, which is not such an amusing thing to do either, they say; and she began humming a tune, which happened to be

"Why should I not be married, oh why?"

"Why not indeed?" said she. And she made up her mind to marry, if she could find a husband who had an answer ready when a question was put to him. She called all the court ladies together, and when they heard what she wanted they were delighted.

'"I like that now," they said. "I was thinking the same thing myself the other day."

'Every word I say is true,' said the crow, 'for I have a tame sweetheart who goes about the palace whenever she likes. She told me the whole story.'

---

[1] Children have a kind of language, or gibberish, formed by adding letters or syllables to every word, which is called 'crow's language.'

Of course his sweetheart was a crow, for 'birds of a feather flock together,' and one crow always chooses another. The newspapers all came out immediately with borders of hearts and the Princess's initials. They gave notice that any young man who was handsome enough might go up to the Palace to speak to the Princess. The one who spoke as if he were quite at home, and spoke well, would be chosen by the Princess as her husband. Yes, yes, you may believe me, it's as true as I sit here,' said the crow. 'The people came crowding in; there was such running, and crushing, but no one was fortunate enough to be chosen, either on the first day, or on the second. They could all of them talk well enough in the street, but when they entered the castle gates, and saw the guard in silver uniforms, and when they went up the stairs through rows of lackeys in gold embroidered liveries, their courage forsook them. When they reached the brilliantly lighted reception-rooms, and stood in front of the throne where the Princess was seated, they could think of nothing to say, they only echoed her last words, and of course that was not what she wanted.

'It was just as if they had all taken some kind of sleeping-powder, which made them lethargic; they did not recover themselves until they got out into the street again, and then they had plenty to say. There was quite a long line of them, reaching from the town gates up to the Palace.

'I went to see them myself,' said the crow. 'They were hungry and thirsty, but they got nothing at the Palace, not even as much as a glass of tepid water. Some of the wise ones had taken sandwiches with them, but they did not share them with their neighbours; they thought if the others went in to the Princess looking hungry, that there would be more chance for themselves.'

'But Kay, little Kay!' asked Gerda; 'when did he come? was he amongst the crowd?'

'Give me time, give me time! we are just coming to him. It was on the third day that a little personage came marching cheerfully along, without either carriage or horse. His eyes sparkled like yours, and he had beautiful long hair, but his clothes were very shabby.'

'Oh, that was Kay!' said Gerda gleefully; 'then I have found him!' and she clapped her hands.

'He had a little knapsack on his back!' said the crow.

'No, it must have been his sledge; he had it with him when he went away!' said Gerda.

'It may be so,' said the crow; 'I did not look very particularly; but I know from my sweetheart, that when he entered the Palace gates, and saw the life-guards in their silver uniforms, and the lackeys on the stairs in their gold-laced liveries, he was not the least bit abashed. He just nodded to them and said, "It must be very tiresome to stand upon the stairs. I am going inside!" The rooms were blazing with lights. Privy councillors and excellencies without number were walking about barefoot carrying golden vessels; it was enough to make you solemn! His boots creaked fearfully too, but he wasn't a bit upset.'

'Oh, I am sure that was Kay!' said Gerda; 'I know he had a pair of new boots, I heard them creaking in grandmother's room.'

'Yes, indeed they did creak!' said the crow. 'But nothing daunted, he went straight up to the Princess, who was sitting on a pearl as big as a spinning-wheel. Poor, simple boy! all the court ladies and their attendants; the courtiers, and their gentlemen, each attended by a page, were standing round. The nearer the door they stood, so much the greater was their haughtiness; till the footman's boy, who always wore slippers and stood in the doorway, was almost too proud even to be looked at.'

'It must be awful!' said little Gerda, 'and yet Kay has won the Princess!'

'If I had not been a crow, I should have taken her myself, notwithstanding that I am engaged. They say he spoke as well as I could have done myself, when I speak crow-language; at least so my sweetheart says. He was a picture of good looks and gallantry, and then, he had not come with any idea of wooing the Princess, but simply to hear her wisdom. He admired her just as much as she admired him!'

'Indeed it was Kay then,' said Gerda; 'he was so clever he could do mental arithmetic up to fractions. Oh, won't you take me to the Palace?'

'It's easy enough to talk,' said the crow; 'but how are we to manage it? I will talk to my tame sweetheart about it; she will have some advice to give us I daresay, but I am bound to tell you that a little girl like you will never be admitted!'

'Oh, indeed I shall,' said Gerda; 'when Kay hears that I am here, he will come out at once to fetch me.'

'Wait here for me by the stile,' said the crow, then he wagged his head and flew off.

The evening had darkened in before he came back. 'Caw, caw,' he said, 'she sends you greeting. And here is a little roll for you; she got it out of the kitchen where there is bread enough, and I daresay you are hungry! It is not possible for you to get into the Palace; you have bare feet; the guards in silver and the lackeys in gold would never allow you to pass. But don't cry, we shall get you in somehow; my sweetheart knows a little back staircase which leads up to the bedroom, and she knows where the key is kept.'

Then they went into the garden, into the great avenue where the leaves were dropping, softly one by one; and when the Palace lights went out, one after the other, the crow led little Gerda to the back door, which was ajar.

Oh, how Gerda's heart beat with fear and longing! It was just as if she was about to do something wrong, and yet she only wanted to know if this really was little Kay. Oh, it must be him, she thought, picturing to herself his clever eyes and his long hair. She could see his very smile when they used to sit under the rose-trees at home. She thought he would be very glad to see her, and to hear what a long way she had come to find him, and to hear how sad they had all been at home when he did not come back. Oh, it was joy mingled with fear.

They had now reached the stairs, where a little lamp was burning on a shelf. There stood the tame sweetheart, twisting and turning her head to look at Gerda, who made a curtsy, as grandmother had taught her.

'My betrothed has spoken so charmingly to me about you, my little miss!' she said; 'your life, " *Vita*," as it is called, is most touching! If you will take the lamp, I will go on in front. We shall take the straight road here, and we shall meet no one.'

'It seems to me that some one is coming behind us,' said Gerda, as she fancied something rushed past her, throwing a shadow on the walls; horses with flowing manes and slender legs; huntsmen, ladies and gentlemen on horseback.

'Oh, those are only the dreams!' said the crow; 'they come to take the thoughts of the noble ladies and gentlemen out hunting. That's a good thing, for you will be able to see them all the better in bed. But don't forget, when you are taken into favour, to show a grateful spirit.'

'Now, there's no need to talk about that,' said the crow from the woods.

They came now into the first apartment; it was hung with rose-coloured satin embroidered with flowers. Here again the dreams overtook them, but they flitted by so quickly that Gerda could not distinguish them. The apartments became one more beautiful than the other; they were enough to bewilder anybody. They now reached the bedroom. The ceiling was like a great palm with crystal leaves, and in the middle of the room two beds, each like a lily hung from a golden stem. One was white, and in it lay the Princess; the other was red, and there lay he whom Gerda had come to seek — little Kay! She bent aside one of the crimson leaves, and she saw a little brown neck. It was Kay. She called his name aloud, and held the lamp close to him. Again the dreams rushed through the room on horseback — he awoke, turned his head — and it was not little Kay.

It was only the Prince's neck which was like his; but he was young and handsome. The Princess peeped out of her lily-white bed, and asked what was the matter. Then little Gerda cried and told them all her story, and what the crows had done to help her.

'You poor little thing!' said the Prince and Princess. And they praised the crows, and said that they were not at all angry with them, but they must not do it again. Then they gave them a reward.

'Would you like your liberty?' said the Princess, 'or would you prefer permanent posts about the court as court crows, with perquisites from the kitchen?'

Both crows curtsied and begged for the permanent posts, for they thought of their old age, and said 'it was so good to have something for the old man,' as they called it.

The Prince got up and allowed Gerda to sleep in his bed, and he could not have done more. She folded her little hands, and thought 'how good the people and the animals are'; then she shut her eyes and fell fast asleep. All the dreams came flying back again; this time they looked like angels, and they were dragging a little sledge with Kay sitting on it, and he nodded. But it was only a dream; so it all vanished when she woke.

Next day she was dressed in silk and velvet from head to foot; they asked her to stay at the Palace and have a good time, but she only begged them to give her a little carriage and horse, and a little pair of boots, so that she might drive out into the wide world to look for Kay.

They gave her a pair of boots and a muff. She was beautifully dressed, and when she was ready to start, there before the door stood a new chariot of pure gold. The Prince's and Princess's coat of arms were emblazoned on it, and shone like a star. Coachman, footman, and outrider, for there was even an outrider, all wore golden crowns. The Prince and Princess themselves helped her into the carriage and wished her joy. The wood crow, who was now married, accompanied her for the first three miles; he sat beside Gerda, for he could not ride with his back to the horses. The other crow stood at the door and flapped her wings; she did not go with them, for she suffered from headache since she had become a kitchen pensioner — the consequence of eating too much. The chariot was stored with sugar biscuits, and there were fruit and ginger nuts under the seat. 'Good-bye, good-bye,' cried the Prince and Princess; little Gerda wept, and the crow wept too. At the end of the first few miles the crow said good-bye, and this was the hardest parting of all. It flew up into a tree and flapped its big black wings as long as it could see the chariot, which shone like the brightest sunshine.

FIFTH STORY

THE LITTLE ROBBER GIRL

They drove on through a dark wood, where the chariot lighted up the way and blinded the robbers by its glare; it was more than they could bear.

'It is gold, it is gold!' they cried, and darting forward, seized the horses, and killed the postilions, the coachman, and footman. They then dragged little Gerda out of the carriage.

'She is fat, and she is pretty; she has been fattened on nuts!' said the old robber woman, who had a long beard, and eyebrows that hung down over her eyes. 'She is as good as a fat lamb, and how nice she will taste!' She drew out her sharp knife as she said this; it glittered horribly. 'Oh!' screamed the old woman at the same moment, for her little daughter had come up behind her, and she was biting her ear. She hung on her back, as wild and as savage a little animal as you could wish to find. 'You bad, wicked child!' said her mother, but she was prevented from killing Gerda on this occasion.

'She shall play with me,' said the little robber girl; 'she shall give me her muff, and her pretty dress, and she shall sleep in my bed.' Then she bit her mother again and made her dance. All the robbers laughed and said, 'Look at her dancing with her cub!'

'I want to get into the carriage,' said the little robber girl, and she always had her own way because she was so spoilt and stubborn. She and Gerda got into the carriage, and then they drove over stubble and stones further and further into the wood. The little robber girl was as big as Gerda, but much stronger; she had broader shoulders, and darker skin, her eyes were quite black, with almost a melancholy expression. She put her arm round Gerda's waist and said —

'They shan't kill you as long as I don't get angry with you; you must surely be a Princess!'

'No,' said little Gerda, and then she told her all her adventures, and how fond she was of Kay.

The robber girl looked earnestly at her, gave a little nod, and said, 'They shan't kill you even if I am angry with you. I will do it myself.' Then she dried Gerda's eyes, and stuck her own hands into the pretty muff, which was so soft and warm.

At last the chariot stopped: they were in the courtyard of a robber's castle, the walls of which were cracked from top to bottom. Ravens and crows flew in and out of every hole, and big bulldogs, which each looked ready to devour somebody, jumped about as high as they could, but they did not bark, for it was not allowed. A big fire was burning in the middle of the stone floor of the smoky old hall. The smoke all went up to the ceiling, where it had to find a way out for itself. Soup was boiling in a big caldron over the fire, and hares and rabbits were roasting on the spits.

'You shall sleep with me and all my little pets to-night,' said the robber girl.

When they had something to eat and drink they went along to one corner which was spread with straw and rugs. There were nearly a hundred pigeons roosting overhead on the rafters and beams. They seemed to be asleep, but they fluttered about a little when the children came in.

'They are all mine,' said the little robber girl, seizing one of the nearest. She held it by the legs and shook it till it flapped its wings. 'Kiss it,' she cried, dashing it at Gerda's face. 'Those are the wood pigeons,' she added, pointing to some laths fixed across a big hole high up on the walls; 'they are a regular rabble; they would fly away directly if they were not locked in. And here is my old sweetheart Be,' dragging forward a reindeer by the horn; it was tied up, and it had a bright copper ring round its neck. 'We have to keep him close too, or he would run off. Every single night I tickle his neck with my bright knife, he is so frightened of it.' The little girl produced a long knife out of a hole in the wall and drew it across the reindeer's neck. The poor animal laughed and kicked, and the robber girl laughed and pulled Gerda down into the bed with her.

'Do you have that knife by you while you are asleep?' asked Gerda, looking rather frightened.

'I always sleep with a knife,' said the little robber girl. 'You never know what will happen. But now tell me again

247

what you told me before about little Kay, and why you went out into the world.' So Gerda told her all about it again, and the wood pigeons cooed up in their cage above them; the other pigeons were asleep. The little robber girl put her arm round Gerda's neck and went to sleep with the knife in her other hand, and she was soon snoring. But Gerda would not close her eyes; she did not know whether she was to live or to die. The robbers sat round the fire, eating and drinking, and the old woman was turning somersaults. This sight terrified the poor little girl. Then the wood pigeons said, 'Coo, coo, we have seen little Kay; his sledge was drawn by a white chicken, and he was sitting in the Snow Queen's sledge; it was floating low down over the trees, while we were in our nests. She blew upon us young ones, and they all died except we two; coo, coo.'

'What are you saying up there?' asked Gerda. 'Where was the Snow Queen going? Do you know anything about it?'

'She was most likely going to Lapland, because there is always snow and ice there! Ask the reindeer who is tied up there.'

'There is ice and snow, and it's a splendid place,' said the reindeer. 'You can run and jump about where you like on those big glittering plains. The Snow Queen has her summer tent there, but her permanent castle is up at the North Pole, on the island which is called Spitzbergen!'

'Oh Kay, little Kay!' sighed Gerda.

'Lie still, or I shall stick the knife into you!' said the robber girl.

In the morning Gerda told her all that the wood pigeons had said, and the little robber girl looked quite solemn, but she nodded her head and said, 'No matter, no matter! Do you know where Lapland is?' she asked the reindeer.

'Who should know better than I,' said the animal, its eyes dancing. 'I was born and brought up there, and I used to leap about on the snowfields.'

'Listen,' said the robber girl. 'You see that all our men folks are away, but mother is still here, and she will stay; but later on in the morning she will take a drink out of the big bottle there, and after that she will have a nap — then I will do something for you.' Then she jumped out of bed, ran along to her mother and pulled her beard, and said, 'Good morning, my own dear nanny-goat!' And her mother filliped her nose till it was red and blue; but it was all affection.

As soon as her mother had had her draught from the bottle and had dropped asleep, the little robber girl went along to the reindeer, and said, 'I should have the greatest pleasure in the world in keeping you here, to tickle you with my knife, because you are such fun then; however, it does not matter. I will untie your halter and help you outside so that you may run away to Lapland, but you must put your best foot foremost, and take this little girl for me to the Snow Queen's palace, where her playfellow is. I have no doubt you heard what she was telling me, for she spoke loud enough, and you are generally eavesdropping!'

The reindeer jumped into the air for joy. The robber girl lifted little Gerda up, and had the forethought to tie her on, nay, even to give her a little cushion to sit upon. 'Here, after all, I will give you your fur boots back, for it will be very cold, but I will keep your muff, it is too pretty to part with. Still you shan't be cold. Here are my mother's big mittens for you, they will reach up to your elbows; here, stick your hands in! Now your hands look just like my nasty mother's!'

Gerda shed tears of joy.

'I don't like you to whimper!' said the little robber girl. 'You ought to be looking delighted; and here are two loaves and a ham for you, so that you shan't starve.'

These things were tied on to the back of the reindeer; the little robber girl opened the door, called in all the big dogs, and then she cut the halter with her knife, and said to the reindeer, 'Now run, but take care of my little girl!'

Gerda stretched out her hands in the big mittens to the robber girl and said good-bye; and then the reindeer darted off over briars and bushes, through the big wood, over swamps and plains, as fast as it could go. The wolves howled and the ravens screamed, while the red lights quivered up in the sky.

'There are my old northern lights,' said the reindeer; 'see how they flash!' and on it rushed faster than ever, day and night. The loaves were eaten, and the ham too, and then they were in Lapland.

SIXTH STORY

THE LAPP WOMAN AND THE FINN WOMAN

They stopped by a little hut, a very poverty-stricken one; the roof sloped right down to the ground, and the door was so low that the people had to creep on hands and knees when they wanted to go in or out. There was nobody at home here but an old Lapp woman, who was frying fish over a train-oil lamp. The reindeer told her all Gerda's story, but it told its own first; for it thought it was much the most important. Gerda was so overcome by the cold that she could not speak at all.

'Oh, you poor creatures!' said the Lapp woman; 'you've got a long way to go yet; you will have to go hundreds of miles into Finmark, for the Snow Queen is paying a country visit there, and she burns blue lights every night. I will write a few words on a dried stock-fish, for I have no paper. I will give it to you to take to the Finn woman up there. She will be better able to direct you than I can.'

So when Gerda was warmed, and had eaten and drunk something, the Lapp woman wrote a few words on a dried stock-fish and gave it to her, bidding her take good care of it. Then she tied her on to the reindeer again, and off they flew. Flicker, flicker, went the beautiful blue northern lights up in the sky all night long; — at last they came to Finmark, and knocked on the Finn woman's chimney, for she had no door at all.

There was such a heat inside that the Finn woman went about almost naked; she was little and very grubby. She at once loosened Gerda's things, and took off the mittens and the boots, or she would have been too hot. Then she put a piece of ice on the reindeer's head, and after that she read what was written on the stock-fish. She read it three times, and then she knew it by heart, and put the fish into the pot for dinner; there was no reason why it should not be eaten, and she never wasted anything.

Again the reindeer told his own story first, and then little Gerda's. The Finn woman blinked with her wise eyes, but she said nothing.

'You are so clever,' said the reindeer, 'I know you can bind all the winds of the world with a bit of sewing cotton. When a skipper unties one knot he gets a good wind, when he unties two it blows hard, and if he undoes the third and the fourth he brings a storm about his head wild enough to blow down the forest trees. Won't you give the little girl a drink, so that she may have the strength of twelve men to overcome the Snow Queen?'

'The strength of twelve men,' said the Finn woman. 'Yes, that will be about enough.'

She went along to a shelf and took down a big folded skin, which she unrolled. There were curious characters written on it, and the Finn woman read till the perspiration poured down her forehead.

But the reindeer again implored her to give Gerda something, and Gerda looked at her with such beseeching eyes, full of tears, that the Finn woman began blinking again, and drew the reindeer along into a corner, where she whispered to it, at the same time putting fresh ice on its head.

'Little Kay is certainly with the Snow Queen, and he is delighted with everything there. He thinks it is the best place in the world, but that is because he has got a splinter of glass in his heart and a grain of glass in his eye. They will have to come out first, or he will never be human again, and the Snow Queen will keep him in her power!'

'But can't you give little Gerda something to take which will give her power to conquer it all?'

'I can't give her greater power than she already has. Don't you see how great it is? Don't you see how both man and beast have to serve her? How she has got on as well as she has on her bare feet? We must not tell her what power she has; it is in her heart, because she is such a sweet innocent child. If she can't reach the Snow Queen herself, then we can't help her. The Snow Queen's gardens begin just two miles from here; you can carry the little girl as far as that. Put her down by the big bush standing there in the snow covered with red berries. Don't stand gossiping, but hurry back to me!' Then the Finn woman lifted Gerda on the reindeer's back, and it rushed off as hard as it could.

'Oh, I have not got my boots, and I have not got my mittens!' cried little Gerda.

She soon felt the want of them in that cutting wind, but the reindeer did not dare to stop. It ran on till it came to the bush with the red berries. There it put Gerda down, and kissed her on the mouth, while big shining tears trickled down its face. Then it ran back again as fast as ever it could. There stood poor little Gerda, without shoes or gloves, in the middle of freezing icebound Finmark.

She ran forward as quickly as she could. A whole regiment of snow-flakes came towards her; they did not fall from the sky, for it was quite clear, with the northern lights shining brightly. No; these snow-flakes ran along the ground, and the nearer they came the bigger they grew. Gerda remembered well how big and ingenious they looked under the magnifying glass. But the size of these was monstrous. They were alive; they were the Snow Queen's advanced guard, and they took the most curious shapes. Some looked like big, horrid porcupines, some like bundles of knotted snakes with their heads sticking out. Others, again, were like fat little bears with bristling hair, but all were dazzling white and living snow-flakes.

Then little Gerda said the Lord's Prayer, and the cold was so great that her breath froze as it came out of her mouth, and she could see it like a cloud of smoke in front of her. It grew thicker and thicker, till it formed itself into bright little angels, who grew bigger and bigger when they touched the ground. They all wore helmets, and carried shields and spears in their hands. More and more of them appeared, and when Gerda had finished her prayer she was surrounded by a whole legion. They pierced the snow-flakes with their spears and shivered them into a hundred pieces, and little Gerda walked fearlessly and undauntedly through them. The angels touched her hands and her feet, and then she hardly felt how cold it was, but walked quickly on towards the Palace of the Snow Queen.

Now we must see what Kay was about. He was not thinking about Gerda at all, least of all that she was just outside the Palace.

SEVENTH STORY

WHAT HAPPENED IN THE SNOW QUEEN'S PALACE AND AFTERWARDS

The Palace walls were made of drifted snow, and the windows and doors of the biting winds. There were over a hundred rooms in it, shaped just as the snow had drifted. The biggest one stretched for many miles. They were all lighted by the strongest northern lights. All the rooms were immensely big and empty, and glittering in their iciness. There was never any gaiety in them; not even so much as a ball for the little bears, when the storms might have turned up as the orchestra, and the polar bears might have walked about on their hind legs and shown off their grand manners. There was never even a little game-playing party, for such games as 'touch last' or 'the biter bit' — no, not even a little gossip over the coffee cups for the white fox misses. Immense, vast, and cold were the Snow Queen's halls. The northern lights came and went with such regularity that you could count the seconds between their coming and going. In the midst of these never-ending snow-halls was a frozen lake. It was broken up on the surface into a thousand bits, but each piece was so exactly like the others that the whole formed a perfect work of art. The Snow Queen sat in the very middle of it when she sat at home. She then said that she was sitting on 'The Mirror of Reason,' and that it was the best and only one in the world.

Little Kay was blue with cold, nay, almost black; but he did not know it, for the Snow Queen had kissed away the icy shiverings, and his heart was little better than a lump of ice. He went about dragging some sharp, flat pieces of ice, which he placed in all sorts of patterns, trying to make something out of them; just as when we at home have little tablets of wood, with which we make patterns, and call them a 'Chinese puzzle.'

Kay's patterns were most ingenious, because they were the 'Ice Puzzles of Reason.' In his eyes they were first-rate and of the greatest importance: this was because of the grain of glass still in his eye. He made many patterns forming words, but he never could find out the right way to place them for one particular word, a word he was most anxious to make. It was 'Eternity.' The Snow Queen had said to him that if he could find out this word he should be his own master, and she would give him the whole world and a new pair of skates. But he could not discover it.

'Now I am going to fly away to the warm countries,' said the Snow Queen. 'I want to go and peep into the black caldrons!' She meant the volcanoes Etna and Vesuvius by this. 'I must whiten them a little; it does them good, and the lemons and the grapes too!' And away she flew.

Kay sat quite alone in all those many miles of empty ice halls. He looked at his bits of ice, and thought and thought, till something gave way within him. He sat so stiff and immovable that one might have thought he was frozen to death.

Then it was that little Gerda walked into the Palace, through the great gates in a biting wind. She said her evening prayer, and the wind dropped as if lulled to sleep, and she walked on into the big empty hall. She saw Kay, and knew him at once; she flung her arms round his neck, held him fast, and cried, 'Kay, little Kay, have I found you at last?'

But he sat still, rigid and cold.

Then little Gerda shed hot tears; they fell upon his breast and penetrated to his heart. Here they thawed the lump of ice, and melted the little bit of the mirror which was in it. He looked at her, and she sang:

'Where roses deck the flowery vale, There, Infant Jesus, we thee hail!'

Then Kay burst into tears; he cried so much that the grain of glass was washed out of his eye. He knew her, and shouted with joy, 'Gerda, dear little Gerda! where have you been for such a long time? And where have I been?' He looked round and said, 'How cold it is here; how empty and vast!' He kept tight hold of Gerda, who laughed and cried for joy. Their happiness was so heavenly that even the bits of ice danced for joy around them; and when they settled down, there they lay! just in the very position the Snow Queen had told Kay he must find out, if he was to become his own master and have the whole world and a new pair of skates.

Gerda kissed his cheeks and they grew rosy, she kissed his eyes and they shone like hers, she kissed his hands and his feet, and he became well and strong. The Snow Queen might come home whenever she liked, his order of release was written there in shining letters of ice.

They took hold of each other's hands and wandered out of the big Palace. They talked about grandmother, and about the roses upon the roof. Wherever they went the winds lay still and the sun broke through the clouds. When they reached the bush with the red berries they found the reindeer waiting for them, and he had brought another young reindeer with him, whose udders were full. The children drank her warm milk and kissed her on the mouth. Then they carried Kay and Gerda, first to the Finn woman, in whose heated hut they warmed themselves and received directions about the homeward journey. Then they went on to the Lapp woman; she had made new clothes for them and prepared her sledge. Both the reindeer ran by their side, to the boundaries of the country; here the first green buds appeared, and they said 'Good-bye' to the reindeer and the Lapp woman. They heard the first little birds twittering and saw the buds in the forest. Out of it came riding a young girl on a beautiful horse, which Gerda knew, for it had drawn the golden chariot. She had a scarlet cap on her head and pistols in her belt; it was the little robber girl, who was tired of being at home. She was riding northwards to see how she liked it before she tried some other part of the world. She knew them again, and Gerda recognised her with delight.

'You are a nice fellow to go tramping off!' she said to little Kay. 'I should like to know if you deserve to have somebody running to the end of the world for your sake!'

But Gerda patted her cheek, and asked about the Prince and Princess.

'They are travelling in foreign countries,' said the robber girl.

'But the crow?' asked Gerda.

'Oh, the crow is dead!' she answered. 'The tame sweetheart is a widow, and goes about with a bit of black wool tied round her leg. She pities herself bitterly, but it's all nonsense! But tell me how you got on yourself, and where you found him.'

Gerda and Kay both told her all about it.

'Snip, snap, snurre, it's all right at last then!' she said, and she took hold of their hands and promised that if she ever passed through their town she would pay them a visit. Then she rode off into the wide world. But Kay and Gerda walked on, hand in hand, and wherever they went they found the most delightful spring and blooming flowers. Soon they recognised the big town where they lived, with its tall towers, in which the bells still rang their merry peals. They went straight on to grandmother's door, up the stairs and into her room. Everything was just as they had left it, and the old clock ticked in the corner, and the hands pointed to the time. As they went through the door into the room they perceived that they were grown up. The roses clustered round the open window, and there stood their two little chairs. Kay and Gerda sat down upon them, still holding each other by the hand. All the cold empty grandeur of the Snow Queen's palace had passed from their memory like a bad dream. Grandmother sat in God's warm sunshine reading from her Bible.

'Without ye become as little children ye cannot enter into the Kingdom of Heaven.'

Kay and Gerda looked into each other's eyes, and then all at once the meaning of the old hymn came to them.

'Where roses deck the flowery vale, There, Infant Jesus, we thee hail!'

And there they both sat, grown up and yet children, children at heart; and it was summer — warm, beautiful summer.

THE NIGHTINGALE

In China, as you know, the Emperor is a Chinaman, and all the people around him are Chinamen too. It is many years since the story I am going to tell you happened, but that is all the more reason for telling it, lest it should be forgotten. The emperor's palace was the most beautiful thing in the world; it was made entirely of the finest porcelain, very costly, but at the same time so fragile that it could only be touched with the very greatest care. There were the most extraordinary flowers to be seen in the garden; the most beautiful ones had little silver bells tied to them, which tinkled perpetually, so that one should not pass the flowers without looking at them. Every little detail in the garden had been most carefully thought out, and it was so big, that even the gardener himself did not know where it ended. If one went on walking, one came to beautiful woods with lofty trees and deep lakes. The wood extended to the sea, which was deep and blue, deep enough for large ships to sail up right under the branches of the trees. Among these trees lived a nightingale, which sang so deliciously, that even the poor fisherman, who had plenty of other things to do, lay still to listen to it, when he was out at night drawing in his nets. 'Heavens, how beautiful it is!' he said, but then he had to attend to his business and forgot it. The next night when he heard it again he would again exclaim, 'Heavens, how beautiful it is!'

Travellers came to the emperor's capital, from every country in the world; they admired everything very much, especially the palace and the gardens, but when they heard the nightingale they all said, 'This is better than anything!'

When they got home they described it, and the learned ones wrote many books about the town, the palace and the garden; but nobody forgot the nightingale, it was always put above everything else. Those among them who were poets wrote the most beautiful poems, all about the nightingale in the woods by the deep blue sea. These books went all over the world, and in course of time some of them reached the emperor. He sat in his golden chair reading and reading, and nodding his head, well pleased to hear such beautiful descriptions of the town, the palace and the garden. 'But the nightingale is the best of all,' he read.

'What is this?' said the emperor. 'The nightingale? Why, I know nothing about it. Is there such a bird in my kingdom, and in my own garden into the bargain, and I have never heard of it? Imagine my having to discover this from a book?'

Then he called his gentleman-in-waiting, who was so grand that when any one of a lower rank dared to speak to him, or to ask him a question, he would only answer 'P,' which means nothing at all.

'There is said to be a very wonderful bird called a nightingale here,' said the emperor. 'They say that it is better than anything else in all my great kingdom! Why have I never been told anything about it?'

'I have never heard it mentioned,' said the gentleman-in-waiting. 'It has never been presented at court.'

'I wish it to appear here this evening to sing to me,' said the emperor. 'The whole world knows what I am possessed of, and I know nothing about it!'

'I have never heard it mentioned before,' said the gentleman-in-waiting. 'I will seek it, and I will find it!' But where was it to be found? The gentleman-in-waiting ran upstairs and downstairs and in and out of all the rooms and corridors. No one of all those he met had ever heard anything about the nightingale; so the gentleman-in-waiting ran back to the emperor, and said that it must be a myth, invented by the writers of the books. 'Your imperial majesty must not believe everything that is written; books are often mere inventions, even if they do not belong to what we call the black art!'

'But the book in which I read it is sent to me by the powerful Emperor of Japan, so it can't be untrue. I will hear this nightingale; I insist upon its being here to-night. I extend my most gracious protection to it, and if it is not forthcoming, I will have the whole court trampled upon after supper!'

'Tsing-pe!' said the gentleman-in-waiting, and away he ran again, up and down all the stairs, in and out of all the rooms and corridors; half the court ran with him, for they none of them wished to be trampled on. There was much questioning about this nightingale, which was known to all the outside world, but to no one at court. At last they found a poor little maid in the kitchen. She said, 'Oh heavens, the nightingale? I know it very well. Yes, indeed it can sing. Every evening I am allowed to take broken meat to my poor sick mother: she lives down by the shore. On my way back, when I am tired, I rest awhile in the wood, and then I hear the nightingale. Its song brings the tears into my eyes; I feel as if my mother were kissing me!'

'Little kitchen-maid,' said the gentleman-in-waiting, 'I will procure you a permanent position in the kitchen, and permission to see the emperor dining, if you will take us to the nightingale. It is commanded to appear at court to-night.'

Then they all went out into the wood where the nightingale usually sang. Half the court was there. As they were going along at their best pace a cow began to bellow.

'Oh!' said a young courtier, 'there we have it. What wonderful power for such a little creature; I have certainly heard it before.'

'No, those are the cows bellowing; we are a long way yet from the place.' Then the frogs began to croak in the marsh.

'Beautiful!' said the Chinese chaplain, 'it is just like the tinkling of church bells.'

'No, those are the frogs!' said the little kitchen-maid. 'But I think we shall soon hear it now!'

Then the nightingale began to sing.

'There it is!' said the little girl. 'Listen, listen, there it sits!' and she pointed to a little grey bird up among the branches.

'Is it possible?' said the gentleman-in-waiting. 'I should never have thought it was like that. How common it looks! Seeing so many grand people must have frightened all its colours away.'

'Little nightingale!' called the kitchen-maid quite loud, 'our gracious emperor wishes you to sing to him!'

'With the greatest of pleasure!' said the nightingale, warbling away in the most delightful fashion.

'It is just like crystal bells,' said the gentleman-in-waiting. 'Look at its little throat, how active it is. It is extraordinary that we have never heard it before! I am sure it will be a great success at court!'

'Shall I sing again to the emperor?' said the nightingale, who thought he was present.

'My precious little nightingale,' said the gentleman-in-waiting, 'I have the honour to command your attendance at a court festival to-night, where you will charm his gracious majesty the emperor with your fascinating singing.'

'It sounds best among the trees,' said the nightingale, but it went with them willingly when it heard that the emperor wished it.

The palace had been brightened up for the occasion. The walls and the floors, which were all of china, shone by the light of many thousand golden lamps. The most beautiful flowers, all of the tinkling kind, were arranged in the corridors; there was hurrying to and fro, and a great draught, but this was just what made the bells ring; one's ears were full of the tinkling. In the middle of the large reception-room where the emperor sat a golden rod had been fixed, on which the nightingale was to perch. The whole court was assembled, and the little kitchen-maid had been permitted to stand behind the door, as she now had the actual title of cook. They were all dressed in their best; everybody's eyes were turned towards the little grey bird at which the emperor was nodding. The nightingale sang delightfully, and the tears came into the emperor's eyes, nay, they rolled down his cheeks; and then the nightingale sang more beautifully than ever, its notes touched all hearts. The emperor was charmed, and said the nightingale should have his gold slipper to wear round its neck. But the nightingale declined with thanks; it had already been sufficiently rewarded.

'I have seen tears in the eyes of the emperor; that is my richest reward. The tears of an emperor have a wonderful power! God knows I am sufficiently recompensed!' and then it again burst into its sweet heavenly song.

'That is the most delightful coquetting I have ever seen!' said the ladies, and they took some water into their mouths to try and make the same gurgling when any one spoke to them, thinking so to equal the nightingale. Even the lackeys and the chambermaids announced that they were satisfied, and that is saying a great deal; they are always the most difficult people to please. Yes, indeed, the nightingale had made a sensation. It was to stay at court now, and to have its own cage, as well as liberty to walk out twice a day, and once in the night. It always had twelve footmen, with each one holding a ribbon which was tied round its leg. There was not much pleasure in an outing of that sort.

The whole town talked about the marvellous bird, and if two people met, one said to the other 'Night,' and the other answered 'Gale,' and then they sighed, perfectly understanding each other. Eleven cheesemongers' children were called after it, but they had not got a voice among them.

One day a large parcel came for the emperor; outside was written the word 'Nightingale.'

'Here we have another new book about this celebrated bird,' said the emperor. But it was no book; it was a little work of art in a box, an artificial nightingale, exactly like the living one, but it was studded all over with diamonds, rubies and sapphires.

When the bird was wound up it could sing one of the songs the real one sang, and it wagged its tail, which glittered with silver and gold. A ribbon was tied round its neck on which was written, 'The Emperor of Japan's nightingale is very poor compared to the Emperor of China's.'

Everybody said, 'Oh, how beautiful!' And the person who brought the artificial bird immediately received the title of Imperial Nightingale-Carrier in Chief.

'Now, they must sing together; what a duet that will be.'

Then they had to sing together, but they did not get on very well, for the real nightingale sang in its own way, and the artificial one could only sing waltzes.

'There is no fault in that,' said the music-master; 'it is perfectly in time and correct in every way!'

Then the artificial bird had to sing alone. It was just as great a success as the real one, and then it was so much prettier to look at; it glittered like bracelets and breast-pins.

'That is the most delightful coquetting I have ever seen!' said the ladies, and they took some water into their mouths to try and make the same gurgling, thinking so to equal the nightingale.

It sang the same tune three and thirty times over, and yet it was not tired; people would willingly have heard it from the beginning again, but the emperor said that the real one must have a turn now — but where was it? No one had noticed that it had flown out of the open window, back to its own green woods.

'But what is the meaning of this?' said the emperor.

All the courtiers railed at it, and said it was a most ungrateful bird.

'We have got the best bird though,' said they, and then the artificial bird had to sing again, and this was the thirty-fourth time that they heard the same tune, but they did not know it thoroughly even yet, because it was so difficult.

The music-master praised the bird tremendously, and insisted that it was much better than the real nightingale, not only as regarded the outside with all the diamonds, but the inside too.

'Because you see, my ladies and gentlemen, and the emperor before all, in the real nightingale you never know what you will hear, but in the artificial one everything is decided beforehand! So it is, and so it must remain, it can't be otherwise. You can account for things, you can open it and show the human ingenuity in arranging the waltzes, how they go, and how one note follows upon another!'

'Those are exactly my opinions,' they all said, and the music-master got leave to show the bird to the public next Sunday. They were also to hear it sing, said the emperor. So they heard it, and all became as enthusiastic over it as if they had drunk themselves merry on tea, because that is a thoroughly Chinese habit.

Then they all said 'Oh,' and stuck their forefingers in the air and nodded their heads; but the poor fishermen who had heard the real nightingale said, 'It sounds very nice, and it is very like the real one, but there is something wanting, we don't know what.' The real nightingale was banished from the kingdom.

The artificial bird had its place on a silken cushion, close to the emperor's bed: all the presents it had received of gold and precious jewels were scattered round it. Its title had risen to be 'Chief Imperial Singer of the Bed-Chamber,' in rank number one, on the left side; for the emperor reckoned that side the important one, where the heart was seated. And even an emperor's heart is on the left side. The music-master wrote five-and-twenty volumes about the artificial bird; the treatise was very long and written in all the most difficult Chinese characters. Everybody said they had read and understood it, for otherwise they would have been reckoned stupid, and then their bodies would have been trampled upon.

Things went on in this way for a whole year. The emperor, the court, and all the other Chinamen knew every little gurgle in the song of the artificial bird by heart; but they liked it all the better for this, and they could all join in the song themselves. Even the street boys sang 'zizizi' and 'cluck, cluck, cluck,' and the emperor sang it too.

But one evening when the bird was singing its best, and the emperor was lying in bed listening to it, something gave way inside the bird with a 'whizz.' Then a spring burst, 'whirr' went all the wheels, and the music stopped. The emperor jumped out of bed and sent for his private physicians, but what good could they do? Then they sent for the watchmaker, and after a good deal of talk and examination he got the works to go again somehow; but he said it would have to be saved as much as possible, because it was so worn out, and he could not renew the works so as to be sure of the tune. This was a great blow! They only dared to let the artificial bird sing once a year, and hardly that; but then the music-master made a little speech, using all the most difficult words. He said it was just as good as ever, and his saying it made it so.

Five years now passed, and then a great grief came upon the nation, for they were all very fond of their emperor, and he was ill and could not live, it was said. A new emperor was already chosen, and people stood about in the street, and asked the gentleman-in-waiting how their emperor was going on.

'P,' answered he, shaking his head.

The emperor lay pale and cold in his gorgeous bed, the courtiers thought he was dead, and they all went off to

271

pay their respects to their new emperor. The lackeys ran off to talk matters over, and the chambermaids gave a great coffee-party. Cloth had been laid down in all the rooms and corridors so as to deaden the sound of footsteps, so it was very, very quiet. But the emperor was not dead yet. He lay stiff and pale in the gorgeous bed with its velvet hangings and heavy golden tassels. There was an open window high above him, and the moon streamed in upon the emperor, and the artificial bird beside him.

The poor emperor could hardly breathe, he seemed to have a weight on his chest, he opened his eyes, and then he saw that it was Death sitting upon his chest, wearing his golden crown. In one hand he held the emperor's golden sword, and in the other his imperial banner. Round about, from among the folds of the velvet hangings peered many curious faces: some were hideous, others gentle and pleasant. They were all the emperor's good and bad deeds, which now looked him in the face when Death was weighing him down.

'Do you remember that?' whispered one after the other; 'Do you remember this?' and they told him so many things that the perspiration poured down his face.

'I never knew that,' said the emperor. 'Music, music, sound the great Chinese drums!' he cried, 'that I may not hear what they are saying.' But they went on and on, and Death sat nodding his head, just like a Chinaman, at everything that was said.

'Music, music!' shrieked the emperor. 'You precious little golden bird, sing, sing! I have loaded you with precious stones, and even hung my own golden slipper round your neck; sing, I tell you, sing!'

But the bird stood silent; there was nobody to wind it up, so of course it could not go. Death continued to fix the great empty sockets of his eyes upon him, and all was silent, so terribly silent.

Suddenly, close to the window, there was a burst of lovely song; it was the living nightingale, perched on a branch outside. It had heard of the emperor's need, and had come to bring comfort and hope to him. As it sang the faces round became fainter and fainter, and the blood coursed with fresh vigour in the emperor's veins and through his feeble limbs. Even Death himself listened to the song and said, 'Go on, little nightingale, go on!'

'Yes, if you give me the gorgeous golden sword; yes, if you give me the imperial banner; yes, if you give me the emperor's crown.'

And Death gave back each of these treasures for a song, and the nightingale went on singing. It sang about the quiet churchyard, when the roses bloom, where the elder flower scents the air, and where the fresh grass is ever moistened anew by the tears of the mourner. This song brought to Death a longing for his own garden, and, like a cold grey mist, he passed out of the window.

'Thanks, thanks!' said the emperor; 'you heavenly little bird, I know you! I banished you from my kingdom, and yet you have charmed the evil visions away from my bed by your song, and even Death away from my heart! How can I ever repay you?'

'You have rewarded me,' said the nightingale. 'I brought the tears to your eyes, the very first time I ever sang to you, and I shall never forget it! Those are the jewels which gladden the heart of a singer; — but sleep now, and wake up fresh and strong! I will sing to you!'

Then it sang again, and the emperor fell into a sweet refreshing sleep. The sun shone in at his window, when he woke refreshed and well; none of his attendants had yet come back to him, for they thought he was dead, but the nightingale still sat there singing.

'You must always stay with me!' said the emperor. 'You shall only sing when you like, and I will break the artificial bird into a thousand pieces!'

'Don't do that!' said the nightingale, 'it did all the good it could! keep it as you have always done! I can't build my nest and live in this palace, but let me come whenever I like, then I will sit on the branch in the evening, and sing to you. I will sing to cheer you and to make you thoughtful too; I will sing to you of the happy ones, and of those that suffer too. I will sing about the good and the evil, which are kept hidden from you. The little singing bird flies far and wide, to the poor fisherman, and the peasant's home, to numbers who are far from you and your court. I love your heart more than your crown, and yet there is an odour of sanctity round the crown too! — I will come, and I will sing to you! — But you must promise me one thing! —

'Everything!' said the emperor, who stood there in his imperial robes which he had just put on, and he held the sword heavy with gold upon his heart.

'One thing I ask you! Tell no one that you have a little bird who tells you everything; it will be better so!'

Then the nightingale flew away. The attendants came in to see after their dead emperor, and there he stood, bidding them 'Good morning!'

THE REAL PRINCESS

There was once a prince, and he wanted a princess, but then she must be a *real* Princess. He travelled right round the world to find one, but there was always something wrong. There were plenty of princesses, but whether they were real princesses he had great difficulty in discovering; there was always something which was not quite right about them. So at last he had to come home again, and he was very sad because he wanted a real princess so badly.

One evening there was a terrible storm; it thundered and lightened and the rain poured down in torrents; indeed it was a fearful night.

In the middle of the storm somebody knocked at the town gate, and the old King himself went to open it.

It was a princess who stood outside, but she was in a terrible state from the rain and the storm. The water streamed out of her hair and her clothes; it ran in at the top of her shoes and out at the heel, but she said that she was a real princess.

'Well we shall soon see if that is true,' thought the old Queen, but she said nothing. She went into the bedroom, took all the bedclothes off and laid a pea on the bedstead: then she took twenty mattresses and piled them on the top of the pea, and then twenty feather beds on the top of the mattresses. This was where the princess was to sleep that night. In the morning they asked her how she had slept.

'Oh terribly badly!' said the princess. 'I have hardly closed my eyes the whole night! Heaven knows what was in the bed. I seemed to be lying upon some hard thing, and my whole body is black and blue this morning. It is terrible!'

They saw at once that she must be a real princess when she had felt the pea through twenty mattresses and twenty feather beds. Nobody but a real princess could have such a delicate skin.

So the prince took her to be his wife, for now he was sure that he had found a real princess, and the pea was put into the Museum, where it may still be seen if no one has stolen it.

Now this is a true story.

THE GARDEN OF PARADISE

There was once a king's son; nobody had so many or such beautiful books as he had. He could read about everything which had ever happened in this world, and see it all represented in the most beautiful pictures. He could get information about every nation and every country; but as to where the Garden of Paradise was to be found, not a word could he discover, and this was the very thing he thought most about. His grandmother had told him, when he was quite a little fellow and was about to begin his school life, that every flower in the Garden of Paradise was a delicious cake, and that the pistils were full of wine. In one flower history was written, in another geography or tables; you had only to eat the cake and you knew the lesson. The more you ate, the more history, geography and tables you knew. All this he believed then; but as he grew older and wiser and learnt more, he easily perceived that the delights of the Garden of Paradise must be far beyond all this.

'Oh, why did Eve take of the tree of knowledge? Why did Adam eat the forbidden fruit? If it had only been I it would not have happened! never would sin have entered the world!'

278

This is what he said then, and he still said it when he was seventeen; his thoughts were full of the Garden of Paradise.

He walked into the wood one day; he was alone, for that was his greatest pleasure. Evening came on, the clouds drew up and it rained as if the whole heaven had become a sluice from which the water poured in sheets; it was as dark as it is otherwise in the deepest well. Now he slipped on the wet grass, and then he fell on the bare stones which jutted out of the rocky ground. Everything was dripping, and at last the poor Prince hadn't got a dry thread on him. He had to climb over huge rocks where the water oozed out of the thick moss. He was almost fainting; just then he heard a curious murmuring and saw in front of him a big lighted cave. A fire was burning in the middle, big enough to roast a stag, which was in fact being done; a splendid stag with its huge antlers was stuck on a spit, being slowly turned round between the hewn trunks of two fir trees. An oldish woman, tall and strong enough to be a man dressed up, sat by the fire throwing on logs from time to time.

'Come in, by all means!' she said; 'sit down by the fire so that your clothes may dry!'

'There is a shocking draught here,' said the Prince, as he sat down on the ground.

'It will be worse than this when my sons come home!' said the woman. 'You are in the cavern of the winds; my sons are the four winds of the world! Do you understand?'

'Who are your sons?' asked the Prince.

'Well that's not so easy to answer when the question is stupidly put,' said the woman. 'My sons do as they like; they are playing rounders now with the clouds up there in the great hall,' and she pointed up into the sky.

'Oh indeed!' said the Prince. 'You seem to speak very harshly, and you are not so gentle as the women I generally see about me!'

'Oh, I daresay they have nothing else to do! I have to be harsh if I am to keep my boys under control! But I can do it, although they are a stiff-necked lot! Do you see those four sacks hanging on the wall? They are just as frightened of them as you used to be of the cane behind the looking-glass. I can double the boys up, I can tell you, and then they have to go into the bag; we don't stand upon ceremony, and there they have to stay; they can't get out to play their tricks till it suits me to let them. But here we have one of them.' It was the Northwind who came in with an icy blast; great hailstones peppered about the floor and snow-flakes drifted in. He was dressed in bearskin trousers and jacket, and he had a sealskin cap drawn over his ears. Long icicles were hanging from his beard, and one hailstone after another dropped down from the collar of his jacket.

'Don't go straight to the fire,' said the Prince. 'You might easily get chilblains!'

'Chilblains!' said the Northwind with a loud laugh. 'Chilblains! they are my greatest delight! What sort of a feeble creature are you? How did you get into the cave of the winds?'

'He is my guest,' said the old woman, 'and if you are not pleased with that explanation you may go into the bag! Now you know my opinion!'

This had its effect, and the Northwind told them where he came from, and where he had been for the last month.

'I come from the Arctic seas,' he said. 'I have been on Behring Island with the Russian walrus-hunters. I sat at the helm and slept when they sailed from the north cape, and when I woke now and then the stormy petrels were flying about my legs. They are queer birds; they give a brisk flap with their wings and then keep them stretched out and motionless, and even then they have speed enough.'

'Pray don't be too long-winded,' said the mother of the winds. 'So at last you got to Behring Island!'

'It's perfectly splendid! There you have a floor to dance upon, as flat as a pancake, half-thawed snow, with moss. There were bones of whales and Polar bears lying about; they looked like the legs and arms of giants covered with green mould. One would think that the sun had never shone on them. I gave a little puff to the fog so that one could see the shed. It was a house built of wreckage and covered with the skins of whales; the flesh side was turned outwards; it was all red and green; a living Polar bear sat on the roof growling. I went to the shore and looked at the birds' nests, looked at the unfledged young ones screaming and gaping; then I blew down thousands of their throats and they learnt to shut their mouths. Lower down the walruses were rolling about like monster maggots with pigs' heads and teeth a yard long!'

'You're a good story-teller, my boy!' said his mother. 'It makes my mouth water to hear you!'

'Then there was a hunt! The harpoons were plunged into the walruses' breasts, and the steaming blood spurted out of them like fountains over the ice. Then I remembered my part of the game! I blew up and made my ships, the mountain-high icebergs, nip the boats; whew! how they whistled and how they screamed, but I whistled louder. They were obliged to throw the dead walruses, chests and ropes out upon the ice! I shook the snow-flakes over them and let them drift southwards to taste the salt water. They will never come back to Behring Island!'

'Then you've been doing evil!' said the mother of the winds.

'What good I did, the others may tell you,' said he. 'But here we have my brother from the west; I like him best of all; he smells of the sea and brings a splendid cool breeze with him!'

'Is that the little Zephyr?' asked the Prince.

'Yes, certainly it is Zephyr, but he is not so little as all that. He used to be a pretty boy once, but that's gone by!'

He looked like a wild man of the woods, but he had a padded hat on so as not to come to any harm. He carried a mahogany club cut in the American mahogany forests. It could not be anything less than that.

'Where do you come from?' asked his mother.

'From the forest wildernesses!' he said, 'where the thorny creepers make a fence between every tree, where the

282

water-snake lies in the wet grass, and where human beings seem to be superfluous!'

'What did you do there?'

'I looked at the mighty river, saw where it dashed over the rocks in dust and flew with the clouds to carry the rainbow. I saw the wild buffalo swimming in the river, but the stream carried him away; he floated with the wild duck, which soared into the sky at the rapids; but the buffalo was carried over with the water. I liked that and blew a storm, so that the primaeval trees had to sail too, and they were whirled about like shavings.'

'And you have done nothing else?' asked the old woman.

'I have been turning somersaults in the Savannahs, patting the wild horse, and shaking down cocoanuts! Oh yes, I have plenty of stories to tell! But one need not tell everything. You know that very well, old woman!' and then he kissed his mother so heartily that she nearly fell backwards; he was indeed a wild boy.

The Southwind appeared now in a turban and a flowing bedouin's cloak.

'It is fearfully cold in here,' he said, throwing wood on the fire; 'it is easy to see that the Northwind got here first!'

'It is hot enough here to roast a polar bear,' said the Northwind.

'You are a polar bear yourself!' said the Southwind.

'Do you want to go into the bag?' asked the old woman. 'Sit down on that stone and tell us where you have been.'

'In Africa, mother!' he answered. 'I have been chasing the lion with the Hottentots in Kaffirland! What grass there is on those plains! as green as an olive. The gnu was dancing about, and the ostriches ran races with me, but I am still the fastest. I went to the desert with its yellow sand. It looks like the bottom of the sea. I met a caravan! They were killing their last camel to get water to drink, but it wasn't much they got. The sun was blazing above, and the sand burning below. There were no limits to the outstretched desert. Then I burrowed into the fine loose sand and whirled it up in great columns — that was a dance! You should have seen how despondently the dromedaries stood, and the merchant drew his caftan over his head. He threw himself down before me as if I had been Allah, his god. Now they are buried, and there is a pyramid of sand over them all; when I blow it away, sometime the sun will bleach their bones, and then travellers will see that people have been there before, otherwise you would hardly believe it in the desert!'

'Then you have only been doing harm!' said the mother. 'Into the bag you go!' And before he knew where he was she had the Southwind by the waist and in the bag; it rolled about on the ground, but she sat down upon it and then it had to be quiet.

'Your sons are lively fellows!' said the Prince.

'Yes, indeed,' she said; 'but I can master them! Here comes the fourth.'

It was the Eastwind, and he was dressed like a Chinaman.

'Oh, have you come from that quarter?' said the mother. 'I thought you had been in the Garden of Paradise.'

'I am only going there to-morrow!' said the Eastwind. 'It will be a hundred years to-morrow since I have been there. I have just come from China, where I danced round the porcelain tower till all the bells jingled. The officials were flogged in the streets, the bamboo canes were broken over their shoulders, and they were all people ranging from the first to the ninth rank. They shrieked "Many thanks, Father and benefactor," but they didn't mean what they said, and I went on ringing the bells and singing "Tsing, tsang, tsu!"'

'You're quite uproarious about it!' said the old woman. 'It's a good thing you are going to the Garden of Paradise to-morrow; it always has a good effect on your behaviour. Mind you drink deep of the well of wisdom, and bring a little bottleful home to me.'

'That I will,' said the Eastwind, 'But why have you put my brother from the south into the bag? Out with him. He must tell me about the phoenix; the Princess always wants to hear about that bird when I call every hundred years. Open the bag! then you'll be my sweetest mother, and I'll give you two pockets full of tea as green and fresh as when I picked it!'

'Well, for the sake of the tea, and because you are my darling, I will open my bag!'

She did open it and the Southwind crept out, but he was quite crestfallen because the strange Prince had seen his disgrace.

'Here is a palm leaf for the Princess!' said the Southwind. 'The old phoenix, the only one in the world, gave it to me. He has scratched his whole history on it with his bill, for the hundred years of his life, and she can read it for herself. I saw how the phoenix set fire to his nest himself and sat on it while it burnt, like the widow of a Hindoo. Oh, how the dry branches crackled, how it smoked, and what a smell there was! At last it all burst into flame; the old bird was burnt to ashes, but his egg lay glowing in the fire; it broke with a loud bang and the young one flew out. Now it rules over all the birds, and it is the only phoenix in the world. He bit a hole in the leaf I gave you; that is his greeting to the Princess.'

'Let us have something to eat now!' said the mother of the winds; and they all sat down to eat the roast stag, and the Prince sat by the side of the Eastwind, so they soon became good friends.

'I say,' said the Prince, 'just tell me who is this Princess, and where is the Garden of Paradise?'

'Oh ho!' said the Eastwind, 'if that is where you want to go you must fly with me to-morrow. But I may as well tell you that no human being has been there since Adam and Eve's time. You know all about them I suppose from your Bible stories?'

'Of course,' said the Prince.

'When they were driven away the Garden of Eden sank into the ground, but it kept its warm sunshine, its mild air, and all its charms. The queen of the fairies lives there. The Island of Bliss, where death never enters, and where living is a delight, is there. Get on my back to-morrow and I will take you with me; I think I can manage it! But you mustn't talk now, I want to go to sleep.'

When the Prince woke up in the early morning, he was not a little surprised to find that he was already high above the clouds. He was sitting on the back of the Eastwind, who was holding him carefully; they were so high up that woods and fields, rivers and lakes, looked like a large coloured map.

'Good morning,' said the Eastwind. 'You may as well sleep a little longer, for there is not much to be seen in this flat country below us, unless you want to count the churches. They look like chalk dots on the green board.'

He called the fields and meadows 'the green board.'

'It was very rude of me to leave without saying good-bye to your mother and brothers,' said the Prince.

'One is excused when one is asleep!' said the Eastwind, and they flew on faster than ever. You could mark their flight by the rustling of the trees as they passed over the woods; and whenever they crossed a lake, or the sea, the waves rose and the great ships dipped low down in the water, like floating swans. Towards evening the large towns were amusing as it grew dark, with all their lights twinkling now here, now there, just as when one burns a piece of paper and sees all the little sparks like children coming home from school. The Prince clapped his hands, but the Eastwind told him he had better leave off and hold tight, or he might fall and find himself hanging on to a church steeple.

The eagle in the great forest flew swiftly, but the Eastwind flew more swiftly still. The Kossack on his little horse sped fast over the plains, but the Prince sped faster still.

'Now you can see the Himalayas!' said the Eastwind. 'They are the highest mountains in Asia; we shall soon reach the Garden of Paradise.'

They took a more southerly direction, and the air became scented with spices and flowers. Figs and pomegranates grew wild, and the wild vines were covered with blue and green grapes. They both descended here and stretched themselves on the soft grass, where the flowers nodded to the wind, as much as to say, 'Welcome back.'

'Are we in the Garden of Paradise now?' asked the Prince.

'No, certainly not!' answered the Eastwind. 'But we shall soon be there. Do you see that wall of rock and the great cavern where the wild vine hangs like a big curtain? We have to go through there! Wrap yourself up in your cloak, the sun is burning here, but a step further on it is icy cold. The bird which flies past the cavern has one wing out here in the heat of summer, and the other is there in the cold of winter.'

'So that is the way to the Garden of Paradise!' said the Prince.

Now they entered the cavern. Oh, how icily cold it was; but it did not last long. The Eastwind spread his wings, and they shone like the brightest flame; but what a cave it was! Large blocks of stone, from which the water dripped, hung over them in the most extraordinary shapes; at one moment it was so low and narrow that they had to crawl on hands and knees, the next it was as wide and lofty as if they were in the open air. It looked like a chapel of the dead, with mute organ pipes and petrified banners.

'We seem to be journeying along Death's road to the Garden of Paradise!' said the Prince, but the Eastwind never answered a word, he only pointed before them where a beautiful blue light was shining. The blocks of stone above them grew dimmer and dimmer, and at last they became as transparent as a white cloud in the moonshine. The air was also deliciously soft, as fresh as on the mountain-tops and as scented as down among the roses in the valley.

A river ran there as clear as the air itself, and the fish in it were like gold and silver. Purple eels, which gave out blue sparks with every curve, gambolled about in the water; and the broad leaves of the water-lilies were tinged with the hues of the rainbow, while the flower itself was like a fiery orange flame, nourished by the water, just as oil keeps a lamp constantly burning. A firm bridge of marble, as delicately and skilfully carved as if it were lace and glass beads, led over the water to the Island of Bliss, where the Garden of Paradise bloomed.

The Eastwind took the Prince in his arms and bore him over. The flowers and leaves there sang all the beautiful old songs of his childhood, but sang them more wonderfully than any human voice could sing them.

Were these palm trees or giant water plants growing here? The Prince had never seen such rich and mighty trees. The most wonderful climbing plants hung in wreaths, such as are only to be found pictured in gold and colours on the margins of old books of the Saints or entwined among their initial letters. It was the most extraordinary combination of birds, flowers and scrolls.

Close by on the grass stood a flock of peacocks with their brilliant tails outspread. Yes, indeed, it seemed so, but when the Prince touched them he saw that they were not birds but plants. They were big dock leaves, which shone like peacocks' tails. Lions and tigers sprang like agile cats among the green hedges, which were scented with the blossom of the olive, and the lion and the tiger were tame. The wild dove, glistening like a pearl, beat the lion's mane with his wings; and the antelope, otherwise so shy, stood by nodding, just as if he wanted to join the game.

The Fairy of the Garden now advanced to meet them; her garments shone like the sun, and her face beamed like that of a happy mother rejoicing over her child. She was young and very beautiful, and was surrounded by a band of lovely girls, each with a gleaming star in her hair.

When the Eastwind gave her the inscribed leaf from the Phoenix her eyes sparkled with delight. She took the Prince's hand and led him into her palace, where the walls were the colour of the brightest tulips in the sunlight. The ceiling was one great shining flower, and the longer one gazed into it the deeper the calyx seemed to be. The Prince went to the window, and looking through one of the panes saw the Tree of Knowledge, with the Serpent, and Adam and Eve standing by.

'Are they not driven out?' he asked, and the Fairy smiled, and explained that Time had burned a picture into each pane, but not of the kind one usually sees; they were alive, the leaves on the trees moved, and people came and went like the reflections in a mirror.

Then he looked through another pane, and he saw Jacob's dream, with the ladder going straight up into heaven, and angels with great wings were fluttering up and down. All that had ever happened in this world lived and moved on these window panes; only Time could imprint such wonderful pictures.

The Fairy smiled and led him into a large, lofty room, the walls of which were like transparent paintings of faces, one more beautiful than the other. These were millions of the Blessed who smiled and sang, and all their songs melted into one perfect melody. The highest ones were so tiny that they seemed smaller than the very smallest rosebud, no bigger than a pinpoint in a drawing. In the middle of the room stood a large tree, with handsome drooping branches; golden apples, large and small, hung like oranges among its green leaves. It was the Tree of Knowledge, of whose fruit Adam and Eve had eaten. From every leaf hung a shining red drop of dew; it was as if the tree wept tears of blood.

'Now let us get into the boat,' said the Fairy. 'We shall find refreshment on the swelling waters. The boat rocks, but it does not move from the spot; all the countries of the world will pass before our eyes.'

It was a curious sight to see the whole coast move. Here came lofty snow-clad Alps, with their clouds and dark fir trees. The horn echoed sadly among them, and the shepherd yodelled sweetly in the valleys. Then banian trees bent their long drooping branches over the boat, black swans floated on the water, and the strangest animals and flowers appeared on the shore. This was New Holland, the fifth portion of the world, which glided past them with a view of its blue mountains. They heard the song of priests, and saw the dances of the savages to the sound of drums and pipes of bone. The pyramids of Egypt reaching to the clouds, with fallen columns, and Sphinxes half buried in sand, next sailed past them. Then came the Aurora Borealis blazing over the peaks of the north; they were fireworks which could not be imitated. The Prince was so happy, and he saw a hundred times more than we have described.

'Can I stay here always?' he asked.

'That depends upon yourself,' answered the Fairy. 'If you do not, like Adam, allow yourself to be tempted to do what is forbidden, you can stay here always.'

'I will not touch the apples on the Tree of Knowledge,' said the Prince. 'There are thousands of other fruits here as beautiful.'

'Test yourself, and if you are not strong enough, go back with the Eastwind who brought you. He is going away now, and will not come back for a hundred years; the time will fly in this place like a hundred hours, but that is a long time for temptation and sin. Every evening when I leave you I must say, "Come with me," and I must beckon to you, but stay behind. Do not come with me, for with every step you take your longing will grow stronger. You will reach the hall where grows the Tree of Knowledge; I sleep beneath its fragrant drooping branches. You will bend over me and I must smile, but if you press a kiss upon my lips Paradise will sink deep down into the earth, and it will be lost to you. The sharp winds of the wilderness will whistle round you, the cold rain will drop from your hair. Sorrow and labour will be your lot.'

'I will remain here!' said the Prince.

And the Eastwind kissed him on the mouth and said: 'Be strong, then we shall meet again in a hundred years. Farewell! Farewell!' And the Eastwind spread his great wings; they shone like poppies at the harvest time, or the Northern Lights in a cold winter.

'Good-bye! good-bye!' whispered the flowers. Storks and pelicans flew in a line like waving ribbons, conducting him to the boundaries of the Garden.

'Now we begin our dancing!' said the Fairy; 'at the end when I dance with you, as the sun goes down you will see me beckon to you and cry, "Come with me", but do not come. I have to repeat it every night for a hundred years. Every time you resist, you will grow stronger, and at last you will not even think of following. To-night is the first time. Remember my warning!'

And the Fairy led him into a large hall of white transparent lilies, the yellow stamens in each formed a little golden harp which echoed the sound of strings and flutes. Lovely girls, slender and lissom, dressed in floating gauze, which revealed their exquisite limbs, glided in the dance, and sang of the joy of living — that they would never die — and that the Garden of Paradise would bloom for ever.

The sun went down and the sky was bathed in golden light which gave the lilies the effect of roses; and the Prince drank of the foaming wine handed to him by the maidens. He felt such joy as he had never known before; he saw the background of the hall opening where the Tree of Knowledge stood in a radiancy which blinded him. The song proceeding from it was soft and lovely, like his mother's voice, and she seemed to say, 'My child, my beloved child!'

Then the Fairy beckoned to him and said so tenderly, 'Come with me,' that he rushed towards her, forgetting his promise, forgetting everything on the very first evening that she smiled and beckoned to him.

The fragrance in the scented air around grew stronger, the harps sounded sweeter than ever, and it seemed as if the millions of smiling heads in the hall where the Tree grew nodded and sang, 'One must know everything. Man is lord of the earth.' They were no longer tears of blood which fell from the Tree; it seemed to him that they were red shining stars.

'Come with me, come with me,' spoke those trembling tones, and at every step the Prince's cheeks burnt hotter and hotter and his blood coursed more rapidly.

'I must go,' he said, 'it is no sin; I must see her asleep; nothing will be lost if I do not kiss her, and that I will not do. My will is strong.'

The Fairy dropped her shimmering garment, drew back the branches, and a moment after was hidden within their depths.

'I have not sinned yet!' said the Prince, 'nor will I'; then he drew back the branches. There she lay asleep already, beautiful as only the Fairy in the Garden of Paradise can be. She smiled in her dreams; he bent over her and saw the tears welling up under her eyelashes.

'Do you weep for me?' he whispered. 'Weep not, beautiful maiden. I only now understand the full bliss of

Paradise; it surges through my blood and through my thoughts. I feel the strength of the angels and of everlasting life in my mortal limbs! If it were to be everlasting night to me, a moment like this were worth it!' and he kissed away the tears from her eyes; his mouth touched hers.

Then came a sound like thunder, louder and more awful than any he had ever heard before, and everything around collapsed. The beautiful Fairy, the flowery Paradise sank deeper and deeper. The Prince saw it sink into the darkness of night; it shone far off like a little tiny twinkling star. The chill of death crept over his limbs; he closed his eyes and lay long as if dead.

The cold rain fell on his face, and the sharp wind blew around his head, and at last his memory came back. 'What have I done?' he sighed. 'I have sinned like Adam, sinned so heavily that Paradise has sunk low beneath the earth!' And he opened his eyes; he could still see the star, the far-away star, which twinkled like Paradise; it was the morning star in the sky. He got up and found himself in the wood near the cave of the winds, and the mother of the winds sat by his side. She looked angry and raised her hand.

'So soon as the first evening!' she said. 'I thought as much; if you were my boy, you should go into the bag!'

'Ah, he shall soon go there!' said Death. He was a strong old man, with a scythe in his hand and great black wings. 'He shall be laid in a coffin, but not now; I only mark him and then leave him for a time to wander about on the earth to expiate his sin and to grow better. I will come some time. When he least expects me, I shall come back, lay him in a black coffin, put it on my head, and fly to the skies. The Garden of Paradise blooms there too, and if he is good and holy he shall enter into it; but if his thoughts are wicked and his heart still full of sin, he will sink deeper in his coffin than Paradise sank, and I shall only go once in every thousand years to see if he is to sink deeper or to rise to the stars, the twinkling stars up there.'

THE MERMAID

Far out at sea the water is as blue as the bluest cornflower, and as clear as the clearest crystal; but it is very deep, too deep for any cable to fathom, and if many steeples were piled on the top of one another they would not reach from the bed of the sea to the surface of the water. It is down there that the Mermen live.

Now don't imagine that there are only bare white sands at the bottom; oh no! the most wonderful trees and plants grow there, with such flexible stalks and leaves, that at the slightest motion of the water they move just as if they were alive. All the fish, big and little, glide among the branches just as, up here, birds glide through the air. The palace of the Merman King lies in the very deepest part; its walls are of coral and the long pointed windows of the clearest amber, but the roof is made of mussel shells which open and shut with the lapping of the water. This has a lovely effect, for there are gleaming pearls in every shell, any one of which would be the pride of a queen's crown.

The Merman King had been for many years a widower, but his old mother kept house for him; she was a clever woman, but so proud of her noble birth that she wore twelve oysters on her tail, while the other grandees were only allowed six. Otherwise she was worthy of all praise, especially because she was so fond of the little mermaid princesses, her grandchildren. They were six beautiful children, but the youngest was the prettiest of all; her skin was as soft and delicate as a roseleaf, her eyes as blue as the deepest sea, but like all the others she had no feet, and instead of legs she had a fish's tail.

All the livelong day they used to play in the palace in the great halls, where living flowers grew out of the walls. When the great amber windows were thrown open the fish swam in, just as the swallows fly into our rooms when we open the windows, but the fish swam right up to the little princesses, ate out of their hands, and allowed themselves to be patted.

Outside the palace was a large garden, with fiery red and deep blue trees, the fruit of which shone like gold, while the flowers glowed like fire on their ceaselessly waving stalks. The ground was of the finest sand, but it was of a blue phosphorescent tint. Everything was bathed in a wondrous blue light down there; you might more readily have supposed yourself to be high up in the air, with only the sky above and below you, than that you were at the bottom of the ocean. In a dead calm you could just catch a glimpse of the sun like a purple flower with a stream of light radiating from its calyx.

Each little princess had her own little plot of garden, where she could dig and plant just as she liked. One made her flower-bed in the shape of a whale; another thought it nice to have hers like a little mermaid; but the youngest made hers quite round like the sun, and she would only have flowers of a rosy hue like its beams. She was a curious child, quiet and thoughtful, and while the other sisters decked out their gardens with all kinds of extraordinary objects which they got from wrecks, she would have nothing besides the rosy flowers like the sun up above, except a statue of a beautiful boy. It was hewn out of the purest white marble and had gone to the bottom from some wreck. By the statue she planted a rosy red weeping willow which grew splendidly, and the fresh delicate branches hung round and over it, till they almost touched the blue sand where the shadows showed violet, and were ever moving like the branches. It looked as if the leaves and the roots were playfully interchanging kisses.

Nothing gave her greater pleasure than to hear about the world of human beings up above; she made her old grandmother tell her all that she knew about ships and towns, people and animals. But above all it seemed strangely beautiful to her that up on the earth the flowers were scented, for they were not so at the bottom of the sea; also that the woods were green, and that the fish which were to be seen among the branches could sing so loudly and sweetly that it was a delight to listen to them. You see the grandmother called little birds fish, or the mermaids would not have understood her, as they had never seen a bird.

'When you are fifteen,' said the grandmother, 'you will be allowed to rise up from the sea and sit on the rocks in the moonlight, and look at the big ships sailing by, and you will also see woods and towns.'

One of the sisters would be fifteen in the following year, but the others, — well, they were each one year younger than the other, so that the youngest had five whole years to wait before she would be allowed to come up from the bottom, to see what things were like on earth. But each one promised the others to give a full account of all that she had seen, and found most wonderful on the first day. Their grandmother could never tell them enough, for there were so many things about which they wanted information.

None of them was so full of longings as the youngest, the very one who had the longest time to wait, and who was so quiet and dreamy. Many a night she stood by the open windows and looked up through the dark blue water which the fish were lashing with their tails and fins. She could see the moon and the stars, it is true; their light was pale, but they looked much bigger through the water than they do to our eyes. When she saw a dark shadow glide between her and them, she knew that it was either a whale swimming above her, or else a ship laden with human beings. I am certain they never dreamt that a lovely little mermaid was standing down below, stretching up her white hands towards the keel.

The eldest princess had now reached her fifteenth birthday, and was to venture above the water. When she came back she had hundreds of things to tell them, but the most delightful of all, she said, was to lie in the moonlight, on a sandbank in a calm sea, and to gaze at the large town close to the shore, where the lights twinkled like hundreds of stars; to listen to music and the noise and bustle of carriages and people, to see the many church towers and spires, and to hear the bells ringing; and just because she could not go on shore she longed for that most of all.

Oh, how eagerly the youngest sister listened! and when, later in the evening she stood at the open window and looked up through the dark blue water, she thought of the big town with all its noise and bustle, and fancied that she could even hear the church bells ringing.

The year after, the second sister was allowed to mount up through the water and swim about wherever she liked. The sun was just going down when she reached the surface, the most beautiful sight, she thought, that she had ever seen. The whole sky had looked like gold, she said, and as for the clouds! well, their beauty was beyond description; they floated in red and violet splendour over her head, and, far faster than they went, a flock of wild swans flew like a long white veil over the water towards the setting sun; she swam towards it, but it sank and all the rosy light on clouds and water faded away.

The year after that the third sister went up, and, being much the most venturesome of them all, swam up a broad river which ran into the sea. She saw beautiful green, vine-clad hills; palaces and country seats peeping through splendid woods. She heard the birds singing, and the sun was so hot that she was often obliged to dive, to cool her burning face. In a tiny bay she found a troop of little children running about naked and paddling in the water; she wanted to play with them, but they were frightened and ran away. Then a little black animal came up; it was a dog, but she had never seen one before; it barked so furiously at her that she was frightened and made for the open sea. She could never forget the beautiful woods, the green hills and the lovely children who could swim in the water although they had no fishes' tails.

The fourth sister was not so brave; she stayed in the remotest part of the ocean, and, according to her account, that was the most beautiful spot. You could see for miles and miles around you, and the sky above was like a great glass dome. She had seen ships, but only far away, so that they looked like sea-gulls. There were grotesque dolphins turning somersaults, and gigantic whales squirting water through their nostrils like hundreds of fountains on every side.

Now the fifth sister's turn came. Her birthday fell in the winter, so that she saw sights that the others had not seen on their first trips. The sea looked quite green, and large icebergs were floating about, each one of which looked like a pearl, she said, but was much bigger than the church towers built by men. They took the most wonderful shapes, and sparkled like diamonds. She had seated herself on one of the largest, and all the passing ships sheered off in alarm when they saw her sitting there with her long hair streaming loose in the wind.

In the evening the sky became overcast with dark clouds; it thundered and lightened, and the huge icebergs glittering in the bright lightning, were lifted high into the air by the black waves. All the ships shortened sail, and there was fear and trembling on every side, but she sat quietly on her floating iceberg watching the blue lightning flash in zigzags down on to the shining sea.

The first time any of the sisters rose above the water she was delighted by the novelties and beauties she saw; but once grown up, and at liberty to go where she liked, she became indifferent and longed for her home; in the course of a month or so they all said that after all their own home in the deep was best, it was so cosy there.

Many an evening the five sisters interlacing their arms would rise above the water together. They had lovely voices, much clearer than any mortal, and when a storm was rising, and they expected ships to be wrecked, they would sing in the most seductive strains of the wonders of the deep, bidding the seafarers have no fear of them. But the sailors could not understand the words, they thought it was the voice of the storm; nor could it be theirs to see this Elysium of the deep, for when the ship sank they were drowned, and only reached the Merman's palace in death. When the elder sisters rose up in this manner, arm-in-arm, in the evening, the youngest remained behind quite alone, looking after them as if she must weep; but mermaids have no tears, and so they suffer all the more.

'Oh! if I were only fifteen!' she said, 'I know how fond I shall be of the world above, and of the mortals who dwell there.'

At last her fifteenth birthday came.

'Now we shall have you off our hands,' said her grandmother, the old queen-dowager. 'Come now, let me adorn you like your other sisters!' and she put a wreath of white lilies round her hair, but every petal of the flowers was half a pearl; then the old queen had eight oysters fixed on to the princess's tail to show her high rank.

'But it hurts so!' said the little mermaid.

'You must endure the pain for the sake of the finery!' said her grandmother.

But oh! how gladly would she have shaken off all this splendour, and laid aside the heavy wreath. Her red flowers in her garden suited her much better, but she did not dare to make any alteration. 'Good-bye,' she said, and mounted as lightly and airily as a bubble through the water.

The sun had just set when her head rose above the water, but the clouds were still lighted up with a rosy and golden splendour, and the evening star sparkled in the soft pink sky, the air was mild and fresh, and the sea as calm as a millpond. A big three-masted ship lay close by with only a single sail set, for there was not a breath of wind, and the sailors were sitting about the rigging, on the cross-trees, and at the mast-heads. There was music and singing on board, and as the evening closed in hundreds of gaily coloured lanterns were lighted — they looked like the flags of all nations waving in the air. The little mermaid swam right up to the cabin windows, and every time she was lifted by the swell she could see through the transparent panes crowds of gaily dressed people. The handsomest of them all was the young prince with large dark eyes; he could not be much more than sixteen, and all these festivities were in honour of his birthday. The sailors danced on deck, and when the prince appeared among them hundreds of rockets were let off making it as light as day, and frightening the little mermaid so much that she had to dive under the water. She soon ventured up again, and it was just as if all the stars of heaven were falling in showers round about her. She had never seen such magic fires. Great suns whirled round, gorgeous fire-fish hung in the blue air, and all was reflected in the calm and glassy sea. It was so light on board the ship that every little rope could be seen, and the people still better. Oh, how handsome the prince was! how he laughed and smiled as he greeted his guests, while the music rang out in the quiet night.

It got quite late, but the little mermaid could not take her eyes off the ship and the beautiful prince. The coloured lanterns were put out, no more rockets were sent up, and the cannon had ceased its thunder, but deep down in the sea there was a dull murmuring and moaning sound. Meanwhile she was rocked up and down on the waves, so that she could look into the cabin; but the ship got more and more way on, sail after sail was filled by the wind, the waves grew stronger, great clouds gathered, and it lightened in the distance. Oh, there was going to be a fearful storm! and soon the sailors had to shorten sail. The great ship rocked and rolled as she dashed over the angry sea, the black waves rose like mountains, high enough to overwhelm her, but she dived like a swan through them and rose again and again on their towering crests. The little mermaid thought it a most amusing race, but not so the sailors. The ship creaked and groaned; the mighty timbers bulged and bent under the heavy blows; the water broke over the decks, snapping the main mast like a reed; she heeled over on her side, and the water rushed into the hold.

Now the little mermaid saw that they were in danger, and she had for her own sake to beware of the floating beams and wreckage. One moment it was so pitch dark that she could not see at all, but when the lightning flashed it became so light that she could see all on board. Every man was looking out for his own safety as best he could; but she more particularly followed the young prince with her eyes, and when the ship went down she saw him sink in the deep sea. At first she was quite delighted, for now he was coming to be with her, but then she remembered that human beings could not live under water, and that only if he were dead could he go to her father's palace. No! he must not die; so she swam towards him all among the drifting beams and planks, quite forgetting that they might crush her. She dived deep down under the water, and came up again through the waves, and at last reached the young prince just as he was becoming unable to swim any further in the stormy sea. His limbs were numbed, his beautiful eyes were closing, and he must have died if the little mermaid had not come to the rescue. She held his head above the water and let the waves drive them whithersoever they would.

By daybreak all the storm was over, of the ship not a trace was to be seen; the sun rose from the water in radiant brilliance, and his rosy beams seemed to cast a glow of life into the prince's cheeks, but his eyes remained closed. The mermaid kissed his fair and lofty brow, and stroked back the dripping hair; it seemed to her that he was like the marble statue in her little garden; she kissed him again and longed that he might live.

At last she saw dry land before her, high blue mountains on whose summits the white snow glistened as if a flock of swans had settled there; down by the shore were beautiful green woods, and in the foreground a church or temple, she did not quite know which, but it was a building of some sort. Lemon and orange trees grew in the garden, and lofty palms stood by the gate. At this point the sea formed a little bay where the water was quite calm, but very deep, right up to the cliffs; at their foot was a strip of fine white sand to which she swam with the beautiful prince, and laid him down on it, taking great care that his head should rest high up in the warm sunshine.

The bells now began to ring in the great white building, and a number of young maidens came into the garden. Then the little mermaid swam further off behind some high rocks and covered her hair and breast with foam, so that no one should see her little face, and then she watched to see who would discover the poor prince.

It was not long before one of the maidens came up to him. At first she seemed quite frightened, but only for a moment, and then she fetched several others, and the mermaid saw that the prince was coming to life, and that he smiled at all those around him, but he never smiled at her. You see he did not know that she had saved him. She felt so sad that when he was led away into the great building she dived sorrowfully into the water and made her way home to her father's palace.

Always silent and thoughtful, she became more so now than ever. Her sisters often asked her what she had seen on her first visit to the surface, but she never would tell them anything.

Many an evening and many a morning she would rise to the place where she had left the prince. She saw the fruit in the garden ripen, and then gathered, she saw the snow melt on the mountain-tops, but she never saw the prince, so she always went home still sadder than before. At home her only consolation was to sit in her little garden with her arms twined round the handsome marble statue which reminded her of the prince. It was all in gloomy shade now, as she had ceased to tend her flowers, and the garden had become a neglected wilderness of long stalks and leaves entangled with the branches of the tree.

At last she could not bear it any longer, so she told one of her sisters, and from her it soon spread to the others, but to no one else except to one or two other mermaids who only told their dearest friends. One of these knew all about the prince; she had also seen the festivities on the ship; she knew where he came from and where his kingdom was situated.

'Come, little sister!' said the other princesses, and, throwing their arms round each other's shoulders, they rose from the water in a long line, just in front of the prince's palace.

It was built of light yellow glistening stone, with great marble staircases, one of which led into the garden. Magnificent gilded cupolas rose above the roof, and the spaces between the columns which encircled the building were filled with life-like marble statues. Through the clear glass of the lofty windows you could see gorgeous halls adorned with costly silken hangings, and the pictures on the walls were a sight worth seeing. In the midst of the central hall a large fountain played, throwing its jets of spray upwards to a glass dome in the roof, through which the sunbeams lighted up the water and the beautiful plants which grew in the great basin.

She knew now where he lived, and often used to go there in the evenings and by night over the water. She swam much nearer the land than any of the others dared; she even ventured right up the narrow channel under the splendid marble terrace which threw a long shadow over the water. She used to sit here looking at the young prince, who thought he was quite alone in the clear moonlight.

She saw him many an evening sailing about in his beautiful boat, with flags waving and music playing; she used to peep through the green rushes, and if the wind happened to catch her long silvery veil and any one saw it, they only thought it was a swan flapping its wings.

Many a night she heard the fishermen, who were fishing by torchlight, talking over the good deeds of the young prince; and she was happy to think that she had saved his

308

life when he was drifting about on the waves, half dead, and she could not forget how closely his head had pressed her breast, and how passionately she had kissed him; but he knew nothing of all this, and never saw her even in his dreams.

She became fonder and fonder of mankind, and longed more and more to be able to live among them; their world seemed so infinitely bigger than hers; with their ships they could scour the ocean, they could ascend the mountains high above the clouds, and their wooded, grass-grown lands extended further than her eye could reach. There was so much that she wanted to know, but her sisters could not give an answer to all her questions, so she asked her old grandmother, who knew the upper world well, and rightly called it the country above the sea.

'If men are not drowned,' asked the little mermaid, 'do they live for ever? Do they not die as we do down here in the sea?'

'Yes,' said the old lady, 'they have to die too, and their lifetime is even shorter than ours. We may live here for three hundred years, but when we cease to exist we become mere foam on the water and do not have so much as a grave among our dear ones. We have no immortal souls; we have no future life; we are just like the green sea-weed, which, once cut down, can never revive again! Men, on the other hand, have a soul which lives for ever, lives after the body has become dust; it rises through the clear air, up to the shining stars! Just as we rise from the water to see the land of mortals, so they rise up to unknown beautiful regions which we shall never see.'

'Why have we no immortal souls?' asked the little mermaid sadly. 'I would give all my three hundred years to be a human being for one day, and afterwards to have a share in the heavenly kingdom.'

'You must not be thinking about that,' said the grandmother; 'we are much better off and happier than human beings.'

'Then I shall have to die and to float as foam on the water, and never hear the music of the waves or see the beautiful flowers or the red sun! Is there nothing I can do to gain an immortal soul?'

'No,' said the grandmother; 'only if a human being so loved you that you were more to him than father or mother, if all his thoughts and all his love were so centred in you that he would let the priest join your hands and would vow to be faithful to you here, and to all eternity; then your body would become infused with his soul. Thus, and only thus, could you gain a share in the felicity of mankind. He would give you a soul while yet keeping his own. But that can never happen! That which is your greatest beauty in the sea, your fish's tail, is thought hideous up on earth, so little do they understand about it; to be pretty there you must have two clumsy supports which they call legs!'

Then the little mermaid sighed and looked sadly at her fish's tail.

'Let us be happy,' said the grandmother; 'we will hop and skip during our three hundred years of life; it is surely a long enough time; and after it is over we shall rest all the better in our graves. There is to be a court ball to-night.'

This was a much more splendid affair than we ever see on earth. The walls and the ceiling of the great ballroom

310

were of thick but transparent glass. Several hundreds of colossal mussel shells, rose red and grass green, were ranged in order round the sides holding blue lights, which illuminated the whole room and shone through the walls, so that the sea outside was quite lit up. You could see countless fish, great and small, swimming towards the glass walls, some with shining scales of crimson hue, while others were golden and silvery. In the middle of the room was a broad stream of running water, and on this the mermaids and mermen danced to their own beautiful singing. No earthly beings have such lovely voices. The little mermaid sang more sweetly than any of them, and they all applauded her. For a moment she felt glad at heart, for she knew that she had the finest voice either in the sea or on land. But she soon began to think again about the upper world, she could not forget the handsome prince and her sorrow in not possessing, like him, an immortal soul. Therefore she stole out of her father's palace, and while all within was joy and merriment, she sat sadly in her little garden. Suddenly she heard the sound of a horn through the water, and she thought, 'Now he is out sailing up there; he whom I love more than father or mother, he to whom my thoughts cling and to whose hands I am ready to commit the happiness of my life. I will dare anything to win him and to gain an immortal soul! While my sisters are dancing in my father's palace I will go to the sea-witch, of whom I have always been very much afraid; she will perhaps be able to advise and help me!'

Thereupon the little mermaid left the garden and went towards the roaring whirlpools at the back of which the witch lived. She had never been that way before; no flowers grew there, no seaweed, only the bare grey sands, stretched towards the whirlpools, which like rushing mill-wheels swirled round, dragging everything that came within reach down to the depths. She had to pass between these boiling eddies to reach the witch's domain, and for a long way the only path led over warm bubbling mud, which the witch called her 'peat bog.' Her house stood behind this in the midst of a weird forest. All the trees and bushes were polyps, half animal and half plant; they looked like hundred-headed snakes growing out of the sand, the branches were long slimy arms, with tentacles like wriggling worms, every joint of which, from the root to the outermost tip, was in constant motion. They wound themselves tightly round whatever they could lay hold of and never let it escape. The little mermaid standing outside was quite frightened, her heart beat fast with terror and she nearly turned back, but then she remembered the prince and the immortal soul of mankind and took courage. She bound her long flowing hair tightly round her head, so that the polyps should not seize her by it, folded her hands over her breast, and darted like a fish through the water, in between the hideous polyps, which stretched out their sensitive arms and tentacles towards her. She could see that every one of them had something or other, which they had grasped with their hundred arms, and which they held as if in iron bands. The bleached bones of men who had perished at sea and sunk below peeped forth from the arms of some, while others clutched rudders and sea-chests, or the skeleton of some land animal; and most horrible of all, a little mermaid whom they had caught and suffocated. Then she came to a large opening in the wood where the ground was all slimy, and where some huge fat water snakes were gambolling about. In the middle of this opening was a house built of the bones of the wrecked; there sat the witch, letting a toad eat out of her mouth, just as mortals let a little canary eat sugar. She called the hideous water snakes her little chickens, and allowed them to crawl about on her unsightly bosom.

'I know very well what you have come here for,' said the witch. 'It is very foolish of you! all the same you shall have your way, because it will lead you into misfortune, my fine princess. You want to get rid of your fish's tail, and instead to have two stumps to walk about upon like human beings, so that the young prince may fall in love with you, and that you may win him and an immortal soul.' Saying this, she gave such a loud hideous laugh that the toad and the snakes fell to the ground and wriggled about there.

'You are just in the nick of time,' said the witch; 'after sunrise to-morrow I should not be able to help you until another year had run its course. I will make you a potion, and before sunrise you must swim ashore with it, seat yourself on the beach and drink it; then your tail will divide and shrivel up to what men call beautiful legs. But it hurts; it is as if a sharp sword were running through you. All who see you will say that you are the most beautiful child of man they have ever seen. You will keep your gliding gait, no dancer will rival you, but every step you take will be as if you were treading upon sharp knives, so sharp as to draw blood. If you are willing to suffer all this I am ready to help you!'

'Yes!' said the little princess with a trembling voice, thinking of the prince and of winning an undying soul.

'But remember,' said the witch, 'when once you have received a human form, you can never be a mermaid again; you will never again be able to dive down through the water to your sisters and to your father's palace. And if you do not succeed in winning the prince's love, so that for your sake he will forget father and mother, cleave to you with his whole heart, let the priest join your hands

313

and make you man and wife, you will gain no immortal soul! The first morning after his marriage with another your heart will break, and you will turn into foam of the sea.'

'I will do it,' said the little mermaid as pale as death.

'But you will have to pay me, too,' said the witch, 'and it is no trifle that I demand. You have the most beautiful voice of any at the bottom of the sea, and I daresay that you think you will fascinate him with it; but you must give me that voice; I will have the best you possess in return for my precious potion! I have to mingle my own blood with it so as to make it as sharp as a two-edged sword.'

'But if you take my voice,' said the little mermaid, 'what have I left?'

'Your beautiful form,' said the witch, 'your gliding gait, and your speaking eyes; with these you ought surely to be able to bewitch a human heart. Well! have you lost courage? Put out your little tongue, and I will cut it off in payment for the powerful draught.'

'Let it be done,' said the little mermaid, and the witch put on her caldron to brew the magic potion. 'There is nothing like cleanliness,' said she, as she scoured the pot with a bundle of snakes; then she punctured her breast and let the black blood drop into the caldron, and the steam took the most weird shapes, enough to frighten any one. Every moment the witch threw new ingredients into the pot, and when it boiled the bubbling was like the sound of crocodiles weeping. At last the potion was ready and it looked like the clearest water.

'There it is,' said the witch, and thereupon she cut off the tongue of the little mermaid, who was dumb now and could neither sing nor speak.

'If the polyps should seize you, when you go back through my wood,' said the witch, 'just drop a single drop of this liquid on them, and their arms and fingers will burst into a thousand pieces.' But the little mermaid had no need to do this, for at the mere sight of the bright liquid, which sparkled in her hand like a shining star, they drew back in terror. So she soon got past the wood, the bog, and the eddying whirlpools.

She saw her father's palace; the lights were all out in the great ballroom, and no doubt all the household was asleep, but she did not dare to go in now that she was dumb and about to leave her home for ever. She felt as if her heart would break with grief. She stole into the garden and plucked a flower from each of her sisters' plots, wafted with her hand countless kisses towards the palace, and then rose up through the dark blue water.

The sun had not risen when she came in sight of the prince's palace and landed at the beautiful marble steps. The moon was shining bright and clear. The little mermaid drank the burning, stinging draught, and it was like a sharp, two-edged sword running through her tender frame; she fainted away and lay as if she were dead. When the sun rose on the sea she woke up and became conscious of a sharp pang, but just in front of her stood the handsome young prince, fixing his coal black eyes on her; she cast hers down and saw that her fish's tail was gone, and that she had the prettiest little white legs any maiden could desire; but she was quite naked, so she wrapped her long thick hair around her. The prince asked who she was and how she came there. She looked at him tenderly and with a sad expression in her dark blue eyes, but could not speak. Then he took her by the hand and led her into the palace. Every step she took was, as the witch had warned her beforehand, as if she were treading on sharp knives and spikes, but she bore it gladly; led by the prince, she moved as lightly as a bubble, and he and every one else marvelled at her graceful gliding gait.

Clothed in the costliest silks and muslins she was the greatest beauty in the palace, but she was dumb, and could neither sing nor speak. Beautiful slaves clad in silks and gold came forward and sang to the prince and his royal parents; one of them sang better than all the others, and the prince clapped his hands and smiled at her; that made the little mermaid very sad, for she knew that she used to sing far better herself. She thought, 'Oh! if he only knew that for the sake of being with him I had given up my voice for ever!' Now the slaves began to dance, graceful undulating dances to enchanting music; thereupon the little mermaid, lifting her beautiful white arms and raising herself on tiptoe, glided on the floor with a grace which none of the other dancers had yet attained. With every motion her grace and beauty became more apparent, and her eyes appealed more deeply to the heart than the songs of the slaves. Every one was delighted with it, especially the prince, who called her his little foundling; and she danced on and on, notwithstanding that every time her foot touched the ground it was like treading on sharp knives. The prince said that she should always be near him, and she was allowed to sleep outside his door on a velvet cushion.

He had a man's dress made for her, so that she could ride about with him. They used to ride through scented woods, where the green branches brushed her shoulders, and little birds sang among the fresh leaves. She climbed up the highest mountains with the prince, and although her delicate feet bled so that others saw it, she only laughed and followed him until they saw the clouds sailing below them like a flock of birds, taking flight to distant lands.

At home in the prince's palace, when at night the others were asleep, she used to go out on to the marble steps; it cooled her burning feet to stand in the cold sea-water, and at such times she used to think of those she had left in the deep.

One night her sisters came arm in arm; they sang so sorrowfully as they swam on the water that she beckoned to them, and they recognised her, and told her how she had grieved them all. After that they visited her every night, and one night she saw, a long way out, her old grandmother (who for many years had not been above the water), and the Merman King with his crown on his head; they stretched out their hands towards her, but did not venture so close to land as her sisters.

Day by day she became dearer to the prince; he loved her as one loves a good sweet child, but it never entered his head to make her his queen; yet unless she became his wife she would never win an everlasting soul, but on his wedding morning would turn to sea-foam.

'Am I not dearer to you than any of them?' the little mermaid's eyes seemed to say when he took her in his arms and kissed her beautiful brow.

'Yes, you are the dearest one to me,' said the prince, 'for you have the best heart of them all, and you are fondest of me; you are also like a young girl I once saw, but whom I never expect to see again. I was on board a ship

317

which was wrecked; I was driven on shore by the waves close to a holy Temple where several young girls were ministering at a service; the youngest of them found me on the beach and saved my life; I saw her but twice. She was the only person I could love in this world, but you are like her, you almost drive her image out of my heart. She belongs to the holy Temple, and therefore by good fortune you have been sent to me; we will never part!'

'Alas! he does not know that it was I who saved his life,' thought the little mermaid. 'I bore him over the sea to the wood where the Temple stands. I sat behind the foam and watched to see if any one would come. I saw the pretty girl he loves better than me.' And the mermaid heaved a bitter sigh, for she could not weep.

'The girl belongs to the holy Temple, he has said; she will never return to the world, they will never meet again. I am here with him; I see him every day. Yes! I will tend him, love him, and give up my life to him.'

But now the rumour ran that the prince was to be married to the beautiful daughter of a neighbouring king, and for that reason was fitting out a splendid ship. It was given out that the prince was going on a voyage to see the adjoining countries, but it was without doubt to see the king's daughter; he was to have a great suite with him. But the little mermaid shook her head and laughed; she knew the prince's intentions much better than any of the others. 'I must take this voyage,' he had said to her; 'I must go and see the beautiful princess; my parents demand that, but they will never force me to bring her home as my bride; I can never love her! She will not be like the lovely girl in the Temple whom you resemble. If ever I had to choose a bride it would sooner be you with your speaking eyes, my sweet, dumb foundling!' And he kissed her rosy mouth, played with her long hair, and laid his head upon her heart, which already dreamt of human joys and an immortal soul.

'You are not frightened of the sea, I suppose, my dumb child?' he said, as they stood on the proud ship which was to carry them to the country of the neighbouring king; and he told her about storms and calms, about curious fish in the deep, and the marvels seen by divers; and she smiled at his tales, for she knew all about the bottom of the sea much better than any one else.

At night, in the moonlight, when all were asleep, except the steersman who stood at the helm, she sat at the side of the ship trying to pierce the clear water with her eyes, and fancied she saw her father's palace, and above it her old grandmother with her silver crown on her head, looking up through the cross currents towards the keel of the ship. Then her sisters rose above the water; they gazed sadly at her, wringing their white hands. She beckoned to them, smiled, and was about to tell them that all was going well and happily with her, when the cabin-boy approached, and the sisters dived down, but he supposed that the white objects he had seen were nothing but flakes of foam.

The next morning the ship entered the harbour of the neighbouring king's magnificent city. The church bells rang and trumpets were sounded from every lofty tower, while the soldiers paraded with flags flying and glittering bayonets. There was a *fete* every day, there was a succession of balls, and receptions followed one after the other, but the princess was not yet present; she was being brought up a long way off, in a holy Temple they said, and was learning all the royal virtues. At last she came. The little mermaid stood eager to see her beauty, and she was obliged to confess that a lovelier creature she had never beheld. Her complexion was exquisitely pure and delicate, and her trustful eyes of the deepest blue shone through their dark lashes.

'It is you,' said the prince, 'you who saved me when I lay almost lifeless on the beach?' and he clasped his blushing bride to his heart. 'Oh! I am too happy!' he exclaimed to the little mermaid.

'A greater joy than I had dared to hope for has come to pass. You will rejoice at my joy, for you love me better than any one.' Then the little mermaid kissed his hand, and felt as if her heart were broken already.

His wedding morn would bring death to her and change her to foam.

All the church bells pealed and heralds rode through the town proclaiming the nuptials. Upon every altar throughout the land fragrant oil was burnt in costly silver lamps. Amidst the swinging of censers by the priests the bride and bridegroom joined hands and received the bishop's blessing. The little mermaid dressed in silk and gold stood holding the bride's train, but her ears were deaf to the festal strains, her eyes saw nothing of the sacred ceremony; she was thinking of her coming death and of all that she had lost in this world.

That same evening the bride and bridegroom embarked, amidst the roar of cannon and the waving of banners. A royal tent of purple and gold softly cushioned was raised amidships where the bridal pair were to repose during the calm cool night.

The sails swelled in the wind and the ship skimmed lightly and almost without motion over the transparent sea.

At dusk lanterns of many colours were lighted and the sailors danced merrily on deck. The little mermaid could not help thinking of the first time she came up from the sea and saw the same splendour and gaiety; and she now threw herself among the dancers, whirling, as a swallow skims through the air when pursued. The onlookers cheered her in amazement, never had she danced so divinely; her delicate feet pained her as if they were cut with knives, but she did not feel it, for the pain at her heart was much sharper. She knew that it was the last night that she would breathe the same air as he, and would look upon the mighty deep, and the blue starry heavens; an endless night without thought and without dreams awaited her, who neither had a soul, nor could win one. The joy and revelry on board lasted till long past midnight; she went on laughing and dancing with the thought of death all the time in her heart. The prince caressed his lovely bride and she played with his raven locks, and with their arms entwined they retired to the gorgeous tent. All became hushed and still on board the ship, only the steersman stood at the helm; the little mermaid laid her white arms on the gunwale and looked eastwards for the pink-tinted dawn; the first sunbeam, she knew, would be her death. Then she saw her sisters rise from the water; they were as pale as she was; their beautiful long hair no longer floated on the breeze, for it had been cut off.

'We have given it to the witch to obtain her help, so that you may not die to-night! She has given us a knife; here it is, look how sharp it is! Before the sun rises, you must plunge it into the prince's heart, and when his warm

321

blood sprinkles your feet they will join together and grow into a tail, and you will once more be a mermaid; you will be able to come down into the water to us, and to live out your three hundred years before you are turned into dead, salt sea-foam. Make haste! you or he must die before sunrise! Our old grandmother is so full of grief that her white hair has fallen off as ours fell under the witch's scissors. Slay the prince and come back to us! Quick! Quick! do you not see the rosy streak in the sky? In a few minutes the sun will rise and then you must die!' saying this they heaved a wondrous deep sigh and sank among the waves.

The little mermaid drew aside the purple curtain from the tent and looked at the beautiful bride asleep with her head on the prince's breast. She bent over him and kissed his fair brow, looked at the sky where the dawn was spreading fast, looked at the sharp knife, and again fixed her eyes on the prince, who, in his dream called his bride by name. Yes! she alone was in his thoughts! For a moment the knife quivered in her grasp, then she threw it far out among the waves, now rosy in the morning light, and where it fell the water bubbled up like drops of blood.

Once more she looked at the prince, with her eyes already dimmed by death, then dashed overboard and fell, her body dissolving into foam.

Now the sun rose from the sea and with its kindly beams warmed the deadly cold foam, so that the little mermaid did not feel the chill of death. She saw the bright sun, and above her floated hundreds of beauteous ethereal beings, through which she could see the white ship and the rosy heavens; their voices were melodious, but so spirit-like that no human ear could hear them, any more than earthly eye could see their forms. Light as bubbles they floated through the air without the aid of wings. The little mermaid perceived that she had a form like theirs; it gradually took shape out of the foam. 'To whom am I coming?' said she, and her voice sounded like that of the other beings, so unearthly in its beauty that no music of ours could reproduce it.

'To the daughters of the air!' answered the others; 'a mermaid has no undying soul, and can never gain one without winning the love of a human being. Her eternal life must depend upon an unknown power. Nor have the daughters of the air an everlasting soul, but by their own good deeds they may create one for themselves. We fly to the tropics where mankind is the victim of hot and pestilent winds; there we bring cooling breezes. We diffuse the scent of flowers all around, and bring refreshment and healing in our train. When, for three hundred years, we have laboured to do all the good in our power, we gain an undying soul and take a part in the everlasting joys of mankind. You, poor little mermaid, have with your whole heart struggled for the same thing as we have struggled for. You have suffered and endured, raised yourself to the spirit-world of the air, and now, by your own good deeds you may, in the course of three hundred years, work out for yourself an undying soul.'

Then the little mermaid lifted her transparent arms towards God's sun, and for the first time shed tears.

On board ship all was again life and bustle. She saw the prince with his lovely bride searching for her; they looked sadly at the bubbling foam, as if they knew that she had thrown herself into the waves. Unseen she kissed the bride on her brow, smiled at the prince, and rose aloft with the other spirits of the air to the rosy clouds which sailed above.

'In three hundred years we shall thus float into Paradise.'

'We might reach it sooner,' whispered one. 'Unseen we flit into those homes of men where there are children, and for every day that we find a good child who gives pleasure to its parents and deserves their love God shortens our time of probation. The child does not know when we fly through the room, and when we smile with pleasure at it one year of our three hundred is taken away. But if we see a naughty or badly disposed child, we cannot help shedding tears of sorrow, and every tear adds a day to the time of our probation.'

THE EMPEROR'S NEW CLOTHES

Many years ago there was an Emperor, who was so excessively fond of new clothes that he spent all his money on them. He cared nothing about his soldiers, nor for the theatre, nor for driving in the woods except for the sake of showing off his new clothes. He had a costume for every hour in the day, and instead of saying, as one does about any other king or emperor, 'He is in his council chamber,' here one always said, 'The Emperor is in his dressing-room.'

Life was very gay in the great town where he lived; hosts of strangers came to visit it every day, and among them one day two swindlers. They gave themselves out as weavers, and said that they knew how to weave the most beautiful stuffs imaginable. Not only were the colours and patterns unusually fine, but the clothes that were made of the stuffs had the peculiar quality of becoming invisible to every person who was not fit for the office he held, or if he was impossibly dull.

'Those must be splendid clothes,' thought the Emperor. 'By wearing them I should be able to discover which men in my kingdom are unfitted for their posts. I shall distinguish the wise men from the fools. Yes, I certainly must order some of that stuff to be woven for me.'

He paid the two swindlers a lot of money in advance so that they might begin their work at once.

They did put up two looms and pretended to weave, but they had nothing whatever upon their shuttles. At the outset they asked for a quantity of the finest silk and the purest gold thread, all of which they put into their own bags, while they worked away at the empty looms far into the night.

'I should like to know how those weavers are getting on with the stuff,' thought the Emperor; but he felt a little queer when he reflected that any one who was stupid or unfit for his post would not be able to see it. He certainly thought that he need have no fears for himself, but still he thought he would send somebody else first to see how it was getting on. Everybody in the town knew what wonderful power the stuff possessed, and every one was anxious to see how stupid his neighbour was.

'I will send my faithful old minister to the weavers,' thought the Emperor. 'He will be best able to see how the stuff looks, for he is a clever man, and no one fulfils his duties better than he does!'

So the good old minister went into the room where the two swindlers sat working at the empty loom.

'Heaven preserve us!' thought the old minister, opening his eyes very wide. 'Why, I can't see a thing!' But he took care not to say so.

Both the swindlers begged him to be good enough to step a little nearer, and asked if he did not think it a good pattern and beautiful colouring. They pointed to the empty loom, and the poor old minister stared as hard as he could, but he could not see anything, for of course there was nothing to see.

'Good heavens!' thought he, 'is it possible that I am a fool. I have never thought so, and nobody must know it. Am I not fit for my post? It will never do to say that I cannot see the stuffs.'

'Well, sir, you don't say anything about the stuff,' said the one who was pretending to weave.

'Oh, it is beautiful! quite charming!' said the old minister, looking through his spectacles; 'this pattern and these colours! I will certainly tell the Emperor that the stuff pleases me very much.'

'We are delighted to hear you say so,' said the swindlers, and then they named all the colours and described the peculiar pattern. The old minister paid great attention to what they said, so as to be able to repeat it when he got home to the Emperor.

Then the swindlers went on to demand more money, more silk, and more gold, to be able to proceed with the weaving; but they put it all into their own pockets — not a single strand was ever put into the loom, but they went on as before weaving at the empty loom.

The Emperor soon sent another faithful official to see how the stuff was getting on, and if it would soon be ready. The same thing happened to him as to the

327

minister; he looked and looked, but as there was only the empty loom, he could see nothing at all.

'Is not this a beautiful piece of stuff?' said both the swindlers, showing and explaining the beautiful pattern and colours which were not there to be seen.

'I know I am not a fool!' thought the man, 'so it must be that I am unfit for my good post! It is very strange, though! However, one must not let it appear!' So he praised the stuff he did not see, and assured them of his delight in the beautiful colours and the originality of the design. 'It is absolutely charming!' he said to the Emperor. Everybody in the town was talking about this splendid stuff.

Now the Emperor thought he would like to see it while it was still on the loom. So, accompanied by a number of selected courtiers, among whom were the two faithful officials who had already seen the imaginary stuff, he went to visit the crafty impostors, who were working away as hard as ever they could at the empty loom.

'It is magnificent!' said both the honest officials. 'Only see, your Majesty, what a design! What colours!' And they pointed to the empty loom, for they thought no doubt the others could see the stuff.

'What!' thought the Emperor; 'I see nothing at all! This is terrible! Am I a fool? Am I not fit to be Emperor? Why, nothing worse could happen to me!'

'Oh, it is beautiful!' said the Emperor. 'It has my highest approval!' and he nodded his satisfaction as he gazed at the empty loom. Nothing would induce him to say that he could not see anything.

The whole suite gazed and gazed, but saw nothing more than all the others. However, they all exclaimed with his Majesty, 'It is very beautiful!' and they advised him to wear a suit made of this wonderful cloth on the occasion of a great procession which was just about to take place. 'It is magnificent! gorgeous! excellent!' went from mouth to mouth; they were all equally delighted with it. The Emperor gave each of the rogues an order of knighthood to be worn in their buttonholes and the title of 'Gentlemen weavers.'

The swindlers sat up the whole night, before the day on which the procession was to take place, burning sixteen candles; so that people might see how anxious they were to get the Emperor's new clothes ready. They pretended to take the stuff off the loom. They cut it out in the air with a huge pair of scissors, and they stitched away with needles without any thread in them. At last they said: 'Now the Emperor's new clothes are ready!'

The Emperor, with his grandest courtiers, went to them himself, and both the swindlers raised one arm in the air, as if they were holding something, and said: 'See, these are the trousers, this is the coat, here is the mantle!' and so on. 'It is as light as a spider's web. One might think one had nothing on, but that is the very beauty of it!'

'Yes!' said all the courtiers, but they could not see anything, for there was nothing to see.

'Will your imperial majesty be graciously pleased to take off your clothes,' said, the impostors, 'so that we may put on the new ones, along here before the great mirror?'

The Emperor took off all his clothes, and the impostors pretended to give him one article of dress after the other of the new ones which they had pretended to make. They pretended to fasten something round his waist and to tie on something; this was the train, and the Emperor turned round and round in front of the mirror.

'How well his majesty looks in the new clothes! How becoming they are!' cried all the people round. 'What a design, and what colours! They are most gorgeous robes!'

'The canopy is waiting outside which is to be carried over your majesty in the procession,' said the master of the ceremonies.

'Well, I am quite ready,' said the Emperor. 'Don't the clothes fit well?' and then he turned round again in front of the mirror, so that he should seem to be looking at his grand things.

The chamberlains who were to carry the train stooped and pretended to lift it from the ground with both hands, and they walked along with their hands in the air. They dared not let it appear that they could not see anything.

Then the Emperor walked along in the procession under the gorgeous canopy, and everybody in the streets and at the windows exclaimed, 'How beautiful the Emperor's new clothes are! What a splendid train! And they fit to perfection!' Nobody would let it appear that he could see nothing, for then he would not be fit for his post, or else he was a fool.

None of the Emperor's clothes had been so successful before.

'But he has got nothing on,' said a little child.

'Oh, listen to the innocent,' said its father; and one person whispered to the other what the child had said. 'He has nothing on; a child says he has nothing on!'

'But he has nothing on!' at last cried all the people.

The Emperor writhed, for he knew it was true, but he thought 'the procession must go on now,' so held himself stiffer than ever, and the chamberlains held up the invisible train.

THE WIND'S TALE

ABOUT WALDEMAR DAA AND HIS DAUGHTERS

When the wind sweeps across a field of grass it makes little ripples in it like a lake; in a field of corn it makes great waves like the sea itself: this is the wind's frolic. Then listen to the stories it tells; it sings them aloud, one kind of song among the trees of the forest, and a very different one when it is pent up within walls with all their cracks and crannies. Do you see how the wind chases the white fleecy clouds as if they were a flock of sheep? Do you hear the wind down there, howling in the open doorway like a watchman winding his horn? Then, too, how he whistles in the chimneys, making the fire crackle and sparkle. How cosy it is to sit in the warm glow of the fire listening to the tales it has to tell! Let the wind tell its own story! It can tell you more adventures than all of us put together. Listen now: —

'Whew! — Whew! — Fare away!' That was the refrain of his song.

'Close to the Great Belt stands an old mansion with thick red walls,' says the wind. 'I know every stone of it; I knew them before when they formed part of Marsk Stig's Castle on the Ness. It had to come down. The stones were used again, and made a new wall of a new castle in another place — Borreby Hall as it now stands.

'I have watched the highborn men and women of all the various races who have lived there, and now I am going to tell you about Waldemar Daa and his daughters!

'He held his head very high, for he came of a royal stock! He knew more than the mere chasing of a stag, or the emptying of a flagon; he knew how to manage his affairs, he said himself.

'His lady wife walked proudly across the brightly polished floors, in her gold brocaded kirtle; the tapestries in the rooms were gorgeous, and the furniture of costly carved woods. She had brought much gold and silver plate into the house with her, and the cellars were full of German ale, when there was anything there at all. Fiery black horses neighed in the stables; Borreby Hall was a very rich place when wealth came there.

'Then there were the children, three dainty maidens, Ida, Johanna and Anna Dorothea. I remember their names well.

'They were rich and aristocratic people, and they were born and bred in wealth! Whew! — whew! — fare away!' roared the wind, then he went on with his story.

'I did not see here, as in other old noble castles the highborn lady sitting among her maidens in the great hall turning the spinning-wheel. No, she played upon the ringing lute, and sang to its tones. Her songs were not always the old Danish ditties, however, but songs in foreign tongues. All was life and hospitality; noble guests came from far and wide; there were sounds of music and the clanging of flagons, so loud that I could not drown them!' said the wind. 'Here were arrogance and ostentation enough and to spare; plenty of lords, but the Lord had no place there.

'Then came the evening of May-day!' said the wind. 'I came from the west; I had been watching ships being wrecked and broken up on the west coast of Jutland. I tore over the heaths and the green wooded coasts, across the island of Funen and over the Great Belt puffing and blowing. I settled down to rest on the coast of Zealand close to Borreby Hall, where the splendid forest of oaks still stood. The young bachelors of the neighbourhood came out and collected faggots and branches, the longest and driest they could find. These they took to the town, piled them up in a heap, and set fire to them; then the men and maidens danced and sang round the bonfire. I lay still,' said the wind, 'but I softly moved a branch, the one laid by the handsomest young man, and his billet blazed up highest of all. He was the chosen one, he had the name of honour, he became 'Buck of the Street!' and he chose from among the girls his little May-lamb. All was life and merriment, greater far than within rich Borreby Hall.

'The great lady came driving towards the Hall, in her gilded chariot drawn by six horses. She had her three dainty daughters with her; they were indeed three lovely flowers. A rose, a lily and a pale hyacinth. The mother herself was a gorgeous tulip; she took no notice whatever of the crowd, who all stopped in their game to drop their curtsies and make their bows; one might have thought that, like a tulip, she was rather frail in the stalk and feared to bend her back. The rose, the lily, and the pale hyacinth — yes, I saw them all three. Whose May-lambs were they one day to become, thought I; their mates would be proud knights — perhaps even princes!

'Whew! — whew! — fare away! Yes, the chariot bore them away, and the peasants whirled on in their dance. They played at "Riding the Summer into the village," to Borreby village, Tareby village, and many others.

'But that night when I rose,' said the wind, 'the noble lady laid herself down to rise no more; that came to her which comes to every one — there was nothing new about it. Waldemar Daa stood grave and silent for a time; "The proudest tree may bend, but it does not break," said something within him. The daughters wept, and every one else at the Castle was wiping their eyes; but Madam Daa had fared away, and I fared away too! Whew! — whew!' said the wind.

'I came back again; I often came back across the island of Funen and the waters of the Belt, and took up my place on Borreby shore close to the great forest of oaks. The ospreys and the wood pigeons used to build in it, the blue raven and even the black stork! It was early in the year; some of the nests were full of eggs, while in others the young ones were just hatched. What a flying and screaming was there! Then came the sound of the axe, blow upon blow; the forest was to be felled. Waldemar Daa was about to build a costly ship, a three-decked man-of-war, which it was expected the king would buy. So the wood fell, the ancient landmark of the seaman, the home of the birds. The shrike was frightened away; its nest was torn down; the osprey and all the other birds lost their nests too, and they flew about distractedly, shrieking in their terror and anger. The crows and the jackdaws screamed in mockery, Caw! caw! Waldemar Daa and his three daughters stood in the middle of the wood among the workmen. They all laughed at the wild cries of the birds, except Anna Dorothea, who was touched by their distress, and when they were about to fell a tree which was half-dead, and on whose naked branches a black stork had built its nest, out of which the young ones were sticking their heads, she begged them with tears in her eyes to spare it. So the tree with the black stork's nest was allowed to stand. It was only a little thing.

'The chopping and the sawing went on — the three-decker was built. The master builder was a man of humble origin, but of noble loyalty; great power lay in his eyes and on his forehead, and Waldemar Daa liked to listen to him, and little Ida liked to listen too, the eldest fifteen-year-old daughter. But whilst he built the ship for her father, he built a castle in the air for himself, in which he and little Ida sat side by side as man and wife. This might also have happened if his castle had been built of solid stone, with moat and ramparts, wood and gardens. But with all his wisdom the shipbuilder was only a poor bird, and what business has a sparrow in a crane's nest? Whew! whew! I rushed away, and he rushed away, for he dared not stay, and little Ida got over it, as get over it she must.

'The fiery black horses stood neighing in the stables; they were worth looking at, and they were looked at to some purpose too. An admiral was sent from the King to look at the new man-of-war, with a view to purchasing it. The admiral was loud in his admiration of the horses. I heard all he said,' added the wind. 'I went through the open door with the gentlemen and scattered the straw like gold before their feet. Waldemar Daa wanted gold; the admiral wanted the black horses, and so he praised them as he did; but his hints were not taken, therefore the ship remained unsold. There it stood by the shore covered up with boards, like a Noah's Ark which never reached the water. Whew! whew! get along! get along! It was a miserable business. In the winter, when the fields were covered with snow and the Belt was full of ice-floes which I drove up on to the coast,' said the wind, 'the ravens and crows came in flocks, the one blacker than the other, and perched upon the desolate, dead ship by the shore. They screamed themselves hoarse about the forest which had disappeared, and the many precious birds' nests which had been devastated, leaving old and young homeless; and all for the sake of this old piece of lumber, the proud ship which was never to touch the water! I whirled the snow about till it lay in great heaps round the ship. I let it hear my voice, and all that a storm has to say, I know that I did my best to give it an idea of the sea. Whew! whew!'

'The winter passed by; winter and summer passed away! They come and go just as I do. The snow-flakes, the apple blossom, and the leaves fall, each in their turn. Whew! whew! they pass away, as men pass too!

'The daughters were still young. Little Ida, the rose, as lovely to look at as when the shipbuilder turned his gaze upon her. I often took hold of her long brown hair when she stood lost in thought by the apple-tree in the garden. She never noticed that I showered apple-blossom over her loosened hair; she only gazed at the red sunset against the golden background of the sky, and the dark trees and bushes of the garden. Her sister Johanna was like a tall, stately lily; she held herself as stiffly erect as her mother, and seemed to have the same dread of bending her stem. She liked to walk in the long gallery where the family portraits hung. The ladies were painted in velvet and silk, with tiny pearl embroidered caps on their braided tresses.

337

Their husbands were all clad in steel, or in costly cloaks lined with squirrel skins and stiff blue ruffs; their swords hung loosely by their sides. Where would Johanna's portrait one day hang on these walls? What would her noble husband look like? These were her thoughts, and she even spoke them aloud; I heard her as I swept through the long corridor into the gallery, where I veered round again.

'Anna Dorothea, the pale hyacinth, was only a child of fourteen, quiet and thoughtful. Her large blue eyes, as clear as water, were very solemn, but childhood's smile still played upon her lips; I could not blow it away, nor did I wish to do so. I used to meet her in the garden, the ravine, and in the manor fields. She was always picking flowers and herbs, those she knew her father could use for healing drinks and potions. Waldemar Daa was proud and conceited, but he was also learned, and he knew a great deal about many things. One could see that, and many whispers went about as to his learning. The fire blazed in his stove even in summer, and his chamber door was locked. This went on for days and nights, but he did not talk much about it. One must deal silently with the forces of nature. He would soon discover the best of everything, the red, red gold!

'This was why his chimney flamed and smoked and sparkled. Yes, I was there, too,' said the wind.

'Away with you, away! I sang in the back of the chimney. Smoke smoke, embers and ashes, that is all it will come to! You will burn yourself up in it. Whew! whew! away with it! But Waldemar Daa could not let it go.

'The fiery steeds in the stable, where were they? The old gold and silver plate in cupboard and chest, where was

338

that? The cattle, the land, the castle itself? Yes, they could all be melted down in the crucible, but yet no gold would come.

'Barn and larder got emptier and emptier. Fewer servants; more mice. One pane of glass got broken and another followed it. There was no need for me to go in by the doors,' said the wind. 'A smoking chimney means a cooking meal, but the only chimney which smoked here swallowed up all the meals, all for the sake of the red gold.

'I blew through the castle gate like a watchman blowing his horn, but there was no watchman,' said the wind. 'I twisted round the weather-cock on the tower and it creaked as if the watchman up there was snoring, only there was no watchman. Rats and mice were the only inhabitants. Poverty laid the table; poverty lurked in wardrobe and larder. The doors fell off their hinges, cracks and crannies appeared everywhere; I went in and out,' said the wind, 'so I know all about it.

'The hair and the beard of Waldemar Daa grew grey, in the sorrow of his sleepless nights, amid smoke and ashes. His skin grew grimy and yellow, and his eyes greedy for gold, the long expected gold.

'I whistled through the broken panes and fissures; I blew into the daughters' chests where their clothes lay faded and threadbare; they had to last for ever. A song like this had never been sung over the cradles of these children. A lordly life became a woeful life! I was the only one to sing in the castle now,' said the wind. 'I snowed them up, for they said it gave warmth. They had no firewood, for the forest was cut down where they should have got it. There was a biting frost. Even I had to keep rushing through the crannies and passages to keep myself lively. They stayed in bed to keep themselves warm, those noble ladies. Their father crept about under a fur rug. Nothing to bite, and nothing to burn! a lordly life indeed! Whew! whew! let it go! But this was what Waldemar Daa could not do.

'"After winter comes the spring," said he; "a good time will come after a time of need; but they make us wait their pleasure, wait! The castle is mortgaged, we are in extremities — and yet the gold will come — at Easter!"

'I heard him murmur to the spider's web. — "You clever little weaver! You teach me to persevere! If your web is broken, you begin at the beginning again and complete it! Broken again — and cheerfully you begin it over again. That is what one must do, and one will be rewarded!"

'It was Easter morning, the bells were ringing, and the sun was at play in the heavens. Waldemar Daa had watched through the night with his blood at fever pitch; boiling and cooling, mixing and distilling. I heard him sigh like a despairing soul; I heard him pray, and I felt that he held his breath. The lamp had gone out, but he never noticed it; I blew up the embers and they shone upon his ashen face, which took a tinge of colour from their light; his eyes started in their sockets, they grew larger and larger, as if they would leap out.

'Look at the alchemist's glass! something twinkles in it; it is glowing, pure and heavy. He lifted it with a trembling hand and shouted with a trembling voice: "Gold! gold!" He reeled, and I could easily have blown him over,' said the wind, 'but I only blew upon the embers, and followed him to the room where his daughters sat shivering. His coat was powdered with ash, as well as his beard and his matted hair. He drew himself up to his full height and held up his precious treasure, in the fragile glass: "Found! won! gold!" he cried, stretching up his hand with the glass which glittered in the sunbeams: his hand shook, and the alchemist's glass fell to the ground shivered into a thousand atoms. The last bubble of his welfare was shattered too. Whew! whew! fare away! and away I rushed from the goldmaker's home.

'Late in the year, when the days were short and dark up here, and the fog envelops the red berries and bare branches with its cold moisture, I came along in a lively mood clearing the sky and snapping off the dead boughs. This is no great labour, it is true, yet it has to be done. Borreby Hall, the home of Waldemar Daa, was having a clean sweep of a different sort. The family enemy, Ove Ramel from Basness, appeared, holding the mortgage of the Hall and all its contents. I drummed upon the cracked window panes, beat against the decaying doors, and whistled through all the cracks and crannies, whew! I did my best to prevent Herr Ove taking a fancy to stay there. Ida and Anna Dorothea faced it bravely, although they shed some tears; Johanna stood pale and erect and bit her finger till it bled! Much that would help her! Ove Ramel offered to let them stay on at the Castle for Waldemar Daa's lifetime, but he got no thanks for his offer; I was listening. I saw the ruined gentleman stiffen his neck and hold his head higher than ever. I beat against the walls and the old linden trees with such force that the thickest branch broke, although it was not a bit rotten. It fell across the gate like a broom, as if some one was about to sweep; and a sweeping there was indeed to be. I quite expected it. It was a grievous day and a hard time for them, but their wills were as stubborn as their necks were stiff. They had not a possession in the world but the clothes on their backs; yes, one thing — an alchemist's glass which had been bought and filled with the fragments scraped up from the floor. The treasure which promised much and fulfilled nothing. Waldemar Daa hid it in his bosom, took his staff in his hand, and, with his three daughters, the once wealthy gentleman walked out of Borreby Hall for the last time. I blew a cold blast upon his burning cheeks, I fluttered his grey beard and his long white hair; I sang such a tune as only I could sing. Whew! whew! away with them! away with them! This was the end of all their grandeur.

'Ida and Ana Dorothea walked one on each side of him: Johanna turned round in the gateway, but what was the good of that? nothing could make their luck turn. She looked at the red stones of what had once been Marsk Stig's Castle. Was she thinking of his daughters?

'"The elder took the younger by the hand, And out they roamed to a far-off land."

Was she thinking of that song? Here there were three and their father was with them. They walked along the road where once they used to ride in their chariot. They trod it now as vagrants, on their way to a plastered cottage on Smidstrup Heath, which was rented at ten marks yearly. This was their new country seat with its empty walls and its empty vessels. The crows and the magpies wheeled screaming over their heads with their mocking "Caw, caw! Out of the nest, Caw, caw!" just as they screamed in Borreby Forest when the trees were felled.

'Herr Daa and his daughters must have noticed it. I blew into their ears to try and deaden the cries, which after all were not worth listening to.

'So they took up their abode in the plastered cottage on Smidstrup Heath, and I tore off over marshes and meadows, through naked hedges and bare woods, to the open seas and other lands. Whew! whew! away, away! and that for many years.'

What happened to Waldemar Daa? What happened to his daughters? This is what the wind relates.

'The last of them I saw, yes, for the last time, was Anna Dorothea, the pale hyacinth. She was old and bent now; it was half a century later. She lived the longest, she had gone through everything.

'Across the heath, near the town of Viborg, stood the Dean's new, handsome mansion, built of red stone with toothed gables. The smoke curled thickly out of the chimneys. The gentle lady and her fair daughters sat in the bay window looking into the garden at the drooping thorns and out to the brown heath beyond. What were they looking at there? They were looking at a stork's nest on a tumble-down cottage; the roof was covered, as far as there was any roof to cover, with moss and house-leek; but the stork's nest made the best covering. It was the only part to which anything was done, for the stork kept it in repair.

'This house was only fit to be looked at, not to be touched. I had to mind what I was about,' said the wind. 'The cottage was allowed to stand for the sake of the stork's nest; in itself it was only a scarecrow on the heath, but the dean did not want to frighten away the stork, so the hovel was allowed to stand. The poor soul inside was allowed to live in it; she had the Egyptian bird to thank for that; or was it payment for once having pleaded for the nest of his wild black brother in the Borreby Forest? Then, poor thing, she was a child, a delicate, pale hyacinth in a noble flower-garden. Poor Anna Dorothea;

343

she remembered it all! Ah, human beings can sigh as well as the wind when it soughs through the rushes and reeds.

'Oh dear! oh dear! No bells rang over the grave of Waldemar Daa. No schoolboys sang when the former lord of Borreby Castle was laid in his grave. Well, everything must have an end, even misery! Sister Ida became the wife of a peasant, and this was her father's sorest trial. His daughter's husband a miserable serf, who might at any moment be ordered the punishment of the wooden horse by his lord. It is well that the sod covers him now, and you too, Ida! Ah yes! ah yes! Poor me! poor me! I still linger on. In Thy mercy release me, O Christ!'

'This was the prayer of Anna Dorothea, as she lay in the miserable hovel which was only left standing for the sake of the stork.

'I took charge of the boldest of the sisters,' said the wind. 'She had clothes made to suit her manly disposition, and took a place as a lad with a skipper. Her words were few and looks stubborn, but she was willing enough at her work. But with all her will she could not climb the rigging; so I blew her overboard before any one discovered that she was a woman, and I fancy that was not a bad deed of mine!' said the wind.

'On such an Easter morning as that on which Waldemar Daa thought he had found the red gold, I heard from beneath the stork's nest a psalm echoing through the miserable walls. It was Anna Dorothea's last song. There was no window; only a hole in the wall. The sun rose in splendour and poured in upon her; her eyes were glazed and her heart broken! This would have been so this morning whether the sun had shone upon her or not. The stork kept a roof over her head till her death! I sang at her grave,' said the wind, 'and I sang at her father's grave. I know where it is, and hers too, which is more than any one else knows.

'The old order changeth, giving place to the new. The old high-road now only leads to cultivated fields, while peaceful graves are covered by busy traffic on the new road. Soon comes Steam with its row of waggons behind it, rushing over the graves, forgotten, like the names upon them. Whew! whew! Let us be gone! This is the story of Waldemar Daa and his daughters. Tell it better yourselves, if you can,' said the wind, as it veered round. Then it was gone.

www.ingramcontent.com/pod-product-compliance
Lightning Source LLC
Chambersburg PA
CBHW060941030726
47503CB00003B/687